THE
Perfect Recipe

Getting It Right Every Time

Making Our Favorite Dishes
the Absolute Best They Can Be

Pam Anderson

ILLUSTRATIONS BY JUDY LOVE

A Chapters Book

HOUGHTON MIFFLIN COMPANY
Boston New York
1998

For information about permission to reproduce selections from this book, write to Permissions, Houghton Mifflin Company, 215 Park Avenue South, New York, New York 10003.

Grateful acknowledgment is made to *Cook's Illustrated*, where much of the material for this book originally appeared in slightly different form, and to Christopher Kimball for his recipe for Pastry Dough, to Stephen Schmidt for his recipes for Fluffy Buttermilk Biscuits and Baked Macaroni and Cheese, to Nathalie DuPree for her recipe for Batter Fruit Cobbler and to Hugh Carpenter for his recipes for stir-fry sauces.

Library of Congress Cataloging-in-Publication Data

Anderson, Pam. date.
    The perfect recipe: getting it right every time—making your favorite dishes the absolute best they can be / Pam Anderson: illustrations by Judy Love.
      p. cm.
    "A Chapters book."
    Includes index.
    ISBN 0-395-89403-4
    1. Cookery, American. I. Title.
TX715.A566655   1998
641.5973—dc21   98-17821

Printed in the United States of America

Book design by Susan McClellan

RMT 10 9 8 7

To Annie, Della and Juliaette,
who taught me how to cook

CONTENTS

On the Side, but Not Forgotten

Bread Winners

Be-All and End-All Desserts

Acknowledgments

Thanks to:

Christopher Kimball, editor and publisher of *Cook's Illustrated,* who hired a wide-eyed test cook 10 years ago and gave me the chance to trade in my business suit for a full-time apron.

Karen Tack, who was the perfect partner for *The Perfect Recipe.* A gifted cook with a faultless palate, she worked with me until distance and young children made it impossible for us to finish this project together. Our early marathon cooking days are among my happiest memories.

Melissa Hamilton, who picked up where Karen Tack left off and didn't miss a beat.

John Willoughby, Jack Bishop, Mark Bittman, Stephanie Lyness, Adam Ried, Maryellen Driscoll, Susan Logozzo, Anne Yamanaka, Dawn Yanagihara, Eva Katz, Vicki Roland and Anne Tuomey—colleagues, friends and practically family—without whom life would be cottage cheese and dry toast.

Sarah Jane Freymann, my agent and friend, who loved me despite my baggage. Without her, this book might not have left my hard drive.

Rick Kot, who bought this book on faith and shepherded it up to editing. Only a job change kept him from finishing the project.

Rux Martin, who gave the book an enthusiastic home and finally whipped this hodgepodge collection of articles into a real live book.

Stephen Schmidt, colleague and soulmate, whose advice I always trust and whose direction on this book was always enlightening.

Shirley Corriher, who listened to my science questions as if she were Angela Lansbury. On the rare occasion when she didn't know the answers, she either jumped into the lab with me or pointed me in the right direction.

Nach Waxman and Matt Sartwell of Kitchen Arts and Letters, who assisted my research and told me exactly which books I needed to buy (and better yet, which ones I didn't).

All my suppliers: Lena George, Vince Mirack and Jack Ennis at the Thriftway meat department; Greg Heller and Scott Espenshade at Heller's Seafood; and Brian McCabe at Coté and Co.

And finally, David Anderson, my kitchen-table editor, who is always the first to read and comment.

INTRODUCTION

BEFORE DEVELOPING A COLLECTION of truly exceptional recipes—the ones I turn to season after season, year after year—I used to hop around a lot, sampling food from all the latest cookbooks and magazines. The resulting dishes were as erratic as you might expect, given their diverse origins: sometimes great, but often mediocre. I got tired of having to guess whether a recipe would produce a winner or a dud. Although I could spot glaring errors, like most home cooks, I couldn't look at a pancake recipe and tell whether one teaspoon of baking powder was too much or too little. I didn't know if a fruit pie was best thickened with cornstarch, flour, arrowroot or tapioca. I couldn't analyze an ingredient list for muffins and figure out whether they would rise fully and beautifully or be flat-topped and sunken.

I also suspected that the recipes I grew up with—those from standard reliable cookbooks as well as the ones I knew by heart—could do with an update. The roast turkey recipe handed down from my mother always delivered dry breast meat. Without a host of supporting vegetables, my chicken soup lacked flavor. After only a few hours at room temperature, the crust of my lemon meringue pie turned soggy. And I couldn't have told you whether a 450-degree oven was just right or too hot for prime rib.

Who could?—unless you made it a point to study these problems. Most of us roast prime rib only once or twice a year. We're lucky if we have a chance to put on a pot of homemade chicken noodle soup more than a few times each winter. We rely on those who cook and write professionally to do our homework for us.

Rather than continue to guess about the outcome of a recipe or wonder if the method I had always relied on was really the best, I decided to make a study of the dishes I prepared frequently. I wanted a stir-fry formula that I could commit to memory and make with the meat, vegetables and flavorings I had on hand, and with a number of different sauces. I wanted a chicken pot pie that I'd actually have time to put on the table on weeknights, and macaroni and cheese that both my kids and I would eat. I wanted foolproof coleslaw and potato salads that would go with all sorts of dishes, and a cobbler recipe that I could vary with seasonal fruit and top in several different ways. For special occasions, I wanted dishes that would deliver the absolute best: Cornish hens that tasted as good as they looked, pork roast that was juicy and flavorful as well as lean, and rich and creamy cheesecake.

I also wanted answers to the questions that had been dogging me for years. Which cut of beef is best for stew? Why are lobster claws jam-packed with meat one time and limp and scrawny the next? When mashing potatoes, which comes first: the butter or the milk? What is the best filler for a meat loaf? Which apples are best for pie, and what causes the gap that sometimes appears between the crust and the fruit?

I set out to solve these problems one by one. Before heading into the kitchen, I spent some time at the books, studying 50 to 75 recipes—a process that made me realize how many different ways a dish can be prepared. Then I would come up with a composite recipe, a place to begin to test the role of each ingredient as well as the best cooking method.

Together with my colleagues Karen Tack and Melissa Hamilton, I systematically tested each variable in each dish. Although I occasionally found the best method quickly—as with my chicken broth, where I struck gold on the first day—generally, the process took weeks or even months. I roasted more than 40 turkeys, for example, before developing a bird whose breast was as juicy as its thighs. I spent over $600 and six months of time in search of a consistently tender lobster. I cleaned and cooked more than 100 pounds of greens, roasted 20 prime ribs and baked 50 cobblers in my quest for the perfect recipe. Often, when I needed help beyond my library and kitchen, I called on other experts: academics, scientists, industry authorities, restaurateurs, chefs, food boards and councils, fellow cookbook authors, caterers and grandmothers. After these recipes had finally succeeded with my own taste panel, they still had to pass muster in the test kitchens of *Cook's Illustrated,* where they met an even more critical set of palates.

From this book, you'll not only get infallible recipes, you'll learn *why* they work. Once you've had the secret cracked, you'll have a formula you can vary—as well as scores of general principles you can apply to all the dishes you'd love to turn into your own perfect recipes.

I

Taking Stock

Chicken Soup for the Body

CHICKEN SOUP ought to be as delicious as it is restorative. Unfortunately, many chicken soups taste bland and weak. I know because I've made a few lackluster pots myself. I've always managed to salvage them with a can of tomatoes, frozen green peas or mixed vegetables, a few potatoes and a turnip or two. The resulting soup was always delicious, but I hadn't wanted vegetable soup. I wanted to know how to make a pot of chicken soup so good that I'd long for an excuse to be sick.

Obviously my soup's problem was the broth. Standard chicken broths just aren't flavorful enough to produce a robust soup. Besides, it always bothers me to strain out and throw away all the celery, carrots and onions called for in traditional recipes, only to turn around and chop more of the same for the soup. So I started my testing with more offbeat methods to see if I could somehow develop a more potent broth.

It's not unusual for me for try 30 or 40 times before I'm satisfied with the results. Chicken soup was different. After only four tries, I knew I had a winner.

I started with a Chinese method, in Bruce Cost's *Asian Ingredients* (Morrow, 1988). This rich, clear broth is made by first blanching a whole chicken to keep it from releasing foam as it cooks. Foam can cloud the finished broth. The blanched chicken is then placed in a bowl, partially covered with water and set over a pan of barely simmering water for four hours. Cooked this way, the liquid in which the chicken cooks never simmers, and the resulting broth is remarkably refined. This very special broth is perfect for floating dumplings or blanched vegetables, but is much too fine a base for a hearty main-course soup. And such a long cooking time rendered my 4-pound chicken good for nothing but the compost heap. Only special occasions warrant this kind of sacrifice.

A number of recipes promoted roasting chicken bones with the celery, carrot and onion for a rich, full-flavored broth. I gave it a try, roasting 3 pounds of chicken backs, necks and bones for 20 minutes in a 400-degree oven. I then added a small carrot, a medium onion and a small piece of celery to the pan and roasted 40 minutes longer before adding water and simmering for an hour. The resulting broth was dark;

it had a nice roasted-chicken-and-caramelized-onion flavor, but it still wasn't the full-flavored broth I sought.

James Beard believed gizzards made especially good broth. Following his direction, I made a broth of 2¼ pounds chicken backs and wings and ¾ pound gizzards. The result was acceptable, but all the broths made to this point turned out to be the weak cousins of the one I was about to experience.

Liquid Gold

The winning broth took as its starting point the one in Edna Lewis's *In Pursuit of Flavor* (Knopf, 1988). Lewis's broth was different from any I'd ever seen. It was fast and simple—so much so that I was a bit skeptical. In my experience, offbeat methods were fun to try but rarely yielded spectacular results. Hers proved the exception.

Rather than simmering chicken bones, aromatic vegetables and herbs for hours, Lewis's recipe involved sautéing a chicken that had been hacked into small pieces, along with an onion, until the chicken lost its raw color. Lewis then covered the pot and set it over low heat until the chicken and onion released their rich, flavorful juices, a process that took 15 to 20 minutes. Only at that point did she add water, and she simmered the broth for only 20 minutes longer.

I knew I was on to something as I smelled the chicken and onion sautéing,

and the finished broth confirmed what my nose had detected. The broth tasted pleasantly sautéed, not boiled. I had some refining to do, though. For once, I had made too strong a broth; this one had almost demi-glace intensity. And like Cost's recipe, this broth depleted the chicken itself, leaving its meat flavorless after cooking.

I followed Lewis's technique, substituting chicken backs and wing tips for the whole chicken and increasing the water from 3 cups to 2 quarts. The broth had just the right strength and made some of the best chicken soup I've ever tasted. I prepared the broth twice more—once without the onion and once with onion, celery and carrot. The onion added a flavor dimension I liked; the extra vegetables neither added nor detracted from the final soup, so I left them out.

Where to Get the Goods

So how do you come up with useless chicken parts for this broth? The Buffalo chicken wing fad has made wings more expensive than legs and thighs. Some cooks freeze chicken bones as they accumulate them, but unless you're careful about wrapping and marking freezer packages, you may find yourself with an unidentifiable, unusable bag of freezer-burned bones in six months. I came up with four alternatives.

Buying chicken backs is clearly the

most inexpensive way to make broth for soup. My grocery store usually sells them for almost nothing. Although you may not find chicken backs for sale at just any meat counter, most grocery stores and meat markets will obtain them if you request them.

Rather than freeze chicken bones as I acquire them, I often cook them right away. For example, I rarely roast a whole chicken but instead usually remove the backbone and butterfly it (see page 83). That way, I end up with a back, a neck, wing tips and giblets. Once I've removed the back, I put it in the pot with the giblets and make a quick quart of broth while I'm cooking the chicken. You can make a small pot of soup from this amount, or you can go on and freeze the broth, which is much easier to store than a big bag of bones.

I've also discovered that whole legs, which are relatively inexpensive, make incredibly full-flavored broths for soup. In a side-by-side comparison of broth made from backs and broth made from whole legs, I found that the whole-leg broth was more flavorful than the all-bone broth. Just don't try to salvage the meat. After 25 minutes of sweating and another 20 minutes of simmering, it is devoid of flavor.

My favorite method requires a whole chicken. But rather than using the entire bird for the broth, I remove and reserve the breast for use in the final soup. The rest of the bird—the legs, back, wings and giblets—make up the broth. I particularly like this method's tidiness—one bird, one pot of soup.

HACK IT UP

CUTTING THE CHICKEN into small pieces is actually the most difficult part of making this soup. A meat cleaver, a heavy-duty chef's knife or a pair of heavy-duty kitchen shears makes the task fairly simple. Don't worry about precision: the point is to get the pieces small enough to release their flavorful juices in a short period of time.

Follow figures 1 through 7 for Butchering the Bird, page 98. Remove as little breast meat as possible when separating the wings from the breast; omit steps 5 and 6. Set the breasts aside. Cut up the remaining chicken in the following way:

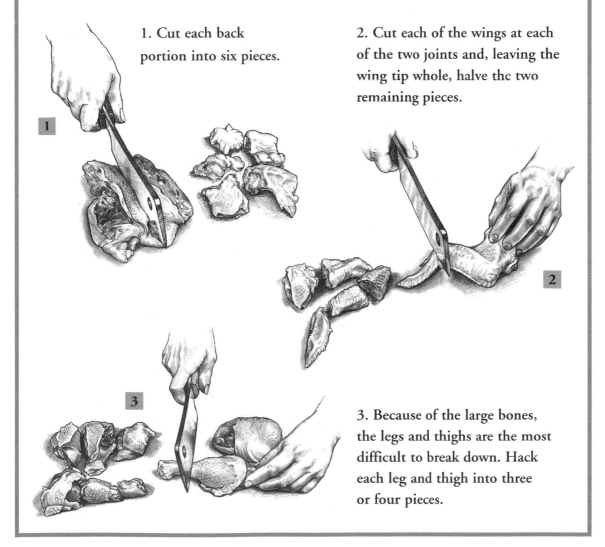

1. Cut each back portion into six pieces.

2. Cut each of the wings at each of the two joints and, leaving the wing tip whole, halve the two remaining pieces.

3. Because of the large bones, the legs and thighs are the most difficult to break down. Hack each leg and thigh into three or four pieces.

Quick Full-Flavored Chicken Broth

Makes scant 2 quarts

YOU CAN MAKE THIS BROTH from a 4-pound chicken instead of the legs and thighs called for here. Simply remove the breast first and reserve for another use. Cut up the back, wings, legs and thighs and proceed with the recipe.

1 tablespoon vegetable oil
1 medium onion, cut into medium dice
3 pounds legs and thighs, trimmed of excess fat and
   cut into 2-inch pieces (see illustrations on page 17)
   or 4 pounds chicken backs and/or bones,
   cut into 2-inch pieces
1 teaspoon salt
2 bay leaves

1. Heat oil in a large, heavy-bottomed soup kettle over medium-high heat. When oil shimmers, add onion and chicken pieces and sauté until no longer pink, 5 to 7 minutes.

2. Reduce heat to low. Cover and cook until chicken releases its juices, about 20 minutes. Increase heat to high; add 2 quarts water (already boiling if you are in a hurry), salt and bay leaves. As soon as water comes to a simmer, immediately reduce heat to low again. Cover and simmer until broth is rich and flavorful, 20 to 30 minutes longer.

3. Strain and discard solids. Broth is ready to use. Or cool to room temperature and refrigerate or freeze.

Hearty Chicken Soup

MAKES ABOUT 3 QUARTS, SERVING 6 TO 8

BOIL THE WATER IN THIS RECIPE only if you are in a hurry. Otherwise, room-temperature water is preferable.

1   tablespoon vegetable oil
2   medium onions, cut into medium dice
1   whole chicken (about 4 pounds), breast removed
    and split; remaining chicken cut into 2-inch pieces
    (see illustrations on page 17)
    Salt
2   bay leaves
1   large carrot, peeled and sliced ¼ inch thick
1   celery stalk, sliced ¼ inch thick
½   teaspoon dried thyme leaves
2   cups (3 ounces) hearty egg noodles
    Ground black pepper
¼   cup minced fresh parsley leaves

1. Heat oil over medium-high heat in a large soup kettle. Add half of chopped onions and all chicken pieces (reserve breast). Sauté until chicken is no longer pink, 5 to 7 minutes. Reduce heat to low, cover and simmer until chicken releases its juices, about 20 minutes. Increase heat to high; add 2 quarts water (already boiling if you are in a hurry) along with the whole chicken breast, 1 teaspoon salt and bay leaves. Bring to a simmer, then cover, reduce heat to low and barely simmer until chicken breast is cooked and broth is rich and flavorful, 20 minutes longer.

2. Remove chicken breast from kettle; set aside. When cool enough to handle, remove skin from breast, then remove meat from bones and shred into bite-size pieces; discard skin and bones. Strain broth into a large bowl and discard any remaining chicken pieces and bones. Skim fat from broth and reserve 2 tablespoons. (Broth and meat can be covered and refrigerated for up to 2 days.)

3. Return soup kettle to medium-high heat. Add reserved chicken fat. Add remaining onion, along with carrot and celery. Sauté until softened, about 5 minutes. Add thyme, broth and shredded chicken. Simmer until vegetables are tender and flavors meld, 10 to 15 minutes. Add noodles and cook until just tender, about 5 minutes. Adjust seasonings, adding salt, if necessary, and pepper, stir in parsley and serve.

Hearty Chicken Soup with Orzo and Spring Vegetables

SERVES 6 TO 8

BECAUSE LEEKS GROW underground, they are often full of dirt. To ensure that the leek is properly cleaned, trim off the dark green leaves. Quarter the trimmed leek lengthwise, then cut it crosswise into ½-inch pieces. Rinse the chopped leek thoroughly in a bowl or sink of cold water, letting the grit fall to the bottom.

- 1   tablespoon vegetable oil
- 1   medium onion, cut into medium dice
- 1   whole chicken (about 4 pounds), breast removed and split; remaining chicken cut into 2-inch pieces
- 1   teaspoon salt
- 2   bay leaves
- 1   medium leek, thoroughly washed and cut into medium dice
- 1   large carrot, peeled and sliced ¼ inch thick
- 1   celery stalk, sliced ¼ inch thick
- ½   teaspoon dried thyme leaves
- ½   cup orzo
- ¼   pound asparagus, trimmed and cut into 1-inch lengths
- ¼   cup peas, fresh or frozen
- 2   tablespoons minced fresh tarragon leaves or 2 teaspoons dried tarragon
  Ground black pepper

1. Follow steps 1 and 2 of recipe for Hearty Chicken Soup (page 19).

2. In step 3, substitute leek for onion. Substitute orzo for egg noodles. Along with orzo, add asparagus and peas. Substitute tarragon for parsley.

Hearty Chicken Soup with Shells, Tomato and Zucchini

Serves 6 to 8

To ensure perfectly cooked pasta, add the shells to the simmering soup at the last minute.

1 tablespoon vegetable oil

2 medium onions, cut into medium dice

1 whole chicken (about 4 pounds), breast removed
   and split; remaining chicken cut into 2-inch pieces

1 teaspoon salt

2 bay leaves

1 large carrot, peeled and sliced ¼ inch thick

1 celery stalk, sliced ¼ inch thick

1 medium zucchini, cut into medium dice

½ cup chopped tomatoes, fresh or canned

½ teaspoon dried thyme leaves

1 cup small shells or macaroni

¼ cup minced fresh basil leaves

Ground black pepper

Grated Parmesan cheese (optional)

1. Follow steps 1 and 2 of recipe for Hearty Chicken Soup (page 19).

2. In step 3, add zucchini to sautéed onions, carrots and celery and sauté for 2 minutes more. Add tomatoes with broth. Substitute small shells or macaroni for egg noodles and simmer until pasta is cooked. Substitute basil for parsley. Season to taste with pepper. Serve with grated Parmesan, if you like.

Hearty Chicken Soup with Leeks, Wild Rice and Mushrooms

SERVES 6 TO 8

WILD RICE BLEND—a mix of wild and brown rice—is a nice substitute for the wild rice in this recipe.

- 1 tablespoon vegetable oil
- 1 medium onion, cut into medium dice
- 1 whole chicken (about 4 pounds), breast removed and split; remaining chicken cut into 2-inch pieces
- 1 teaspoon salt
- 2 bay leaves
- ½ cup wild rice
- ½ cup dried wild mushrooms
- 1 medium leek, thoroughly washed and cut into medium dice
- 1 large carrot, peeled and sliced ¼ inch thick
- ¼ pound mushrooms, sliced (domestic or wild)
- ¼ cup minced fresh parsley leaves

1. Follow steps 1 and 2 of recipe for Hearty Chicken Soup (page 19).

2. While broth simmers, cook wild rice, following package instructions. Soak dried mushrooms in 1 cup of the hot chicken broth until softened, about 20 minutes. Drain and chop wild mushrooms; reserve soaking broth.

3. In step 3, substitute leek for onion; omit celery. When leek and carrot have softened, add fresh mushrooms and sauté until softened, about 5 minutes more. Add dried mushrooms and soaking broth to soup kettle along with chicken broth. Simmer as directed, stirring in rice during last 5 minutes of cooking. Stir in parsley and serve.

Simple Clam Chowder

I LOVE HOMEMADE clam chowder almost as much as I love good chicken soup, but until recently, I rarely made it, turning to the canned variety more often than not. That's a shame, because clam chowder is actually quicker to cook than chicken soup.

I had my reasons for not making it, however. Clams required a trip to the fish market. Although my local grocery store carries small, pricey bags of little-neck clams, using them for a pot of chowder would cost me almost $30. Clams must also be processed fairly quickly or they'll spoil.

Further, many chowder recipes demand that the clams be purged of sand by soaking them in salt water with cornmeal or baking powder—yet another time-consuming step. And once made, chowder is more fragile than most other soups. Unless it is stabilized in some way, it curdles if brought to a boil. And because it is chock-full of potatoes, it doesn't freeze well either.

My goals for this soup, then, were multiple. I wanted to develop a delicious, traditional chowder that was economical, easy and stable. To solve the avail-ability and perishability problems, I wanted to develop a second recipe using canned clams and bottled clam juice. I wanted this everyday chowder to be almost as simple as opening a can.

Clam Digging

Before testing chowder recipes, I explored clam options. There are two varieties—hard-shells and soft-shells. Chowders are typically made with hard-shells, although I found a recipe or two calling for soft-shells as well. Of the hard-shell variety, I purchased (from smallest to largest) cockles, littlenecks, cherrystones and chowder clams, often called quahogs. Another hard-shell variety, top-necks, fall between littlenecks and cherrystones in size. Of the soft-shells, only steamer clams are available to me in the east, but razor clams and geoducks are common on the West Coast.

Although they made delicious chowders, I eliminated littlenecks and cockles, both of which were too expensive to toss into a chowder pot. (I paid almost $40 for 7 pounds of cockles, and the same quantity of littlenecks were $28. At that price, you'd want to serve these two varieties as a first course in the shell. By contrast, 7 pounds of cherry-stones cost $4, and quahogs of the same weight cost a mere $2.)

Chowders made with the cheapest clams, however, weren't really satisfactory either. The quahogs I purchased for testing were large (4 to 5 inches in diameter), tough and strongly flavored. Their oversized bellies gave the chowder a powerful mineral taste, detracting from its smooth, rich flavor. Though only slightly more expensive, cherrystones offered good value and flavor. The chowder made from these slightly smaller clams was distinctly flavored, without an inky aftertaste. Because there are no industry sizing standards for each clam variety (see page 27), you may find some small quahogs labeled as cherrystones or large cherrystones labeled as quahogs. Regardless of designation, clams much over 3 inches in diameter will deliver a distinctly metallic-tasting chowder.

The recipe I followed for soft-shell clam chowder required steaming the clams open, separating the necks and strips from the belly meat, mincing them fine, then adding each to the stew at separate times. In addition to the steamers' sandiness, I found the entire cleaning and separating process tedious. As their name suggests, steamers should be steamed, opened and eaten straight from the shell.

Shucked, Baked or Steamed?

Steaming cherrystones or topnecks open is far easier than shucking them. Five minutes over simmering water and the clams open as naturally as a budding flower. If they are pulled from the pot as soon as they open, and if they aren't cooked too long in the finished chowder, they do not toughen. In addition to steaming, I tried baking them open. Compared to steaming, baking takes longer and is more awkward. I also prefer steaming because of the wonderful broth that results when clam juices combine with the steaming liquid.

The extra step of purging or filtering hard-shell clams is unnecessary. Although soft-shell steamers are a bit sandy, the hard-shells are relatively clean, and what little sediment there is sinks to the bottom of the steaming liquid. Getting rid of the grit is simple: just leave the last few tablespoons of broth in the pan when you pour it from the pot. If you find that your clam broth is still gritty, strain it through a coffee filter.

The Right Texture

After making several pots of chowder, I came to agree with the cookbook author Phillip Schulz, who writes in *As American as Apple Pie* (Simon and Schuster, 1990) that chowders should be "slurpable, yet not watery. Thick, but not stewlike." Older recipes call for thickening the chowder with crumbled biscuits; bread crumbs and crackers are modern stand-ins. Ignoring tradition, however, allowed three more thickening possibilities: I could give the soup body with heavy cream, I could thicken with flour before adding the liquid, or I could thicken in the end with a *beurre manié* (a paste made of equal parts butter and flour).

Traditional bread crumb-thickened chowders failed to impress. I wanted a smooth, creamy soup base for the potatoes, onions and clams. Although I like crumbled crackers in chowder, I want to sprinkle them in at the table for texture, not at the stove as a thickener. No matter how long the chowder is simmered, bread crumbs or crackers never completely dissolve into the cooking liquid.

Heavy cream, by contrast, did not give the chowder enough body, and I discovered fairly quickly that flour is necessary, not only as a thickener but as a stabilizer, because unthickened chowders separate and tend to curdle. Of the two flour methods, I opted to thicken at the beginning of cooking rather than use the *beurre manié* at the end. The final recipe is finished with cream, so the chowder doesn't need the extra butter required to make the flour paste.

Because chowders call for potatoes, some cooks have suggested that starchy baking potatoes could double as a thickener. But the potatoes did not break down sufficiently and instead became soft and mushy. Waxy red boiling potatoes are best for chowders.

I now had two more questions to answer. First, should the chowder include salt pork or bacon and, if bacon, did I need to blanch it? I ended up using such small amounts of this flavoring in the final recipe that either worked fine. Bacon is more readily available and easier to use up. Blanching the bacon makes it taste more like salt pork, but I like the subtle smokiness of the chowder made with unblanched bacon.

Should the chowder be enriched with milk or cream? So much milk was required to make it look and taste creamy that the chowder started to lose its clam flavor and became more like a mild bisque, the clam equivalent of oyster stew. Making the chowder with almost all clam broth, then finishing it with a cup of cream, finally gave me what I was looking for—a rich chowder that tasted distinctly of clams.

Sizing Up Clams

There seems to be no consistent way of measuring clams for chowder. Some recipes call for a certain quantity of shucked clams, giving the cook no idea how many whole clams to buy. Other recipes call for a particular number of "hard-shell clams," apparently not taking into account the incredible difference in size between a quahog and a littleneck.

Likewise, there are no industry standards for the size of each clam variety. One company's cherrystone is another company's quahog. So simply calling for a certain number of cherrystones or quahogs is not a consistent measurement either.

I wondered if calling for pounds of clams, regardless of their size, would yield similar quantities of meat and liquid. Working with 1½-pound quantities, I shucked quahogs, cherrystones and littlenecks. Although the number of clams per pound varied greatly (two quahogs equaled 1½ pounds while it took two dozen littlenecks to equal the same weight), they all fairly consistently yielded a scant ½ cup clams and ⅔ cup juice.

Even though clams are usually sold by the piece at the fish market, I find it more accurate and consistent to give a weight rather than a number. Even most outdoor fish markets have a scale. Regardless of clam size, you'll need about 7 pounds of hard-shells to make the chowder recipe that follows.

New England Clam Chowder

Makes about 2 quarts, serving 6

MOST EVERYBODY KNOWS you shouldn't eat oysters in the "r-less" months of the year (May, June, July, August). During spring and summer, these shellfish spawn, leaving them weak, extremely perishable and off-flavored, with poor texture. For the same reasons, clams and mussels are not at their peak during those months either. Although clams recover from their spawning phase much more quickly than mussels and oysters, you should avoid them from midspring through early summer.

7 pounds medium-size hard-shell clams, such as topneck
  or cherrystone, scrubbed and thoroughly washed

2 slices (about 2 ounces) thick-cut bacon,
  cut into ½-inch pieces

1 large Spanish onion, cut into medium dice (about 2 cups)

3 tablespoons all-purpose flour

3 medium waxy red boiling potatoes, cut into medium dice

1 large bay leaf

¼ teaspoon dried thyme leaves

1 cup heavy cream

2 tablespoons minced fresh parsley

Salt

Ground black or white pepper

1. Bring clams and 3 cups water to a boil in a large covered soup kettle. Steam until clams just start to open, 3 to 5 minutes. Transfer clams to a large bowl; cool slightly. Working with one at a time, pry clam open over bowl to catch any juices. Remove clam from shell and put into a small bowl; discard shells. Mince clams; set aside. Pour clam broth from kettle into a 2-quart liquid measuring cup, holding back the last few tablespoons of broth to avoid adding any sediment. Set broth aside. (You should have about 5 cups.) Rinse and dry kettle; return it to burner.

2. Fry bacon over medium heat in kettle until fat renders and bacon crisps, about 5 minutes.

3. Add onion to bacon and drippings and sauté until softened, about 5 minutes. Add flour; stir until lightly colored, about 1 minute. Gradually whisk in reserved clam broth. Add potatoes, bay leaf and thyme and bring to a simmer. Reduce heat to low and continue to simmer until potatoes are tender, about 10 minutes. Add clams, cream, parsley and salt and pepper to taste; bring to a simmer. Remove from heat and serve.

The Right Canned Clams

From late summer through winter, when clams are plentiful, you'll probably want to make chowder using fresh clams. But when you're short on time or when clams are scarce and expensive, the right canned clams and bottled clam juice deliver a chowder that's at least three notches above canned soup in quality.

But are all canned clams the same? Taste-testing four varieties of minced canned clams (Doxsee, Progresso, Gorton's and Cento) and three kinds of canned whole baby clams (3 Diamonds, Cento and Chicken of the Sea), I discovered dramatic differences.

In the end, I preferred Doxsee minced clams teamed with Doxsee clam juice. For those who prefer whole clams in their chowder, Chicken of the Sea baby clams were best in their category.

Minced Canned Clams

♦ **Cento Minced Clams:** A 6½-ounce can yields ½ cup liquid and a generous ⅓ cup meat. The clams have a uniform minced look, but are gritty. The majority of meat looks like the tough hinge muscle that's been artificially tenderized, and

there are very few strips. Contains no preservatives.

♦ **Doxsee (No MSG) Minced Clams:** A 6½-ounce can yields ½ cup clam juice and ⅓ cup minced clam meat. The meat doesn't have the pinkish orangy color of the other varieties. This is the best of the canned minced clams. Not too tough, not artificially tender.

♦ **Gorton's Chopped Clams:** A 6½-ounce can yields ½ juice and ⅓ cup meat. Because the clams are chopped, not minced, the pieces are uneven, with larger pieces mixed in with smaller. MSG and sodium bisulfate are added to preserve color, and sodium tripolyphosphate to retain moisture. Tastes bland.

♦ **Progresso Recipe Ready, Gourmet Quality Minced Clams:** A 10½-ounce can yields ⅔ cup clam juice and ⅔ cup meat. MSG is added to preserve color, and sodium tripolyphosphate to retain moisture. The final product looks chewed up, and some of the pieces taste chewy. The meat also looks bleached.

SMALL WHOLE CLAMS

♦ **Cento Whole Shelled Baby Clams:** A 10-ounce can yields 1 cup clams and ⅔ cup juice. Contains the same additives as Gorton's and Progresso. Much lighter in color. Looks and tastes washed out. These clams seem to have been cooked longer and do not hold their shape very well.

♦ **Chicken of the Sea Baby Clams:** A 10-ounce can yields 1 cup clams and a scant ⅔ cup juice. My favorite of the baby clam variety. With their soft texture, they don't feel overly cooked. They also look natural, neither too green nor washed out, and taste more clamlike than Cento or 3 Diamonds. Citric acid and calcium disodium EDTA are added to promote color retention, sodium PF and sodium pyrophosphate to maintain flavor and firmness, and sodium sulfite as a preservative.

♦ **3 Diamonds Whole Small Clams:** A 10-ounce can yields a scant cup of clams and ⅔ cup broth. Citric acid and sodium sulfite are added as preservatives. Very strong flavor. Bellies are very green and give the clams a baitlike flavor. A small crab was found in the can.

♦ **Chopped fresh frozen clams** (available at most grocery store fish counters and seafood markets): These clams were as chewy as rubber bands, gritty and almost flavorless.

Quick Clam Chowder

Makes about 2 quarts, serving 6

THIS HOMEMADE CHOWDER is almost as simple to make as opening a can. The next time you are tempted to buy canned clam chowder, pick up some canned clams and bottled clam juice and make your own instead. The flavor will be much better.

2 slices (about 2 ounces) thick-cut bacon,
      cut into ½-inch pieces
1 large Spanish onion, cut into medium dice (about 2 cups)
3 tablespoons all-purpose flour
4 cans (6½ ounces each) minced clams, preferably Doxsee
      (No MSG) Minced Clams; clams and juice separated
2 bottles (8 ounces each) clam juice, preferably Doxsee brand
3 medium waxy red boiling potatoes
1 large bay leaf
¼ teaspoon dried thyme leaves
1 cup heavy cream
2 tablespoons minced fresh parsley leaves
    Salt
    Ground black or white pepper

1. Fry minced bacon over medium heat in a large soup kettle until fat renders and bacon crisps, about 5 minutes.

2. Add onion to bacon and drippings, and sauté until softened, about 5 minutes. Add flour; stir until lightly colored, about 1 minute. Gradually whisk in canned and bottled clam juices and 3 cups water. Add potatoes, bay leaf and thyme, and bring to a simmer. Reduce heat to low and continue to simmer until potatoes are tender, about 10 minutes. Add clams, cream and parsley, and season to taste with salt and pepper. Bring to a simmer. Remove from heat and serve.

How to Make Flavorful Beef Soup

THE BEEF SOUP of my dreams starts with a broth almost as intense as pot roast *jus* or beef stew. With such a flavorful base, only a few vegetables and a handful of noodles or barley are needed for contrasting flavor, color and texture. Unfortunately, a good broth—the key ingredient—is not easy to make and it is impossible to buy. Most traditional recipes require a trip to the butcher for rare bones and demand hours of simmering time. I was determined to make a really great broth in just a couple of hours with beef cuts I could easily find in my grocery store.

To make her beef vegetable soup, my mother would buy a little "stew meat" and cut it into tiny chunks. She didn't brown the meat, but just covered it with a lot of water and simmered it. As the meat cooked, she prepared each of her vegetables—onions, carrots, celery, potatoes, tomatoes, green beans, corn, okra and whatever else happened to be around—adding them to the pot one at a time when they were ready. Her stone-soup approach yielded a delicious pot—

a mélange of vegetables, the meat juices subtly flavoring the broth, the meat itself no more abundant than any one vegetable. This style of soup was wonderfully satisfying and simple, but I wanted a more beefy flavor.

Trying the French Method

In contrast to the simple, straightforward soup of my youth, the classic French method requires much more time and effort. Following the classic recipe, I found a butcher who gave me some meaty knuckle and shin bones. I roasted them, along with celery, carrots and onions. I covered the roasted bones and vegetables with lots of water, brought them to a simmer, adjusted the heat to a mere perk and went to bed. The next morning, I strained and skimmed my precious concoction. I had followed the technique perfectly, but after taking a few sips, I realized my broth tasted like bone-enhanced vegetable liquid.

In an attempt to beef up the broth, I followed the traditional French method again, this time with 4 pounds of beef bones, fortified with a generous 2 pounds of beef as well as celery, carrot, onion, tomato and fresh thyme, all covered with 4 quarts of water. My plan was to taste the broth after 4, 6, 8, 12 and 16 hours of simmering. Not only was I interested in the broth's evolution of flavor, I wanted to keep this traditional broth on hand for taste comparison throughout subsequent tests. Despite my unsuccessful history with the method, I was rooting for it. The simmering roasted bones, meat, vegetables and fresh herbs were earthy and beautiful. Although I wanted to find a quicker alternative technique, I was certain the classic was a must when the best was required.

Strong on Body,
Weak on Flavor

After 4, 6 and even 8 hours, however, the broth was weak and tasted mostly of vegetables. Even though the texture of the 12- and 16-hour broths was richly gelatinous, the flavors of vegetables and bones still predominated. Not willing to give up on this method quite yet, I found a recipe that prescribed roasting, then simmering, beef bones, onions and tomatoes—no celery and carrots—for 12 hours. During the last 3 hours of cooking, I added beef to the fully cooked broth, increasing the amount from 2 to 3 pounds. This broth, I thought, could be the ideal—great body

from the bones, minimal vegetable flavor and generous hunks of beef to enhance the rich, reduced liquids. Once again, however, the broth was beautifully textured but had very little flavor. It was time to look into the question of the beef.

A Better Method,
the Right Beef

Knowing now that it was going to take more meat than bones to get great flavor, I started the next set of tests by making broths with different cuts of meat. In my research, I had found recipes calling for chuck (as well as for neck, a particularly gelatinous and allegedly more flavorful section of the chuck), shank, round, brisket, oxtail and short ribs. I made small pots of broth from each of these meats. In the process, I decided to streamline the method. Instead of roasting the bones, I thoroughly browned 2 pounds of meat and 1 pound of small marrow bones (or, alternatively, 3 pounds bone-in cuts like shank, short ribs and oxtails) and an onion on the stovetop. Then I covered the browned ingredients and let them "sweat" so they softened and cooked in their own juices for 20 minutes, adding only a quart of water to each pot and simmering them until the meat in each pot was done.

With so little water added to the pot, I knew that these broths would be more braiselike than brothlike. But because more traditional methods yielded bland broths, I decided to start with the flavor I was looking for and add water from there.

After an hour and a half of simmering, each of the broths was done, most tasting unmistakably beefy. Upon a blind tasting of each, I chose shank as my favorite, followed by the marrow-bone-enhanced brisket and chuck. Not only was the broth rich, beefy and full of body, the shank meat was soft and gelatinous, perfect for shredding and adding to a pot of soup. Because it appeared that the broth was going to require a generous amount of meat, brisket's high price ($3.99 per pound compared to $1.99 for both the shanks and chuck) knocked it out of the running.

I had hoped that bone-in cuts like oxtails and short ribs would score better. Surprisingly, the oxtail and neck broths were at once gamy and weak. Also, separating the cooked oxtail meat from its bone for soup was fairly difficult. As I continued testing, it became clear that browning the meat well was the key to great flavor. Because of their rough, bony texture, oxtails were difficult to brown thoroughly and evenly, contributing to their unimpressive showing. The short-rib broth was fatty and less flavorful than chuck and shank. To confirm that its weak flavor was not from lack of browning, I made a second

short-rib broth, which was equally as weak as the first pot. The broth made from round was weak as well.

Though not yet perfect, this broth was on its way to fulfilling my requirements. First, it didn't necessitate a trip to the butcher. It could be made from common supermarket cuts like shank, chuck and marrow bones. Second, it didn't take all day. The broth was done in about two and a half hours and was full-flavored as soon as the meat was tender. Unlike traditional broths, which require a roasting pan, stockpot, oven and stove-top burner, this one could be done in one pot on the stovetop. Finally, this broth didn't require a cornucopia of vegetables to make it taste good. The more vegetables, the weaker the beef flavor At this point, my recipe called for one lone onion.

What I sacrificed in vegetables, however, I was apparently going to have to compensate for in meat. The 2 pounds of meat yielded only 1 quart of broth. But now that I had a flavor I liked, I decided to see if I could achieve an equally beefy broth with less meat.

The More Beef, the More Flavor

In order to stretch the meat a bit further, I increased the current ratio of 2 pounds meat and 1 pound bones by half (to 3 pounds and 1½ pounds respectively) and *doubled* the water from 1 to 2 quarts to yield enough broth for a small pot of soup. Unfortunately, the extra water diluted the broth, and though it was better than many versions, I missed the strong beef flavor of the original formula. To intensify flavor, I tried adding 1 pound of ground beef to the 3 pounds of meat, thinking I would throw away the spent meat during straining. Ground beef only fattened up the broth, and its distinctive hamburger flavor muddied the waters. Also, fried ground beef does not brown well, and this burger-enhanced broth further confirmed for me that browning not only deepened the color, but beefed up flavor as well.

I went back to the original proportions, doubling both the meat and bones as well as the water. Not surprisingly, the broth was deeply colored, richly flavored and full-bodied. Though the broth requires more meat than is necessary for the soup, the leftover beef is delicious, good for sandwiches and cold salads.

Livening the Broth

I had followed the method for making chicken broth without giving it much thought—browning, then sweating a generous portion of meat and bones, adding water just to cover and simmering for a relatively short time. I knew my ratio of meat to water was right, but I questioned whether sweating the meat for 20 minutes before adding the water was really a necessary step. Side-by-side tests proved that sweating the meat does result in a richer-flavored broth. Moreover, the "sweated" meat and bones release less foamy scum, thus eliminating the need for frequent skimming.

At this point, the richly flavored broth needed enlivening. Some broth recipes call for a splash of vinegar, others tomato. Although I like tomatoes in many soups, they didn't do much for my broth. And although vinegar was an improvement, red wine makes the broth even better. I ultimately fortified the broth with a modest ½ cup of red wine, adding it to the kettle after browning the meat.

Dozens of tests have convinced me that it takes a generous amount of browned beef and a few small bones to make a good beef broth. Whereas a 3-pound chicken makes a good broth, the same amount of beef yields a watery potion. To make beef soup right, don't skimp on the meat.

Beef Broth in Just One Hour

To see if the pressure cooker could deliver as full-flavored a beef broth in less time, I put the stovetop broth to the test. Following the recipe for Rich Beef Broth for Soup (page 38), I browned beef, bones and an onion in a pressure cooker, skipping the 20-minute "sweating" step to keep the cooking time as short as possible. Once the meat was browned and the kettle deglazed, I added water, but only 1½ quarts rather than the 2 quarts called for in the recipe because the pressure-cooker instructions warned not to fill the kettle more than two-thirds full. After the cooker was brought to pressure, I cooked the broth for 45 minutes, reduced pressure and opened the lid.

The cooked beef chunks were meltingly tender and delicious. And although the pressure-cooker broth tasted of bones and was noticeably less flavorful than the stovetop broth, it was far superior to any commercial brand.

Since the pressure-cooker broth was made with less water, I thought I might be able to dilute it after cooking. Upon tasting it, however, I decided it was not strong enough to stand dilution. Despite minor drawbacks, a good beef broth can be made in the pressure cooker in record time, one and a half to two hours faster than the stovetop method.

Rich Beef Broth for Soup

MAKES SCANT 2 QUARTS

IF YOU PREFER a slightly less rich broth, add a little more water to taste after the broth is fully cooked and skimmed.

2 tablespoons vegetable oil
6 pounds beef shank, meat cut from bone
in large chunks or 4 pounds chuck
and 2 pounds small marrow bones
1 large onion, halved
½ cup dry red wine
½ teaspoon salt

1. Heat 1 tablespoon oil in a large soup kettle over medium-high heat; brown meat, bones and onion halves on all sides in batches, making sure not to overcrowd pan and removing them as soon as they are browned, adding additional oil when necessary. Add red wine to kettle; cook until reduced to a syrup, 1 to 2 minutes. Return browned bones, meat and onion to kettle. Reduce heat to low, then cover and sweat meat and onions until they have released about ¾ cup dark, intensely flavored liquid, about 20 minutes. Increase heat to medium-high, add 2 quarts water and salt. Bring to a simmer, reduce heat to very low, partially cover and barely simmer until meat is tender, 1½ to 2 hours.

2. Strain broth, discard bones and onions and set meat aside, reserving half the meat for another use. (At this point broth and meat can be cooled to room temperature and covered and refrigerated for up to 3 days. Congealed fat from refrigerated broth can be lifted off in sheets and discarded.) Let broth stand until fat rises to the top; skim and discard fat. When meat is cool enough to handle, shred into bite-size pieces. Continue with one of the following soup recipes.

Beef Noodle Soup

SERVES 6

ONCE THE BROTH IS MADE, this soup can be on the table in less than a half hour. I often make the broth and shred the meat ahead of time.

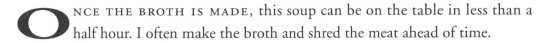

- 1 tablespoon vegetable oil
- 1 medium onion, cut into medium dice
- 2 medium carrots, cut into medium dice
- 1 celery stalk, cut into medium dice
- ½ teaspoon dried thyme leaves or 1½ teaspoons minced fresh thyme
- ½ cup canned tomatoes, cut into medium dice
  Rich Beef Broth for Soup, strained and skimmed of fat, meat shredded into bite-size pieces (page 38)
- 2 cups egg noodles
- ¼ cup minced fresh parsley leaves
  Salt
  Ground black pepper

1. Heat oil over medium-high heat in a Dutch oven or soup kettle. Add onion, carrots and celery, and sauté until softened, about 5 minutes. Add thyme and tomatoes, then beef broth and meat; bring to a simmer. Reduce heat to low, and simmer until vegetables are no longer crunchy and flavors have blended, about 15 minutes.

2. Add noodles and simmer until fully cooked, about 5 minutes longer. Stir in parsley and adjust seasonings, adding salt and pepper to taste, and serve.

Beef Barley Soup
with Mushrooms and Thyme

SERVES 6

WHITE RICE can be substituted for the barley. Just reduce the simmering time from 45 to 20 minutes.

- 2 tablespoons vegetable oil
- 1 medium onion, cut into medium dice
- 2 medium carrots, cut into medium dice
- 12 ounces domestic or wild mushrooms, stems removed, caps wiped clean and thinly sliced
- ½ teaspoon dried thyme leaves or 1½ teaspoons minced fresh thyme
- ½ cup canned tomatoes, cut into medium dice
  Rich Beef Broth for Soup, strained and skimmed of fat, meat shredded into bite-size pieces (page 38)
- ½ cup pearl barley
- ¼ cup minced fresh parsley leaves
  Salt
  Ground black pepper

1. Heat oil over medium-high heat in a Dutch oven or soup kettle. Add onion and carrots, and sauté until almost softened, 3 to 4 minutes. Add mushrooms, and sauté until softened and liquid almost evaporates, 4 to 5 minutes longer.

2. Add thyme and tomatoes, then beef broth, meat and barley, and bring to a simmer. Reduce heat to low, and continue to simmer until barley is just tender, 45 to 50 minutes. Stir in parsley and adjust seasonings, adding salt and pepper to taste, and serve.

Beef Onion Soup

SERVES 6

YOU CAN EASILY USE THIS RECIPE for French onion soup by omitting the meat. Ladle the hot liquid into heatproof bowls, float toasted French bread rounds over it and sprinkle Swiss or Gruyère cheese over the bread. Broil the soup until the cheese melts, and serve immediately.

2 tablespoons olive oil

6 medium onions, halved and thinly sliced

½ teaspoon dried thyme leaves or 1½ teaspoons
   minced fresh thyme
   Rich Beef Broth for Soup, strained and skimmed of fat,
   meat shredded into bite-size pieces (page 38)

¼ cup minced fresh parsley leaves
   Salt
   Ground black pepper

1. Heat oil over medium-high heat in a Dutch oven or soup kettle. Add onions and sauté until fully softened, about 10 minutes. Reduce heat to medium-low, and continue to cook, stirring occasionally, until onions start to caramelize, about 30 minutes longer.

2. Add thyme, beef broth and meat, and bring to a simmer. Reduce heat to low; simmer to blend flavors, about 10 minutes. Stir in parsley and adjust seasonings, adding salt and pepper to taste, and serve.

II

Everyday Classics

The Occidental Stir-Fry

CONSIDERING THAT a stir-fry is all those things the modern cook needs a weekday dish to be—attractive, healthy, economical, quick, complete—why do so few of us prepare it at home? I suspect a lot of cooks don't know how to make it properly—at least I didn't.

I was dependent on my Chinese cookbooks and more overwhelmed than not by the long ingredient lists, especially at 6:30 on a Monday night when I needed dinner on the table by 7:00. Often I'd close the book and think, I'll just sauté those chicken breasts again tonight. Or if I did get past the ingredient list, I was often disappointed with the final dish—my meat stewed or stuck instead of stir-fried, my ginger and garlic burned, my sauce too gloppy or too thin. I started feeling about stir-fries the way a lot of people feel about pizza: let's order takeout.

But unlike first-rate pizza, which requires a fair amount of advance planning and preparation, the stir-fry ideally offers a healthy, robustly flavored, balanced meal with almost no forethought. For those reasons, it is too important a dish not to know how to make for weekday meals.

I wanted to get a handle on the formula and get out from under the recipes. These were my questions: If I intended to serve stir-fry with rice as a one-dish meal, how much protein and vegetables would I need for each person? Was it necessary to marinate the meat, or would sauce stirred in at the end be a sufficient flavoring? If marinating the meat *was* necessary, what was the simplest, most effective mixture? Did I really need cornstarch, sesame oil, soy and vermouth—all common marinating ingredients—when many of those same ingredients would show up in the sauce at the end?

How much of the Asian trio—ginger, scallions and garlic—did I need per recipe, and when was it best to add them? What, if any, vegetables needed precooking before stir-frying? The question that kept nagging me most, though, was how to vary the flavor. Was it possible to develop a one-sauce-fits-all approach? Would simply varying the meats and vegetables used or stirring in some sesame oil or chili paste offer enough flavor variety to keep the dish sufficiently interesting to put it on the menu at least once a week?

My goal was not to create a stir-fry that a purist would regard as authentically Chinese but to come up with an unfailingly delicious and efficient Occidental version. I started testing with ¾ pound of meat or seafood to 1½ pounds of vegetables to serve four, with aromatics consisting of 2 tablespoons scallion, 1 tablespoon garlic and 2 teaspoons ginger. The rest of the formula needed further investigation.

Marinating a Must

Because most recipes begin with cutting and marinating the meat, that's where I started. I tested five stir-fries to determine whether marinating the meat was worth the extra time for a weeknight supper and if so, what was the simplest, best version. In Stir-Fry One, I simply salted and stir-fried chicken breast pieces. (Many Chinese recipes do use salt rather than excessive amounts of soy sauce to season a dish.) I thickened and flavored the cooked meat and vegetables with a generic chicken broth, soy sauce, sherry and cornstarch mixture stirred in at the end. In Stir-Fry Two, I marinated the chicken with soy and sherry, later adding the unabsorbed marinade to the cornstarch-chicken broth mixture and stirring it in at the end of cooking.

On the theory that a cornstarch-soy coating seals in the juices, Stir-Fry Three consisted of chicken tossed with equal parts soy and cornstarch. (The finishing sauce consisted of chicken broth, sherry, additional soy and cornstarch.) Stir-Fry Four was the same as Stir-Fry Three, except for a bit of oil I added to the cornstarch-soy marinade.

The difference between Stir-Fries One and Two was remarkable. Although the sauce in Stir-Fry One was flavorful, the chicken, which had been salted but not marinated, was hopelessly bland. The marinade in Stir-Fry Two, on the other hand, penetrated and nicely flavored the meat. The cornstarch coating on the chicken in Stir-Fry Three stuck to the pan. And because I used cornstarch in the marinade, I added less in the end, so this version lacked the nice glaze of its predecessors. The extra cornstarch on the meat also seemed to absorb a lot of the stir-fry liquid, making for a drier dish. The addition of oil to the marinade in Stir-Fry Four didn't improve the sticking problem enough to justify its presence. I considered trying the traditional Chinese technique of "velveting" the chicken by marinating it in egg white, soy and rice wine for at least a half hour and precooking it in hot oil or water before stir-frying to produce a smooth, velvety coating, but decided that was too time-consuming for a weekday get-it-on-the-table-in-under-30-minutes meal. The simple marinade of Stir-Fry Two proved that less is more.

Precooking the Vegetables

Barbara Tropp, cooking authority and author of *The Modern Art of Chinese Cooking* (William Morrow, 1982), has warned that American stoves aren't hot enough to produce an authentic stir-fry; in Chinese kitchens, the wok is set into a recessed well so it receives direct heat from the flame rather than simply perching on top of the burner. Tropp is right: the domestic electric stove just can't handle large batches of uncooked food. With too many raw vegetables to cook, my wok started chugging like the Little Engine That Could. I realized it worked best first to blanch all the harder vegetables—including asparagus and snow peas—and cook the meat in two batches. While some recipes steam the harder vegetables during the middle of the stir-fry process, I preferred not to change gears once I started to stir-fry.

It proved impossible to add the ginger, scallion and garlic at the very beginning of the cooking process. In theory, if these ingredients are added at the beginning, they flavor the entire dish, but in my experience they always turned to burned bits by the end. I got better results by adding them after I stir-fried and removed the meat, seconds before I tossed in the first batch of vegetables. As soon I heard the aromatics sizzle, in went the vegetables.

After analyzing several stir-fries, I discovered I wasn't tasting the minced scallion at all and decided to add the scallions with the vegetables instead of with the aromatics, cutting them into lengths or shredding them so they would really stand out.

I was approaching the big question: How can the flavor be varied? I had developed a generic stir-fry recipe with a simple soy, dry sherry, ginger and garlic flavoring, but I was tiring of it.

At precisely the height of my stir-fry frustration, I got my answer. The East-West cooking authority and author Hugh Carpenter shared with me eight Chinese flavoring sauces that not only provided exactly the variety I was looking for—spicy tomato, lemon, sweet and sour, black bean, oyster, coconut curry, spicy tangerine and Szechwan—but also worked perfectly with the proportions I had developed. Call it good Karma, a miracle or a gift from the universe, I had found my Way to stir-fry.

STIR-FRY SAVVY

♦ Apply all of your Western culinary common sense to matching stir-fry meats and seafoods to vegetables.

♦ Blanch harder vegetables, like carrots, snow peas, asparagus, green beans, broccoli and cauliflower. Do not blanch vegetables with a high water content, such as onions, scallions, bell peppers and mushrooms. If, however, you shred or cut a hard vegetable into julienne strips, you can skip the blanching step.

♦ Thaw frozen vegetables, like green peas. Drain canned vegetables, like water chestnuts and bamboo shoots. Add them with the blanched vegetables.

♦ If you are using more than one kind of raw vegetable, add the one that takes the longest to cook first. Stagger vegetables with similar cooking times by starting some a little ahead. Don't cook more than ¾ pound vegetables at a time. If possible, use a combination of raw and cooked vegetables.

♦ Cut meats and vegetables uniformly. The stir-fry will cook more evenly, and the finished dish will have more eye appeal.

♦ You can flavor stir-fries with a few ounces of cashews and peanuts. Add them right after removing the second batch of meat and just before adding the aromatics. Leave them in the wok for the remainder of the cooking.

♦ To firm up steak or chicken breasts and make them easier to cut, many recipes suggest freezing the meat for an hour or two. If your meat is already frozen, transfer it from the freezer to the refrigerator in the morning. By evening the steak or chicken should be that perfect not-quite-thawed texture for slicing, cubing, dicing or cutting into julienne strips.

♦ Add the sauce to your stir-fry before the cornstarch mixture, so that the sauce is absorbed into the meat and vegetables.

DESIGNER SAUCES

THE FOLLOWING SAUCES from chef and cookbook author Hugh Carpenter make for an almost infinite number of stir-fry combinations. You can find all of the ingredients in most supermarkets.

Mix sauce ingredients in a small bowl. Set aside until ready to stir-fry.

TOMATO FIREWORKS SAUCE

2 tablespoons dry sherry, 3 tablespoons tomato sauce, 1 tablespoon oyster sauce, 1 tablespoon soy sauce, ½ teaspoon sugar and 1 teaspoon sesame oil.

LEMON SAUCE

¼ cup lemon juice, 3 tablespoons sugar, 2 tablespoons chicken broth, 1 tablespoon soy sauce, ¼ teaspoon salt and 2 teaspoons lemon zest.

SWEET AND SOUR SAUCE

¼ cup red wine vinegar, ¼ cup sugar, 2 tablespoons tomato sauce, 2 tablespoons pineapple juice and ¼ teaspoon salt.

BLACK BEAN SAUCE

3 tablespoons dry sherry, 2 tablespoons chicken broth, 1 tablespoon soy sauce, ½ teaspoon sugar, 1 tablespoon sesame oil and ¼ teaspoon ground black pepper.

Add 1 tablespoon salted black beans, rinsed and chopped, to the ginger and garlic in step 5 on page 51.

OYSTER FLAVORED SAUCE

2 tablespoons oyster sauce, 3 tablespoons dry sherry, 1 tablespoon sesame oil, ½ teaspoon sugar and ¼ teaspoon ground black pepper.

COCONUT CURRY SAUCE

2 tablespoons chicken broth, 2 tablespoons dry sherry, 1 tablespoon soy sauce, 1 tablespoon curry powder, ½ teaspoon sugar, ½ teaspoon salt and ½ cup unsweetened coconut milk (not coconut cream).

SPICY TANGERINE SAUCE

1 tablespoon soy sauce, 1 teaspoon black sweet soy sauce, 3 tablespoons dry sherry, 1 teaspoon red wine vinegar, ½ teaspoon roasted and ground Szechwan peppercorns, 1 tablespoon sesame oil, ¼ teaspoon sugar and ¼ teaspoon salt.

Add 1 tablespoon *each* minced fresh hot chilies and tangerine peel to the ginger and garlic in step 5 on page 51.

SZECHWAN CHILI SAUCE
1 tablespoon soy sauce, 1 tablespoon sesame oil, 3 tablespoons dry sherry, 1 tablespoon chili paste or sauce, 2 teaspoons black sweet soy sauce, ¼ teaspoon toasted and ground Szechwan peppercorns, ¼ teaspoon sugar and ¼ teaspoon salt.

PREPARING VEGETABLES FOR STIR-FRYING

HARD VEGETABLES
Precook:

asparagus
broccoflower
broccoli
broccoli rabe
carrots
cauliflower
green beans
hard squash, such as
    butternut and acorn
potatoes
snow peas
sugar snap peas
turnips (yellow and white)

SOFT VEGETABLES
Don't Precook:

bell peppers (red, green,
    yellow, orange and purple)
bok choy
cabbage (red and green)
celery
fennel
fresh mushrooms
leeks
onions
yellow squash
zucchini

Simple Stir-Fry

SERVES 4

ONCE YOU'VE COOKED this recipe a couple of times, you'll have the formula memorized. After that, you'll need to refer only to the eight Chinese sauce recipes to prepare a meal. Unless you're a stir-fry veteran, glance at "Stir-Fry Savvy" (page 47) before you heat up your wok. You can halve this recipe easily; in fact, it's even easier that way, as it does not involve cooking in batches. The typical wok holds up to 3 quarts water, which will comfortably cook 1 pound of vegetables. If you are blanching all the vegetables, you may want to use a large pot.

¾ pound meat, seafood or poultry, cubed, diced,
   thinly sliced or cut into julienne strips
1 tablespoon soy sauce
1 tablespoon dry sherry
   Salt
1½ pounds vegetables, cut to match size of
   selected meat or seafood (see page 49)
   Designer Sauce of your choice (see page 48)
3 tablespoons peanut or vegetable oil
1 tablespoon minced garlic
2 teaspoons minced ginger
1 tablespoon cornstarch, mixed with 2 tablespoons
   water or chicken broth

Steamed Rice (page 58)

1. Toss meat, poultry or seafood with soy sauce and sherry in a medium bowl; set aside.

2. Meanwhile, heat enough water in a wok or a large skillet (11 to 12 inches) to blanch hard vegetables. Add ¾ teaspoon salt for each quart of water, then hard vegetables. Simmer until vegetables brighten in color and soften slightly. Time will vary based on type and cut of vegetables. Drain under cold running water; set aside. Wipe wok or skillet dry.

3. Prepare Designer Sauce.

4. Heat wok or large skillet until it just starts to smoke. If using wok, drizzle 1 tablespoon oil around lower circumference of pan so that it lightly coats sides. If using skillet, simply swirl oil to coat pan bottom. Scatter half of meat, poultry or seafood around bottom and, if using wok, up sides of pan; stir-fry until seared and just cooked through. Spoon into a serving dish. Add 1 tablespoon oil and repeat with remaining batch; transfer second batch to serving dish.

5. Drizzle in remaining 1 tablespoon oil; add garlic and ginger and almost immediately add raw soft vegetables. Stir-fry until vegetables are just tender-crisp. Add cooked vegetables and stir-fry until all vegetables are sizzling hot. Return cooked meat, poultry or seafood to pan. Stir in Designer Sauce; stir-fry to coat all ingredients. Stir cornstarch mixture and add to wok or skillet; stir-fry until juices become saucy and glossy. If juices look too thick, stir in a tablespoon or so water or chicken broth. Serve immediately with Steamed Rice.

Stir-Fried Lemon Chicken with Snow Peas and Mushrooms

SERVES 4

USING PRESLICED MUSHROOMS saves preparation time in this recipe.

¾ pound boneless, skinless chicken breast,
cut crosswise into ¼-inch strips

1 tablespoon soy sauce

1 tablespoon dry sherry
Salt

½ pound snow peas, stems removed
Lemon Sauce (page 48)

3 tablespoons peanut or vegetable oil

1 tablespoon minced garlic

2 teaspoons minced ginger

1 medium-large onion, halved from root to stem end;
each half quartered

1 package (8 ounces) sliced white mushrooms

1 tablespoon cornstarch, mixed with 2 tablespoons
water or chicken broth

Steamed Rice (page 58)

1. Toss chicken pieces with soy sauce and sherry in a small bowl; set aside.

2. Meanwhile, bring 1 quart water to a boil over high heat in a wok, if using, or in a large saucepan, if you plan to use a skillet. When water comes to a boil, add ¾ teaspoon salt and snow peas, return to a boil and simmer until bright green but crunchy, 2 to 3 minutes. Drain and rinse under cold running water to stop the cooking process; set aside.

3. Prepare Lemon Sauce.

4. Heat wok or large skillet over high heat until it just starts to smoke. Add 1 tablespoon oil, then half of chicken; stir-fry until seared and just cooked through. Spoon cooked chicken into a serving dish, add 1 tablespoon oil to cooking vessel and repeat with remaining chicken, transferring second batch to serving dish.

5. Add remaining 1 tablespoon oil, garlic, ginger and onion and stir-fry until crisp, but starting to soften, about 30 seconds. Add mushrooms and stir-fry until they lose their raw color, about 30 seconds more. Add snow peas and stir-fry until all vegetables are tender-crisp and hot, about 1 minute.

6. Return chicken to cooking vessel, then add Lemon Sauce and stir-fry to coat. Add cornstarch mixture and stir-fry until juices are saucy and glossy. If too thick, stir in 1 tablespoon water or broth. Serve immediately with Steamed Rice.

Beef and Broccoli
with Szechwan Chili Sauce

SERVES 4

FLANK STEAK is an obvious choice for this stir-fry, but a nice piece of sirloin steak would be equally good. If using sirloin, cut the meat against the grain as you would for flank steak, but not at an angle.

¾ pound flank steak, sliced against the grain on a slight angle
  ¼ inch thick, then cut into 1½-inch lengths

1 tablespoon soy sauce

1 tablespoon dry sherry
  Salt

1 pound broccoli florets, trimmed and
  cut into bite-size florets
  Szechwan Chili Sauce (page 49)

3 tablespoons peanut or vegetable oil

1 tablespoon minced garlic

2 teaspoons minced ginger

1 medium onion, halved from root to stem end,
  each half quartered

1 can (8 ounces) water chestnuts, drained

1 tablespoon cornstarch, mixed with 2 tablespoons
  water or chicken broth

Steamed Rice (page 58)

1. Toss beef with soy and sherry in a small bowl; set aside.

2. Meanwhile, bring 1 quart water to a boil over high heat in a wok, if using, or in a large saucepan, if you plan to use a skillet. When water boils, add ¾ teaspoon salt and broccoli, return to a boil and boil until bright green, but still crunchy, 2 to 3 minutes. Drain and rinse under cold running water to stop cooking process; set aside.

3. Prepare Szechwan Chili Sauce.

4. Heat wok or large skillet over high heat until it just starts to smoke. Add 1 tablespoon oil, then half of beef, and stir-fry until meat is seared and just cooked through. Spoon cooked meat into a serving dish, add 1 tablespoon oil to cooking vessel and repeat with remaining beef, transferring second batch to serving dish.

5. Add remaining 1 tablespoon oil, garlic, ginger and onion and stir-fry until crisp, but starting to soften, about 30 seconds. Add water chestnuts and stir-fry for about 30 seconds more. Add broccoli and stir-fry until tender-crisp and hot, about 1 minute.

6. Return beef to cooking vessel, then add Szechwan Chili Sauce and stir-fry to coat. Add cornstarch mixture and stir-fry until juices are saucy and glossy. If too thick, stir in 1 tablespoon water or broth. Serve immediately with Steamed Rice.

Sweet and Sour Pork
with Peppers and Pineapple

SERVES 4

PEELED SHRIMP or boneless, skinless chicken breast, cut into bite-size pieces, can stand in for the pork in this recipe.

¾ pound pork tenderloin, cut crosswise into
  ¼-inch-thick slices
1 tablespoon soy sauce
1 tablespoon dry sherry
  Sweet and Sour Sauce (page 48)
3 tablespoons peanut or vegetable oil
1 tablespoon minced garlic
2 teaspoons minced ginger
4 scallions, trimmed and cut into 1-inch lengths
2 medium bell peppers, preferably 1 yellow and 1 red,
  cut into large dice
½ small pineapple, peeled, cored and cut into large dice
1 tablespoon cornstarch, mixed with 2 tablespoons
  water or chicken broth

Steamed Rice (page 58)

1. Toss pork with soy sauce and sherry in a small bowl; set aside.

2. Prepare Sweet and Sour Sauce.

3. Heat a wok or large skillet over high heat until it just starts to smoke. Add 1 tablespoon oil, then half of pork, and stir-fry until meat is seared and just cooked through. Spoon cooked meat into a serving dish, add 1 tablespoon oil to cooking vessel and repeat with remaining pork, transferring second batch to serving dish.

4. Add remaining 1 tablespoon oil, garlic, ginger and scallions and stir-fry until crisp but starting to soften, about 30 seconds. Add peppers and stir-fry until crunchy but starting to soften, about 1 minute more. Add pineapple and stir-fry until vegetables are tender-crisp and hot, about 1 minute.

5. Return pork to cooking vessel, then add Sweet and Sour Sauce and stir-fry to coat. Add cornstarch mixture and stir-fry until juices are saucy and glossy. If too thick, stir in 1 tablespoon water or broth. Serve immediately with Steamed Rice.

THE RIGHT RICE FOR STIR-FRY

EVEN THOUGH MY STIR-FRY was clearly Occidental, I wondered whether the accompanying rice should be cooked American-style, by boiling the water, adding the rice, covering and cooking. Or was the Asian method for steaming rice—rinsing it, simmering it in water, then letting it stand—more suited for stir-fries? A side-by-side tasting of the two styles of rice confirmed that the steaming method produced a cleaner-flavored, stickier, fluffy but not gummy rice, perfect for stir-fries.

According to Chris O'Brien of the Rice Council, many Americans don't rinse their rice because the bulk of it is "enriched," meaning that the vitamins lost during milling have been added back onto the surface of the grain. Every package of enriched rice displays the same warning, "To retain vitamins, do not rinse before or drain after cooking." When asked how much vitamin loss one could expect from rinsing rice, O'Brien revealed that a mere 5 percent of the recommended daily allowance of vitamin D, riboflavin and calcium is washed away. So don't worry about washing an army of vitamins down the drain.

Steamed Rice

Serves 4 with a stir-fry

BEFORE YOU START your stir-fry, get your rice going. It can stand for up to 20 minutes after its 25-minute preparation. You can halve this recipe, but *don't* halve the water: for 1 cup long-grain rice, use 1¾ cups water. For short- and medium-grain, you'll need 1½ cups water for 1 cup rice. Most any long-, short- or medium-grain rice can be made with this cooking method. Parboiled rice (the most common brand is Uncle Ben's) is the exception. To ensure that the rice grains cook up separately, this rice has undergone a steam-pressure process that causes the grains to harden and its starch to gelatinize. More suited to pilaf, parboiled rice is not what you want if you're looking for a clump of rice to pick up with a pair of chopsticks.

2 cups long-, medium- or short-grain rice

1. Measure rice into a 2-quart saucepan and add cold water to cover. Stir with your hand until water becomes cloudy. Drain rice in a large strainer and return to pan. Repeat rinsing process until water is clear when rice is stirred, about 5 times.

2. Return rice to pan; add 3 cups water if using long-grain rice and 2½ cups water for short- or medium-grain rice. Bring to a boil, then cover and reduce heat to low. Simmer for 15 minutes, remove from heat and let stand for at least 10 and up to 30 minutes longer. Fluff with a fork and serve.

Macaroni and Cheese: The Real MacCoy

M Y WHOLE FAMILY is happy when I make macaroni and cheese for dinner. It's the one dish that everybody—both kids and adults—love. Unfortunately the boxed version, complete with orange cheese powder, is what's most familiar to people.

As I looked over recipes for homemade macaroni and cheese, I determined that there were two distinct styles of preparation. The more common variety is béchamel-based, where macaroni is blanketed with a cheese-flavored white sauce, usually topped with crumbs and baked. The other variety, the kind my mother always made, is custard-based. In this version, a mixture of egg and milk is poured over layers of grated cheese and noodles. As the dish bakes, the egg, milk and cheese set into a custard. This recipe is also topped with bread crumbs and baked, although my mom sprinkled crushed saltine crackers over hers.

Although I was in the béchamel-style camp, I couldn't remember the last time I had made a truly exceptional macaroni and cheese. After a few initial tests, I understood why. Most recipes seemed tired, leaden and uninspired. Others attempted to perk up the dish with silly additions like canned green chilies or black olives. And of course, there were the recipes that tried to lighten it. No one seemed to really appreciate the dish.

Temporarily falling under the influence of modern-day recipe authors, I began to wonder if even *I* loved it as much as I thought I had. Then I came across John Thorne's macaroni and cheese chapter in *Simple Cooking* (Penguin, 1989). "As it happens," he begins, "I'm very fond of macaroni and cheese, and keep a special spot in my heart for cooks who genuinely love it: they are not that many." After reading his four-page essay, I knew I was on the trail of a great recipe.

No Comparison

Thorne's recipe starts with macaroni cooked just shy of al dente. The hot, drained macaroni is tossed with butter in a heatproof pan or bowl. Evaporated milk, hot red pepper sauce, dry mustard, eggs and a large quantity of cheese are stirred into the noodles. The macaroni and cheese is baked for 20 minutes, with cheese and milk additions and a thorough stir every 5 minutes. These frequent stirrings allow the eggs to thicken without setting, resulting in an incredibly smooth sauce. During cooking, the sauce settles into the tubular openings of macaroni, offering a burst of cheese with each bite. I was delighted to get the dish right so early on in the process. This macaroni and cheese was the real thing, all others mere shadows. For once, someone else had done my homework for me.

Just to confirm my findings, I baked the two macaroni and cheese versions I described earlier. Neither the cheese-flavored béchamel sauce nor the custard compared to Thorne's dish. The béchamel-based version was grainy and tasted exactly as Thorne predicted—not like macaroni and cheese but rather like "macaroni with cheese sauce." Whereas Thorne's macaroni and cheese sauce was light and silky, the béchamel dish was heavy.

Because the custard-based macaroni and cheese was simply an easier version of Thorne's recipe, I thought it might work as an alternative to stirring, but a side-by-side tasting proved the two macaroni and cheeses very different. Compared to the luxuriously smooth cheese sauce of the stirred version, the baked egg, milk and cheese base formed a dry custard that set around the noodles.

Putting It to the Test

Having ruled out the competition, I moved forward to study Thorne's recipe a little more closely. I wondered if the dish really required evaporated milk. Was this an idiosyncrasy of the late thirties when the recipe was first published? Wouldn't regular milk or half-and-half work equally well? What other cheeses besides cheddar would suit this dish?

Though the recipe was virtually perfect, I developed a few refinements. First, I found that at the end of 20 minutes, the dish was hot, but hardly piping. By the time a person had consumed a portion, the cheese sauce had cooled slightly and set. I also missed the contrasting textures of crunchy bread crumbs and soft noodles and sauce offered by the baked versions. Thorne's advice to sprinkle the macaroni and cheese with crumbled common crackers was one possibility, but I was looking for something a little more finished. And although I liked the rich, full cheese flavor Thorne achieves with a full pound of cheddar, I found myself full after only a few bites. I wanted to find out if the dish would be just as good with a little less cheese.

After testing the recipe with whole and low-fat milk as well as with half-and-half, I realized that evaporated milk was not an unconsidered holdover. All the macaroni and cheeses made with fresh milk curdled a bit, resulting in a chalky, grainy texture. The one made with evaporated milk was always smooth, undoubtedly because the evaporation and sterilization process stabilizes the milk.

After making the dish with Vermont, New York and Wisconsin cheddars, I preferred the less sharp Wisconsin variety. Because the recipe calls for such a large quantity, a slightly milder cheese is preferable. Testing other varieties of cheese confirmed this point. Macaroni and cheese made with Gruyère was so strong I couldn't eat it, while milder Monterey Jack was a wonderful alternative to cheddar. To my surprise, highly processed cheeses like American performed quite well in this dish. As with the evaporated milk, more processing produces a more stable cheese and hence a creamier dish. For flavor, use cheddar; for texture, buy American.

A Gentle Warming

To remedy the dish's lukewarm temperature, I tried two solutions, both of which worked. To avoid pouring the hot macaroni into a cold dish, I placed my pan in the preheated oven. By the time the noodles were ready to drain, the pan emerged from the oven pot holder-hot.

Warming the milk a bit before mixing it with the pasta also gave the dish a warm head start. (Don't, however, try to make this dish hotter by leaving it in the oven for a longer time: if you exceed the suggested 20 minutes, you run the risk of curdling the eggs, and the dish will start to develop a grainy texture.)

As Thorne suggested, crisp common crackers sprinkled over the macaroni and cheese offer a much-needed foil to the rich, unctuous sauce. As a further refinement, I toasted buttered bread crumbs alongside the heating casserole and put them on top instead.

After I shared this recipe with my friend and cooking colleague Stephen Schmidt, he reported that if you use a heavy-bottomed pot and cook over medium low heat, you can heat the macaroni and cheese on top of the stove rather than in the oven to save even more time. If you can live without the toasted bread crumbs, then, that macaroni and cheese can be made in the same amount of time it takes to make the boxed version.

For once, the real dish is almost as simple as the convenience product. Just a few dollars more buys you the difference between an institutional experience and the real *Mac*Coy.

The Best Macaroni and Cheese

Serves 4 as a main course, 6 to 8 as a side dish

If you're in a hurry or prefer to sprinkle the dish with crumbled common crackers (saltines aren't bad, either), skip the bread crumb step or simply follow instructions for the stovetop version that follows. You can make fresh bread crumbs by grating bread on the large holes of a box grater, but the easiest method, by far, is processing it to coarse crumbs in a food processor fitted with the steel blade.

Toasted Bread Crumbs

1	cup fresh bread crumbs from French or Italian bread
	Pinch salt
1½	tablespoons melted butter

Macaroni and Cheese

	Salt
½	pound elbow macaroni
4	tablespoons butter
2	large eggs
1	can (12 ounces) evaporated milk, heated to warm
¼	teaspoon hot red pepper sauce
	Ground black pepper
1	teaspoon dry mustard, dissolved in 1 teaspoon water
10-12	ounces (3 cups) mild cheddar, American or Monterey Jack cheese

1. Heat oven to 350°F and set a 1½-quart heatproof dish, such as a soufflé pan, in the oven to warm.

2. Bread Crumbs: Mix bread crumb ingredients together in a small baking pan; set aside.

3. Macaroni: Bring 2 quarts water to a boil in a large soup kettle. Add 1½ teaspoons salt and macaroni; cook until almost tender, but still a little firm to the bite. Drain and transfer to preheated dish and stir in butter to melt.

4. Meanwhile, mix eggs, *1 cup* evaporated milk, pepper sauce, ½ teaspoon salt (or ¼ teaspoon if using highly processed cheese like American or even Velveeta), ¼ teaspoon pepper and mustard mixture in a small bowl.

5. Pour egg mixture over noodles along with three-fourths of cheese; stir until thoroughly combined and cheese starts to melt.

6. Place bread crumbs in oven to toast until golden brown, 10 to 15 minutes. Remove from oven and set aside. Place pan of macaroni and cheese in oven too and bake for 5 minutes. Remove pan from oven; thoroughly stir macaroni mixture, adding a little remaining milk and cheese. Return to oven and cook 5 minutes longer. Remove macaroni pan from oven and stir thoroughly so that macaroni and cheese cooks evenly, adding additional cheese and milk if mixture does not look moist and creamy. Return to oven for a total of 20 minutes, removing pan from oven once more to stir in remaining milk and cheese. Serve immediately, sprinkled with bread crumbs.

◆ Stovetop Macaroni and Cheese

SERVES 4 AS A MAIN COURSE, 6 TO 8 AS A SIDE DISH

To make this macaroni and cheese on the stovetop, you need a heavy-bottomed Dutch oven or large saucepan. Otherwise the eggs may curdle and make the cheese sauce slightly grainy.

1. Follow steps 3 and 4 of the Best Macaroni and Cheese (page 62), but when macaroni is cooked, put it in a pot (see above), not a baking dish.

2. Over medium heat, add egg mixture and three-fourths of cheese, stirring constantly until cheese starts to melt. Gradually stir in remaining milk and cheese; continue to stir constantly until sauce thickens and mixture is hot and creamy, about 5 minutes. Serve immediately.

♦ Baked Macaroni and Cheese

SERVES 4 AS A MAIN COURSE, 6 TO 8 AS A SIDE DISH

THIS DISH IS THE CASSEROLE VERSION of macaroni and cheese, portable and perfect for family meals and potluck suppers. You can make it up to eight hours ahead, but you must reheat it over very low heat, adding extra milk if necessary, before pouring it into the baking dish.

1. Heat 4 tablespoons butter in a large skillet over medium heat until foam subsides. Add 2 cups lightly packed soft fresh bread crumbs; cook, tossing to coat with butter, until crumbs just begin to color. Season to taste with salt; set aside.

2. Adjust oven rack 6 inches from heating element; preheat broiler. Follow steps 3 and 4 of recipe for the Best Macaroni and Cheese (page 62), but when macaroni is cooked, put it in a heavy-bottomed Dutch oven or large saucepan, not a baking dish.

3. Over medium heat, add egg mixture and three-fourths of cheese, stirring constantly until cheese starts to melt. Gradually stir in remaining milk and cheese; continue to stir constantly until sauce thickens and mixture is hot and creamy, about 5 minutes.

4. Pour cooked macaroni and cheese into a 9-inch heatproof pan (or another pan of similar surface area). Spread crumbs evenly over top. Broil until crumbs turn deep brown, 1 to 2 minutes. Let macaroni and cheese stand to set a bit, about 5 minutes. Serve.

Fine-tuning Homemade Pizza and Calzones

FOR THOSE WHO DON'T like to cook, it's hard to present a convincing case for home-made pizza. You really have to *enjoy* the process—punching down the swelled dough, then stretching the unruly mass into a thin round, sliding the dressed dough from peel to hot tiles and watching it turn from soft white to crisp dark brown. But there is a significant reward for these efforts: properly made, homemade pizza is superb.

Since lining my oven with quarry tiles for breadmaking a few years back, I started making pizza fairly frequently. But with each session came another question. Can the same dough be used for all different styles of pizza? Can it bake up cracker-crisp, or thick and chewy, depending on how thick or thin it is rolled? Can the same dough be used to make calzones, the popular pizza turnovers? I suspected the answer to all these questions was yes, because most restaurants these days offer an array of pizza thicknesses.

In addition to my questions about dough texture, I had never developed a foolproof method for getting dough from ball to disk, particularly a thin disk. Depending on the stretching method I followed, my dough was either full of holes or incredibly misshapen or had grown tough and leathery before I got it to the right thickness. Of course, I could have used a rolling pin, but rolled dough was a little too perfect for me—it felt like cheating.

I had come to like my wooden peel and quarry tiles. I already knew they produced a darker, thicker, crisper crust than that of dough pressed into a pan. Would a pizza stone be a suitable substitute? Would a pizza screen—a *perforated* pizza pan—work just as well?

I was curious about the sauce and the cheese. When fresh tomatoes weren't in season, I topped my pizzas with a quick-cooked sauce made from canned tomatoes, garlic and oil. But I never forgot an interview with a pizza maker who described how he skipped sauce making altogether, stirring herbs and olive oil into uncooked canned tomatoes and counting on oven time alone to make the sauce. If this method worked, it would obviate one step in the process. And when was it best to sprinkle on the cheese—at the beginning, with everything else, or toward the end of baking?

Bread Flour Makes Good Dough

Carlo Middione (*The Food of Southern Italy*, William Morrow, 1987) was the only author in my research who linked bread and pizza dough. He wrote one recipe for both, instructing the cook to add oil to the dough if it was used for making pizza. Further recipe research confirmed that pizza dough is, in fact, nothing more than bread dough enriched with oil. Based on my previous bread dough experience, as well as a review of scores of pizza recipes, I developed a test recipe that used enough yeast so that rising time would be minimal, I hoped, and in quantities that could be handled by a large food processor:

1½   cups water
1   envelope active dry yeast (an easy amount—no measuring, no leftover half packets)
4   cups flour (the full amount a large food processor could handle)
1½   teaspoons table salt

2   tablespoons oil (an average amount of oil called for in pizza dough recipes, though some were oil-free)

Working from this formula, I substituted different flours and liquids, increased and decreased oil quantity and tried quick-rising and long-rising methods.

Not surprisingly, dough made from bleached all-purpose flour was disastrous in both dough and crust form. The dough was soft and difficult to stretch, threatening to tear with every pull. The resulting crust was tough, leathery and limp rather than crisp and chewy. Although unbleached all-purpose flour was an improvement over bleached, bread flour delivered the best pizza crust. I was partial enough to a cornmeal-flavored crust to make it a variation; a semolina-enriched dough resulted in a respectable but denser crust than the one made with bread flour. Neither dough baked up into an extraordinary pizza.

In working with the various doughs over the first few days of testing, I determined that, indeed, one dough could be stretched a little for a medium-thick pizza or a lot for a thin and crispy one or folded over and made into calzones. The next step was to figure out the best way to get it from a fat little ball to a thin disk.

Stretch, Don't Roll

For many cooks, sliding the pizza from peel to stone is the most difficult step in pizza making. For me, it's stretching the dough. What finally worked was a technique that my colleague Karen Tack had picked up at a cooking class a few years earlier. With this technique, the dough stretches easily because it never leaves the work surface (see figures 1-3, page 73).

The dough can be stretched to a medium thickness (see page 70 for exact dough dimensions). At this point in the process, however, I found that regardless of how much stretching and pulling I did, the dough would mischievously shrink back to its medium-thick size. To get the dough any thinner, you simply have to allow it to rest—just walk away from it. Start flattening another portion of dough, tend to a pizza you may have already popped in the oven, do anything—but leave the dough disk alone for a few minutes. Given a rest, it will easily stretch those extra few inches.

The pizzas that had been rolled with a pin rather than stretched were more uniform in size and thickness, but to my surprise, the crusts were noticeably tougher. I suspect that the rolling action presses air out of the dough, causing it to be denser and, hence, tougher.

Tile Your Oven

After baking pies in a pan, on a stone and on a pizza screen, as well as on quarry tiles, I opted for tiles. Pizzas baked on a perforated screen, let alone a solid pan, just don't crisp up and brown the way they do on stones and tiles. In the end, the quarry tiles consistently delivered pizza with darker, crisper bottoms.

Tile has it over stone for another reason: if you don't slide the pizza—especially a large one—onto the stone just right, part of the pizza hangs off the stone, and toppings fall to the oven floor. Lining an oven rack with quarry tiles allows you to bake on the entire rack. My oven, lined with tiles, is large enough to cook two medium pizzas at a time.

Given that I preferred baking pizza on tiles rather than in pans, I needed to develop a reliably consistent method of getting the dough onto the peel and into the oven. I sprinkle coarse cornmeal on the peel when making bread, so I started off using it for the pizzas as well. What worked for bread, though, didn't work for pizza. Because of the extremely large surface area of pizza, the ratio of coarse cornmeal to crust is too high, and I did not like the coarse, raw grain taste that came with every bite. I switched to a finer grind of cornmeal, but it seemed to attract the moisture from the damp dough, causing some of the pizzas to stick. (Nothing's worse than bringing a pizza to this point, then having it stick to the paddle.) Semolina, with its fine, sandy texture, turned out to be perfect for sprinkling on the peel, for it blends with the dough without absorbing its moisture.

All Dressed Up

Of all the pizzas I made, the ones topped with fresh tomatoes were everyone's favorites. But because good tomatoes are available where I live for only about three months out of the year, I found that jazzing up raw canned tomatoes with fresh herbs, garlic and oil makes a fine tomato sauce for pizza. Not just any canned tomato will do, however. Crushed tomatoes packed in puree are thick enough for an uncooked sauce.

Cheese sprinkled on at the beginning with the other toppings disappeared into the dough. But when you add it during the last few minutes of baking, the cheese remains moist and lush and you need far less.

I particularly hate limp pizza. I don't want to have to use two hands to eat it or, worse yet, have to fold it in half. Before I had quarry tiles, I thought they would solve my problem. I quickly discovered that a crisp-crusted pizza is not necessarily a sturdy one. Making sure not to overtop the pizza is the surest way to get a crisp crust to stay crisp.

For occasions when you are short on time, calzones are an easy alternative to pizza. Unlike pizzas, which must topped and baked one at a time, calzones can be assembled, placed on a cookie sheet and baked all at once. And you can easily transfer individual calzones by hand from the work area to the baking surface—another advantage over pizza.

One Size Fits All

THE PIZZA DOUGH on page 71 will make any of the following dough sizes. You need only adjust the cooking time to fit the pizza. Make sure the oven is preheated to 450°F for a minimum of a half hour. Your tiles or stone need at least that amount of time to heat up. If baked any sooner than that, your pizza crust will be thin, blond and limp.

Once the dough disk is topped, get it off the peel and into the oven as soon as possible. The longer you wait, the greater the chances of sticking. Don't hesitate when sliding topped dough from the peel. Shove it in quickly and with confidence.

Two 14-inch thin pizzas
7 to 8 minutes; add cheese and cook, 2 to 3 minutes longer

Four 11-to-12-inch thin pizzas
6 to 7 minutes; add cheese and cook 2 to 3 minutes longer

Eight 8-inch thin pizzas
4 to 5 minutes; add cheese and cook 2 to 3 minutes longer

Two 12-inch medium-thick pizzas
9 to 10 minutes; add cheese and cook 2 to 3 minutes longer

Four 8-inch medium-thick pizzas
7 to 8 minutes; add cheese and cook 2 to 3 minutes longer

Eight 6-inch medium-thick pizzas
5 to 6 minutes; add cheese and cook 2 to 3 minutes longer

Eight 8-inch calzones
20 to 25 minutes

Pizza Dough

MAKES ALMOST 2 POUNDS

Enough for two 14-inch thin pizzas, two 12-inch medium-thick pizzas,
four 11-to-12-inch thin pizzas, four 8-inch medium-thick pizzas,
eight 8-inch thin pizzas, eight 6-inch medium-thick pizzas or eight 8-inch calzones

FOR WEEKNIGHT PIZZA, when you don't have time to make the dough after work, just add less yeast and make it in the morning. By the time you come home, the dough will have slowly doubled and be ready for shaping. Or if the morning isn't an option, you can speed up the evening process by using quick-rising yeast and letting the dough rise in a warm oven.

You can make crisp-bottomed pizza even if you don't have oven tiles or a pizza stone. The baking time, however, will be longer—usually about a third to twice as long. Simply divide the dough according to pan size and stretch it right on a pizza pan or screen that you have coated with vegetable oil cooking spray. Follow the recipe, sprinkling the dough with the toppings, and adding the cheese about halfway through the baking.

1 envelope (2¼ teaspoons) active dry yeast
2 tablespoons olive oil, plus extra for brushing stretched dough
4 cups bread flour
1½ teaspoons salt
   Semolina for dusting peel

1. Measure ½ cup warm (90°F) water in a 2-cup or larger liquid measuring cup. Sprinkle in yeast, and let stand until yeast dissolves and swells, about 5 minutes. Add 1 cup cool tap water and oil to yeast mixture. Meanwhile, pulse flour and salt to combine in a large food processor fitted with a steel blade. Holding back about 1 tablespoon, pour liquid ingredients over flour; pulse to form a rough ball. If dough does not readily form a ball, stop machine, add remaining liquid and continue to pulse until ball forms. Continue to process until dough is smooth and satiny, about 30 seconds longer.

2. Turn dough onto a lightly floured work surface; knead by hand for a few seconds to form a smooth, round ball. Put dough into a medium-large bowl coated with vegetable cooking spray. Cover with plastic wrap or a damp cloth and let rise at room temperature to double in size, about 2 hours.

3. At least ½ hour before you plan to bake, adjust oven rack to low position and line with quarry tiles, or place a pizza stone on a rack. Preheat oven to 450°F.

4. Lift dough out of bowl and place on a lightly floured work surface. Using a chef's knife or a metal dough scraper, cut dough into halves, quarters or eighths, depending on number of pizzas desired (see "One Size Fits All," page 70). Cover dough balls waiting to be stretched with a damp cloth. Following illustrations on page 73, stretch dough to desired thickness.

5. Continue stretching process until dough is preferred diameter. Transfer dough to a pizza peel that has been lightly coated with either semolina or cornmeal, brush entire surface very lightly with oil, then proceed with topping.

♦ Eight-Hour Dough

1. Follow step 1 of recipe for Pizza Dough (page 71), but use only ½ teaspoon yeast.

2. In step 2, let dough stand at cool room temperature (65° to 70°F) until doubled, about 8 hours. Continue as directed.

♦ One-Hour Dough

1. Follow step 1 of recipe for Pizza Dough (page 71), substituting quick-rising yeast for regular yeast. Preheat oven to 200°F, then turn off.

2. In step 2, let dough rise in oven. (If oven feels too hot, set bowl of dough on a rack lined with a tea towel to protect it from direct heat.) Continue as directed.

STRETCHING THE DOUGH

1. Working with one piece of dough at a time, smack the dough with the palm of your hand to flatten the ball into a disk.

2. Once the dough is flattened to about ½ inch thick, use your fingertips to push the dough from the center toward the edges until the dough is about ¼ inch thick.

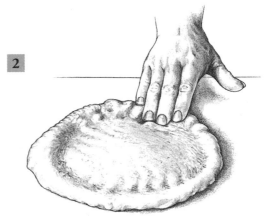

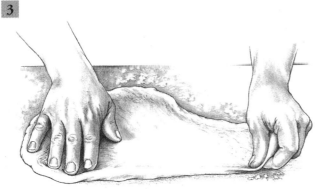

3. For medium-thick pizza, place one hand over the dough while using your other hand to pull it out, turning the dough a quarter turn after each stretch, until it is the correct diameter.

4. For thin pizza, let the stretched dough rest until relaxed, about 5 minutes. Continue the stretching process until the dough is the diameter you want (see page 70).

Quick Tomato Sauce for Pizza

MAKES 3 CUPS

IF YOU'RE USING CRUSHED TOMATOES, I recommend Muir Glen Ground Peeled Tomatoes. Unlike most other canned tomatoes that are full of skins and seeds, this brand contains chunks of tomato in a thick puree. As an alternative, Red Pack crushed tomatoes make a nice base for sauce.

2-3 tablespoons olive oil

2 large garlic cloves, minced

1 can (28 ounces) crushed tomatoes,
   or coarsely chopped tomatoes packed in puree

Salt

Ground black pepper

Mix all ingredients in a medium bowl. Let stand to blend flavors while making pizza. Season to taste with salt and pepper and spoon onto stretched pizza dough just before baking.

Caramelized Onion Pizza with Oil-Cured Olives and Parmesan Cheese

SERVES 4 TO 6 AS A MAIN COURSE, 8 AS A SUBSTANTIAL APPETIZER

THOUGH SUBSTANTIAL ENOUGH to be served as a main course, this pizza is particularly nice stretched thin, cut into small pieces and served as hors d'oeuvres.

Pizza Dough (page 71)
2 tablespoons olive oil
1 pound yellow onions, halved and thinly sliced
1 teaspoon fresh thyme leaves
Salt
Ground black pepper
1½ cups Quick Tomato Sauce (page 74)
⅓ cup oil-cured olives, pitted and quartered
6 anchovies, coarsely chopped (optional)
¼ cup grated Parmesan cheese

1. Make pizza dough as directed in steps 1 and 2.

2. At least ½ hour before you plan to bake, adjust oven rack to low position and line with quarry tiles, or place a pizza stone on a rack. Preheat oven to 450°F.

3. Heat oil over medium-high heat in a large skillet. Add onions and sauté, stirring frequently, until they are softened and somewhat caramelized, about 15 minutes. (You should have about 2 cups.) Stir in thyme and season to taste with salt and pepper.

4. Form and stretch pizza dough to preferred diameter as directed in illustrations (page 73), and top with a portion of Quick Tomato Sauce. Scatter on a portion of cooked onions. Sprinkle on a portion of olives and optional anchovies. Immediately slide dough onto heated tiles or pizza stone. Bake, following "One Size Fits All" (page 70) for cooking time, adding a portion of cheese about halfway through.

Sausage and Bell Pepper Pizza with Basil and Mozzarella

SERVES 4 TO 6 AS A MAIN COURSE, 8 AS A SUBSTANTIAL APPETIZER

IF BULK SAUSAGE is not available, buy cased sausage and remove the casing.

Pizza Dough (page 71)

¾ pound bulk mild Italian sausage, broken into bite-size pieces

About 1½ teaspoons olive oil

1 red or yellow bell pepper, halved, cored, seeded and cut into thin strips

Salt

Ground black pepper

1½ cups Quick Tomato Sauce (page 74)

¼ cup shredded fresh basil leaves

4 ounces mozzarella cheese, shredded (1 cup)

1. Make pizza dough as directed in steps 1 and 2.

2. At least ½ hour before you plan to bake, adjust oven rack to low position and line with quarry tiles, or place a pizza stone on a rack. Preheat oven to 450°F.

3. Put sausage and ¼ cup water in a medium-large skillet. Cook over medium-high heat until water evaporates and sausage cooks through and browns, about 7 minutes. Remove with a slotted spoon. Add enough oil to equal 1 tablespoon. Add pepper and sauté until softened slightly, about 5 minutes. Season to taste with salt and pepper. Remove and set aside.

4. Form and stretch pizza dough to preferred diameter as directed in illustrations (page 73), and top with a portion of Quick Tomato Sauce. Scatter shredded basil, then pieces of sausage and peppers, over sauce. Immediately slide dough onto heated quarry tiles or pizza stone. Bake, following "One Size Fits All" (page 70) for cooking time, adding a portion of cheese about halfway through.

Wild Mushroom Pizza with Sage, Fontina and Parmesan Cheese

SERVES 4 TO 6 AS A MAIN COURSE, 8 AS A SUBSTANTIAL APPETIZER

YOU CAN SUBSTITUTE an equal amount of minced fresh rosemary for the sage. If neither is available, try ½ teaspoon dried thyme leaves.

Pizza Dough (page 71)
2 large garlic cloves, minced
2 tablespoons olive oil
1 pound wild or domestic mushrooms, trimmed and thinly sliced
1 teaspoon minced fresh sage leaves
Salt
Ground black pepper
1 cup Quick Tomato Sauce (page 74)
4 ounces fontina, shredded (1 cup)
¼ cup grated Parmesan cheese

1. Make pizza dough as directed in steps 1 and 2.

2. At least ½ hour before you plan to bake, adjust oven rack to low position and line with quarry tiles, or place a pizza stone on a rack. Preheat oven to 450°F.

3. Heat garlic with oil in a large skillet. When garlic sizzles, add mushrooms and sauté until their liquid nearly evaporates, about 5 minutes. Stir in sage and season to taste with salt and pepper. Set aside.

4. Form and stretch dough to preferred diameter as directed in illustrations (page 73), and top with a portion of Quick Tomato Sauce. Scatter a portion of mushrooms over sauce. Immediately slide dough onto heated quarry tiles or pizza stone. Bake, following "One Size Fits All" (page 70) for cooking time, adding a portion of each cheese about halfway through.

Fresh Tomato Pizza
with Arugula and Prosciutto

SERVES 4 TO 6 AS A MAIN COURSE,
8 AS A SUBSTANTIAL APPETIZER

WHEN TOSSING THE ARUGULA with oil, sprinkle on a touch of balsamic vinegar, if you like.

> Pizza Dough (page 71)
> 1 pound tomatoes, cored and thinly sliced
> Salt
> Ground black pepper
> 4 teaspoons olive oil, plus 2 teaspoons for arugula
> 4 ounces prosciutto, thinly sliced (about 8 slices)
> 4 ounces mozzarella cheese, shredded (1 cup)
> 2 cups arugula, thoroughly washed and spun dry

1. Make pizza dough as directed in steps 1 and 2.

2. At least ½ hour before you plan to bake, adjust oven rack to low position and line with quarry tiles, or place a pizza stone on a rack. Preheat oven to 450°F.

3. Form and stretch pizza dough to preferred diameter as directed in illustrations (page 73). Arrange a portion of tomatoes in concentric circles over prepared dough. Season with salt and ground black pepper. Drizzle with 4 teaspoons oil. Immediately slide dough onto heated quarry tiles or pizza stone. Bake, following "One Size Fits All" (page 70) for cooking time, adding prosciutto, then cheese about halfway through. Toss arugula with remaining oil. As pizza comes out of oven, top with arugula.

Calzones

Makes 8 calzones

YOU CAN MAKE any size calzone you like. I prefer 8-inchers. Larger ones are unwieldy, smaller ones are tedious to form. Also, one 8-inch calzone satisfies the average appetite. Just about any pizza topping doubles as a calzone filling as long as it is not too wet. I spoon a couple of tablespoons of moist tomato sauce over drier ingredients, like sausage or sautéed peppers, then top with mozzarella cheese.

1. Follow steps 1 and 2 of recipe for Pizza Dough (page 71), dividing dough into 8 equal pieces.

2. Preheat oven to 450°F, with oven racks adjusted to low and upper-middle positions. Cover dough balls with a damp cloth.

3. Working with one dough ball at a time and following illustrations below, stretch dough to an 8-inch circle. Place about ½ cup of desired filling on lower half of circle, leaving a ½-inch border. Fold top half of dough over filling, still leaving a ½-inch border around edge. Turn border over and press with fingers to seal.

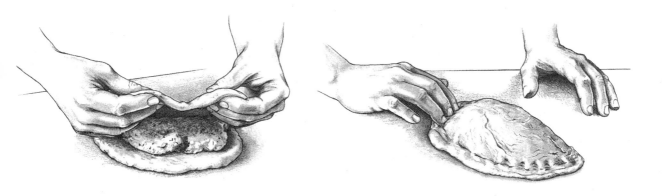

4. Transfer calzones to a large cookie sheet and brush lightly with olive oil. (Four calzones should fit on a large cookie sheet. Don't overcrowd if you are using a smaller sheet.) Put a cookie sheet on each rack and bake, switching the placement of the sheets halfway through baking, until calzones are crisp and golden brown, 20 to 25 minutes.

Chicken in No Time Flat

A FEW YEARS BACK, in the middle of my research on roasting chicken, I discovered that the best way to cook the bird was not whole at all, but flat. By butterflying the chicken—cutting out the back and flattening it—you get all the virtues of a whole bird with the speed and versatility of pieces.

This technique simplifies roasting. Because a butterflied chicken has been butchered and flattened to a virtually even thickness, its breast and legs naturally get done at the same time, while a whole bird requires turning to ensure even cooking. Unlike a whole bird, a butterflied chicken is also a breeze to carve. Once you cut down the breast with kitchen shears, all you have to do is make a few quick snips in the skin to remove the legs from each breast.

After broiling, grilling and cooking chickens on the stovetop, I came to realize that a split and flattened bird can be cooked in ways that a whole one can't. You can't broil or pan-sauté a whole trussed bird. And although you can grill-roast a whole chicken over indirect heat—building a fire on one side of the grill, placing the bird on the other side and covering it—you can't grill one over a bed of hot coals. All these cooking methods are possible with a butterflied bird.

While most recipes call for either splitting or removing the chicken's back, a few suggest splitting them down the breast. To test the advantage of this method, I roasted one of each kind. Splitting a whole chicken breast is hard enough. Trying to split one that's still attached to a whole chicken is awkward and difficult, compared to snipping out the back with a set of kitchen shears. The split-breast chicken looked unnatural when cooked, and its odd shape caused it to brown unevenly. The bird split down the back with shears is much more attractive; it stays flat during cooking and browns evenly.

Tucking the Legs

Tucking the chicken legs into the breast keeps them from bowing and warping, ensuring good presentation. I thought pounding the chicken might decrease cooking time, but it didn't seem to make a noticeable difference, though it was easier to weight a chicken that had been reduced to a uniform thickness than one that had not. Whatever tool you use to pound chicken, make sure it is smooth-sided. (A rolling pin or even a wine bottle will work.) A rough-textured mallet will puncture the skin and tear the flesh.

Seasoning the surface of the chicken with herbs and garlic is pointless because they quickly burn under high heat. But I found that butterflied chickens are easy to season *under* the skin, particularly on the leg and thighs. Including salt and pepper in the herb and garlic mixtures meant that the chicken, not just the skin, was seasoned. At first I added a bit of oil or butter to the seasoning mixtures as well, but soon realized it wasn't necessary. The garlic itself softened the mixture and made spreading easy. Once the cooking began, the fat from the skin and juice from the meat was enough to moisten and transport the flavorings.

Roasting, Pan-Sautéing, Grilling and Broiling

Roasting a butterflied chicken is the simplest of the cooking methods. Once the chicken is butchered (and rubbed with seasonings, if you like), it goes in the oven with no weighting—and very little waiting either. You can forget about it. Thirty minutes later, it's done.

In contrast, many recipes for grilling, broiling and pan-sautéing call for several turns during cooking. I wanted to reduce those to a single turn if possible,

as multiple turns are especially difficult when the bird is weighted. Pan-sautéing a chicken in the skillet with only one turn was a bit tricky at first. Early attempts produced skin that was too dark and meat near the bone that was too pink. Two things helped: first, not allowing the skillet to get too hot before dropping in the chicken (which has, after all, 30 minutes to brown); and, second, reducing the heat from medium-high to a strong medium, which allows the chicken to cook through before browning. For comparison, I tried that method two ways—one with the bird weighted, the other just covered. The weighted chicken browned more evenly and was done a few minutes sooner than the unweighted bird.

Ed Giobbi's tip of using a pot of water to weight the cooking chickens (*Pleasures of the Good Earth*, Knopf, 1991) was one of my happiest finds. I used a soup kettle with a diameter slightly smaller than that of the skillet, covered its bottom with foil to protect it from spattering fat and filled it with 5 quarts of water, for a weight of about 10 pounds. Not only is the soup kettle easier to come up with than bricks or cans, but the setup is simple. When it's time to turn the chicken, simply lift the pot by the handles, flip the bird, then return the pot to the skillet. The pan-sautéed chicken cooks in the same amount of time as roasted, grilled or broiled chickens without the need for preheating.

For grilling, unless you have an old pot in storage that you don't mind damaging with smoke, you'll have to resort to bricks or a heavy stone from the backyard. I use a beat-up jelly roll pan and bricks. Because the chicken cooks over direct heat, I worried about grease fires, but I've never had a single flare-up. I suspect the combination of the grill lid and jelly roll pan prevents oxygen from feeding the fire. As with the pan-sauté method, one turn is enough—12 minutes breast side up and about 15 minutes breast side down produces a stunning chicken. Because of the weights, the grill rack leaves a perfect imprint.

The broiling method also took some fine-tuning, for my first attempts set off two smoke alarms. The key to good chicken broiling is oven-rack position: the chicken must be far enough from the heating element to cook through without burning, which means the top of the chicken must be about 8 inches from the electric element. (The oven rack should be about 12 inches away.) As with grilling and pan-sautéing, only one turn is necessary to cook the chicken properly. If you want a bread crumb or Parmesan cheese coating, though, you do have to give it one more flip to sprinkle on and brown the crumbs or cheese.

Butterflying works with virtually any grilled, broiled, roast or sautéed chicken recipe (excluding boneless, skinless chicken breast). The following recipes will give you some ideas. You can substitute Cornish hens, larger chickens—or even a turkey—as long as you adjust the cooking times. Remember, the cooking time in the recipes that follow is based on 3-pound chickens, so adjust times according to size. As with all poultry, these butterflied chickens are especially flavorful and juicy when brined. If you decide to brine them, use salt and water ratios as for Cornish hens (see page 168) and omit salt from the herb-

BUTTERFLIED CHICKEN

1. Place the chicken breast side down, with the tail end facing you. With kitchen shears, cut along one side of the tail down the entire length of the backbone. With the chicken still breast side down, turn the bird so its neck faces you. Cut along the other side of the backbone and remove it from the chicken; reserve for another use, such as making broth.

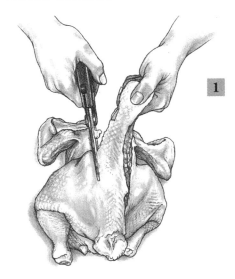

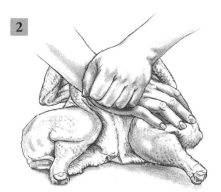

2. Turn the chicken breast side up. Open the chicken up and lay it on work surface. Use the palm of your hand to flatten the breast so that the whole chicken lies flat.

3. Use the smooth side of a mallet to pound the chicken to a more or less even thickness.

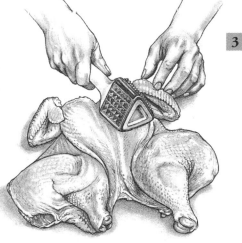

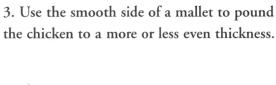

4. Make ½-inch slits on either side of each breast about 1 inch from the tip. Tuck the corresponding leg into each opening.

Roast Butterflied Chicken with Tarragon-Mustard Pan Sauce

Serves 4

I NEVER ROAST a butterflied chicken without throwing a couple of vegetables in the pan—red or sweet potatoes, carrots or parsnips, onions or shallots and turnips or rutabagas—cut into 2-inch chunks. Since the vegetables will be cooked but not browned when the chicken is done, remove the bird from the pan and return the vegetables to the oven while the chicken rests. Don't use more vegetables than will fit in a single layer in the pan. You can deglaze the pan after removing the vegetables.

- 2 teaspoons minced fresh tarragon leaves
- 1 medium garlic clove, minced
  Salt
  Ground black pepper
- 1 whole chicken (3 pounds), butterflied
    (see figures 1-3, page 83)
- 1 teaspoon vegetable oil
- 1 cup homemade chicken broth or
    low-sodium canned broth
- 1 tablespoon Dijon mustard
- 1 tablespoon butter

1. Preheat oven to 500°F.

2. Mix tarragon, garlic, ½ teaspoon salt and ¼ teaspoon pepper into a paste in a small bowl. Following illustration on next page, loosen breast and leg/thigh skin and rub herb-garlic paste over exposed areas. Tuck legs into slits in breast skin, then transfer chicken to a large roasting pan or jelly roll pan, skin side up. Rub skin with oil and very lightly season with salt and pepper. Let chicken stand at room temperature while oven heats.

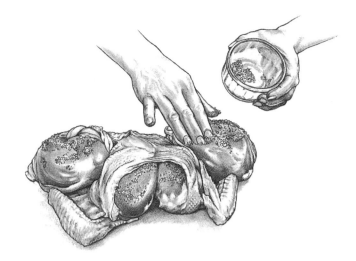

3. Roast until chicken skin is nicely brown and juices run clear, about 30 minutes. Transfer to a serving platter or cutting board, cover with foil and let rest while making sauce.

4. Spoon off all fat from roasting pan. Heat one or two burners (depending on roasting pan size) to medium-high. Pour broth into pan, scraping up any drippings that have stuck to bottom of pan. Pour liquid into a small saucepan and reduce by half, about 4 minutes. Whisk in mustard, then swirl in butter.

5. Halve chicken down breast bone and snip skin between breast and legs/thighs. Serve immediately with sauce passed separately.

Broiled Butterflied Chicken with Parmesan, Lemon and Red Pepper Flakes

SERVES 4

FOR A VARIATION, brush this broiled chicken with Dijon mustard before sprinkling it with the cheese and bread crumbs.

1 teaspoon zest from ½ lemon
1 large garlic clove, minced
  Salt
¼ teaspoon hot red pepper flakes
1 whole chicken (3 pounds), butterflied
  (see figures 1-3, page 83)
1 teaspoon olive oil
  Ground black pepper
2 tablespoons Parmesan cheese
1 tablespoon dried bread crumbs

1. Adjust oven rack so that chicken will be no closer than 8 inches from heating element; preheat broiler.

2. Mix lemon zest, garlic, ½ teaspoon salt and hot red pepper flakes in a small bowl. Following illustration on page 85, loosen breast and leg/thigh skin and rub herb-garlic paste over exposed areas. Tuck legs into slits in breast skin, then transfer chicken to a large roasting pan or jelly roll pan, skin side up. Brush with oil and very lightly season with salt and pepper; let stand while broiler heats. Mix cheese and bread crumbs; set aside.

3. Broil chicken until skin is rich brown, about 15 minutes. Turn chicken over with tongs and continue to broil until juices run clear, about 15 minutes longer. Remove chicken from oven; turn skin side up. Brush skin with pan drippings, then sprinkle with cheese mixture. Return chicken to oven and broil until topping turns golden brown, about 3 minutes longer.

4. Transfer to a serving platter or cutting board, cover with foil and let rest 10 to 15 minutes.

5. Halve chicken down breast bone and snip skin between breast and legs/thighs and serve.

Sautéed Butterflied Chicken with Mushrooms and Sage

Serves 4

To make sure that the chicken skin is not browning too quickly, check it a couple of times during the first half of the cooking time.

- 4 teaspoons minced fresh sage
- 1 medium garlic clove, minced
  Salt
  Ground black pepper
- 1 whole chicken (3 pounds), butterflied (see figures 1-3, page 83)
- 1 tablespoon olive oil
- 2 medium shallots, minced
- 5 ounces assorted wild mushrooms, sliced (about 2 cups)
- 2 tablespoons dry vermouth
- ½ cup homemade chicken broth or low-sodium canned broth
- 1 tablespoon butter

1. Mix 2 teaspoons sage, garlic, ½ teaspoon salt and ¼ teaspoon pepper into a paste in a small bowl. Following illustration on page 85, loosen breast and leg/thigh skin and rub herb-garlic paste over exposed areas. Tuck legs into slits in breast skin. Let stand at room temperature about 15 minutes to allow flavors to meld.

2. Heat oil in an 11- or 12-inch sauté pan. Cover bottom of a soup kettle whose diameter is slightly smaller than sauté pan with foil, then fill with 5 quarts water. Lay chicken skin side down in sauté pan. Set soup kettle on top of the chicken and cook over medium heat, checking once or twice to make sure skin is not browning too quickly, until skin is nicely browned, about 12 minutes. Remove soup kettle; turn chicken skin side up. Set kettle on top of chicken and continue to cook until juices run clear, about 18 minutes longer. Transfer chicken to a serving platter or cutting board; cover with foil while making sauce.

3. Remove all but 1 tablespoon fat from pan; return pan to burner and increase heat to medium-high. Add shallots and sauté until softened, about 2 minutes. Add mushrooms and sauté until their juices release and evaporate. Add vermouth and cook until liquid has almost evaporated. Add chicken broth and boil until thickened to sauce consistency. Stir in remaining 2 teaspoons sage. Remove from heat and swirl in butter.

4. Halve chicken down breast bone and snip skin between breast and legs/thighs. Serve immediately with sauce passed separately.

Grilled Butterflied Chicken with Rosemary, Lemon and Garlic

SERVES 4

ALTHOUGH ALL GRILLS and grilling conditions are different, every time I cook a 3-pound chicken, it is done in less than a half hour—12 minutes for the skin side and 12 to 15 minutes for the other side. Try to avoid checking the chicken before the 12-minute mark. The coals will cool faster, increasing the grilling time. Besides, cooking a chicken this way is like grilling a steak—one turn should do it.

1   teaspoon minced zest from ½ lemon
1   teaspoon minced fresh rosemary leaves
1   large garlic clove, minced
   Salt
   Ground black pepper
1   whole chicken (3 pounds), butterflied
   (see figures 1-3, page 83)
½ cup juice from 2-3 lemons
2   tablespoons olive oil

1. Mix lemon zest, rosemary, garlic, ½ teaspoon salt and ¼ teaspoon pepper into a paste in a small bowl. Following illustration on page 85, loosen breast and leg/thigh skin and rub herb-garlic paste over exposed areas. Tuck legs into slits in breast skin.

2. Heat about 5 quarts of charcoal on grill until covered with gray ash. Spread coals over half of grill and set grill rack in place. Cover and let grill rack heat, about 5 minutes. Place chicken, skin side down, over medium-hot coals. Set a jelly roll pan or other flat pan over chicken. Set 2 bricks on top of jelly roll pan. Cover and grill until chicken skin is deep brown with grill marks, about 12 minutes. Remove grill lid, bricks and jelly roll pan. Turn chicken over with tongs. Replace jelly roll pan, bricks and lid and continue grilling until juices run clear, about 15 minutes longer.

3. Meanwhile, mix lemon juice and olive oil in a shallow pan large enough to hold chicken. Remove chicken from grill and roll on both sides in lemon-oil mixture. Return chicken to cool side of grill and continue to cook, brushing occasionally with remaining lemon mixture until flavors have blended, about 5 minutes longer. Remove from grill.

4. Halve chicken down breast bone and snip skin between breast and legs/thighs and serve.

Rediscovering Fried Chicken

ALL THE HEALTH SCARES over the last few decades have left many of us with frying phobia. We rarely make fried chicken at home anymore. Instead we allow the fast-food restaurants to perform the dirty deed for us. And these days they do little more than pop prebreaded, partially fried frozen chicken into the deep fryer. Every time we buy chicken from run-of-the-mill fast-food operations like these, we forget what the real thing tastes like. I know because it happened to me.

After weeks of research and efforts in the kitchen, I rediscovered just how wonderful this dish can be. I also proved that if chicken is properly fried, most of the oil stays in the skillet and is not absorbed into the bird. Removing the fatty skin before frying does not compromise the quality of the dish and improves its "health profile" even further.

When I started my research, I thought I already knew how to make blue-ribbon fried chicken. Back in the sixties, my matriarchal aunt in Alabama announced to all her younger sisters that she had discovered how to duplicate the fried chicken of a local fast-food chain.

The key was dipping chicken parts in flour, then in water, then back in flour. The first covering of flour and water formed a glue, which caused the second coating of flour to form an unusually thick coating, which fried up hard, thick and crispy. Imitating the fast-food restaurant, the sisters replaced their skillets with Dutch ovens and traded in their shortening for oil. From then on, that's the way my mother and I fried chicken.

But that was before I ran across scores of pan-fried chicken recipes, particularly from the older cookbooks. As I reviewed these recipes, I was suddenly six years old again and back in my grandmother's kitchen. I remembered her cast-iron skillet and the glass lid she borrowed from another pot to cover the frying chicken. I recalled the way she cut the chicken into 10 pieces—the standard eight, plus the pulley bone (or wishbone) piece and the lower meaty back piece—and I could almost taste the tender-crisp quality of her fried chicken.

Was pan-fried chicken better than deep-fried chicken, or was I just romanticizing the past? Shallow-fried versus deep-fried was certainly the big question, but there were other issues to consider. What size chicken was best? Should the chicken parts be soaked before frying, and if so, in what? Was all-purpose flour the best coating, or could corn flour (cornmeal ground to the texture of flour) or even self-rising flour produce a better crust? Was dredging the chicken parts in a pan of flour the best way to get the coating on the chicken, or did the paper-bag method offer better, and perhaps cleaner, results? Should the cook season the chicken, the flour, or both? Was this extra step worth the time? What kind and size of pan and what fat or combination of fats were best for frying chicken? During frying, should the pan be covered, partially covered, covered part of the time, or not at all? How should the fried chicken be drained: on paper towels or paper bags, or did I perhaps have something to learn from the fast-food restaurants?

Smaller Is Better

I've always considered fried chicken a time-consuming project—mainly because it had to be prepared in two batches. Fairly quickly though, I discovered that if the bird was small enough and the pan was big enough, I could fry a whole chicken at one time. The 2½-to-3-pounders were the best fits, but often these smaller birds are not easy to find. If you want to guarantee size, give your butcher or grocery meat depart-

ment a call and place a special order.

I wanted to like the extra-large (13⅜-inch) cast-iron skillet I had specially purchased for this fried chicken testing because it was big enough to hold all 10 pieces of chicken at once. But its size became a handicap—the perimeter of the pan extended far past the burner, with the result that by the time the fat at the sides of the pan was hot enough to fry the chicken properly, the pieces in the center had burned. By the same token, cooking the chicken in the center of the pan resulted in blond-skinned, greasy chicken around the edges. The skillet I came to prefer was a 12-inch cast-iron skillet (a modest $15 investment), though any 12-inch heavy-bottomed skillet will work.

The Coating: Buttermilk Is Best

Of all the stages of preparing the chicken—buying, butchering, seasoning, coating, frying—I found the greatest diversity in how cooks soaked the birds. After testing 13 different soaking methods—from lemon-juice-flavored water and milk to buttermilk and heavy cream—I discovered that dairy-soaked chicken had the most beautifully textured and richly colored skin. Because milk is thicker than water, dairy-based soaking liquids tend to cling to the slippery, raw chicken parts, which, in turn, attract more flour during dredging and fry up into a thick, even coating. Lactose, the sugar found in milk, also causes the chicken to develop its characteristic deep mahogany color during frying. Heavy cream coated the chicken beautifully, but the resulting fried chicken was too rich. A milk-lemon-juice mixture gave the chicken a clean, heightened flavor, but because it was thinner, it didn't cling as well to the chicken and formed a less impressive coating. Buttermilk, on the other hand, is terrific—as viscous as cream and as tangy as the milk-lemon juice, with none of the drawbacks.

You Can't Beat Flour

I was particularly intrigued by two coatings that I had run across in my research—self-rising flour and a combination of all-purpose flour and corn flour. After putting these and other coatings to the test, I found that nothing surpasses reliable all-purpose flour. In fact, most coatings are inferior to it.

The self-rising flour produced a coating that ballooned, then deflated during frying. Once cooked, this crumbly chicken shed its coat. A cornstarch coating produced disastrous-looking and awful-flavored chicken, frying up an unpleasant white with scattered hard spots and a pasty taste. I mixed the cornstarch with flour, which proved more successful, but still no better than the plain flour. I tried other combinations with all-purpose flour—cornmeal, whole wheat flour, corn flour and bread crumbs. The cornmeal coating was pleasant, but didn't adhere as well as straight flour. The whole wheat coating looked grainy. Both the cornmeal and the whole wheat coatings had a coarse, raw taste. And though the corn flour sounded like a good idea, it was barely distinguishable on the fried chicken. Bread crumbs mixed with flour delivered a respectable crust—nice dark brown, fairly crispy, but there was nothing to recommend them over just plain flour.

Brown-Bag It

While determining my favorite coating, I set up a side competition to determine the best way to get that coating on the chicken. I compared dredging the chicken parts in a flour-filled pie tin to shaking the chicken in flour in a brown paper bag. I quickly declared the bag method the winner in both coating consistency and cleanup—though after shaking a thin dusting of flour over the kitchen floor and watching damp, heavy chicken parts threaten to break through the bag, I quickly switched from a single to a double brown bag.

After a number of experiments, I decided that seasoning the flour wasn't sufficient, nor was seasoning the soaking liquid. The sound culinary principle of seasoning all along the way produced the best results. I started off with smaller amounts of salt but discovered that the soaking liquid, much like boiling water for pasta, must be seasoned generously for the chicken to absorb the salt. And because only a portion of seasoned flour clings to the chicken parts, it's just as important that it's heavily seasoned as well.

Into the Frying Pan

I tested every conceivable fat, alone and in combination, and found less dramatic differences in this area. Lard produced gorgeous, deeply tanned chicken, though I disliked the heavy porky smell it gave off as it fried. While this fat seemed to enforce and enhance the chicken's meatiness, it overpowered the flavor of the skin and crust with a rich, heavy taste that grew cloying. I cut the lard with shortening, and still the crust was tainted with the distinctive flavor.

Chicken fried in a butter-vegetable oil combination was sweet and mild but ultimately too rich. It produced chicken with a lighter color than any of the other fats, and it foamed nonstop during frying. This combination also seemed more perishable, making it difficult to store and use again like other fats.

A few of the recipes I came across flavored shortening with bacon drippings. Although I could distinctly smell bacon as the chicken was frying, I could barely identify it during tasting. Vegetable oil worked well, leaving the pieces fast-food-like, but a bit splotchy. Shortening was the winner. Not only does it produce a crisp, light chicken with no heavy overtones of flavor, but it doesn't leave the kitchen smelling like a greasy spoon. That's because shortening is more carefully refined than vegetable oil and has had its odor-causing compounds removed.

Pan-Frying Triumphs

Pan-frying produces superior fried chicken. Deep-fried chicken, attacked on all sides by hot oil, quickly develops a brittle, protective tortoiselike shell right down to the meat. With pan-fried chicken, the coating has the same crunchy exterior, but because the chicken is not totally submerged in hot oil, a moist sublayer has a chance to develop, offering a nice contrast to the crisp surface.

I also wondered if and when fried chicken should be covered. The point of covering the pan during frying is to trap moisture, so if the chicken is left uncovered the entire time, it does not develop the soft desirable undercoating. Covering it from start to finish creates too much steam, leaving the coating too soft and in some cases, causing it to fall off into the oil. Covering during the first half of the cooking time allows the chicken to steam-fry, making it just right.

Chicken drained on paper toweling

gets soggy faster than chicken drained on a paper bag, but both were inferior to a wire rack set over a jelly roll pan. This pan-and-wire-rack setup mimics the draining system used by many fast-food restaurants. Before frying, the rack offers the ideal resting place for the coated chicken. After frying, it keeps the chicken grease-free and crisp. The rack sits safely on the stovetop as well as in a warm oven—not true for either of the paper-draining methods.

With or Without the Skin?

To test whether skinless fried chicken could compare to the traditional kind, I fried three skinned chickens: one simply dusted with seasoned flour; one dipped in flour, then in buttermilk, then back in flour; and finally one soaked in buttermilk and dipped in flour.

The meat of the simple flour-coated chicken was leathery—the flour alone did not sufficiently protect the meat from the boiling oil. The chicken that had been dipped in flour, then in buttermilk and back in flour formed a tough protective coating. It adhered to the chicken, but it ballooned during frying and separated from the meat. Simply coating the buttermilk-soaked chicken with flour provides just the right coating and protection.

Most people did not detect the missing skin, and those who did notice didn't miss it.

The Rest Is Gravy

Years ago, fried chicken was rarely served without mashed potatoes and biscuits, which, of course, are perfect vehicles for lots of hot gravy. To make gravy, the frying oil is poured off. Flour is stirred into the browned bits left in the bottom of the pan to make a roux. Liquid is then added to make a fairly thick gravy, and it is here that recipes part ways.

Many suggest adding milk, others cream or broth enriched with cream. The gravy I grew up on was nothing more than chicken drippings, roux and water. I tested a good number of liquids. The water-based gravy tasted flat and lifeless, while those made with cream and milk were too rich. Gravy made with chicken broth and flavored simply with thyme hits the modern mark. Start the broth while you cut up the chicken and it should be ready for the gravy by the time the chicken is finished. If you don't want to be bothered with broth pots, a can of low-salt chicken broth will work just fine.

A Healthy Surprise

Remember the old Crisco commercials: "It all comes back but 1 tablespoon"? I put this claim to the test with chicken and found it to be absolutely true: when the bird is fried in shortening, virtually all the fat remains in the pan and almost none is absorbed into the meat. I heated 3 cups of fat to 350°F in a 12-inch skillet, pan-fried a whole chicken and measured the fat that was left after frying. I conducted the test a number of times to confirm my findings, each time ending up with the same result: 3 cups of oil before frying and 3 cups after.

According to the food scientist Tina Sieleg, if the water in the food to be fried is kept at the boiling temperature (212°F), the outward pressure of the escaping water vapor keeps the oil from soaking into the food. If the frying oil is not hot enough, on the other hand, it will seep in, making the food greasy. The key is heating the oil hot enough (350°F works well) and maintaining the oil temperature at a sufficiently high level to keep the food, in essence, boiling.

Watching your food roil in a pool of fat may be a turnoff at first, but my testing suggests that we needn't be as concerned about eating properly fried foods as I once thought.

BUTCHERING THE BIRD

THE FOLLOWING METHOD of cutting up chicken results in evenly sized pieces and smaller breast pieces that are more manageable to cook. Although I like the taste of the lower meaty half of the back, I find that it is too unwieldy to fry and crowds the pan, so I usually save it for the stockpot with the other back piece and the giblets. If you're partial to it, though, treat it like a prize and fry it up.

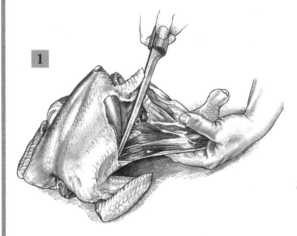

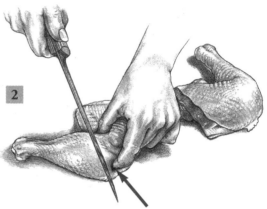

1. Remove the leg/thigh by cutting through the skin where the leg is attached to the breast. As the skin is cut, pull down on the leg until the thigh bone pops out of its socket, then sever the leg/thigh from the body.

2. Separate the leg and thigh at the joint. If you have trouble finding the right cutting position, flex the leg/thigh to feel where the bones connect.

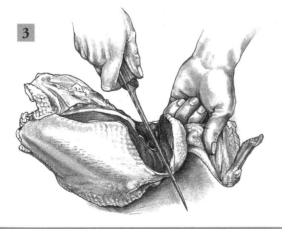

3. Carving a little of the breast meat along with it, remove the wing from the breast at the ball joint. Remove and reserve the wing tips for another use.

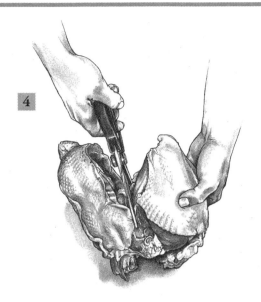

4. Separate the back from the breast by cutting through the rib bones on either side of the breast.

5. Run your fingertip along the breast bone until you feel the bone end and you hit a sudden drop. Then cut straight down about 1½ inches, turn the knife toward the neck end at a slight angle, and continue cutting until the wishbone piece is completely severed from the breast.

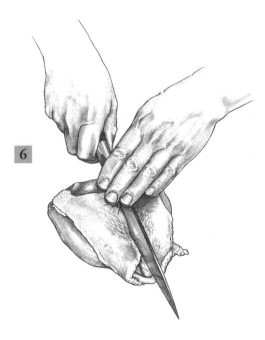

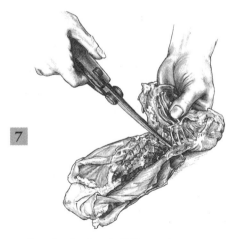

6. Split the breast down the backbone.

7. Break the back. Where it snaps, cut it into 2 pieces. You now have 9 or 10 pieces for frying, depending on whether you decide to fry the lower back. The upper back, wing tips, breast bone, neck and giblets (excluding the liver) are ready to turn into broth.

Buttermilk Fried Chicken with Pan Gravy

Serves 4 to 6

IF YOU PLAN to soak the chicken longer than eight hours, reduce the salt from 1 tablespoon to 2 teaspoons. Even if you skip the gravy, make broth with the neck, back and giblets and reserve it for another time. And if you don't feel like butchering a chicken, you can obviously buy chicken parts of your choice.

To make skinless fried chicken, follow the Buttermilk Fried Chicken recipe, removing the skin from each piece before soaking in buttermilk.

> 1 whole chicken (about 3 pounds), cut into
> 9 or 10 pieces (see illustrations, pages 98-99),
> back, neck, wing tips and giblets reserved
> 1½ cups buttermilk
> Salt
> Ground black pepper

Broth for Pan Gravy

> 1 teaspoon vegetable oil
> Back, neck, wing tips and giblets (excluding liver;
> see illustrations, page 17), hacked into 2-inch pieces
> 1 small onion, quartered
> Salt

> 2 cups all-purpose flour
> Salt
> Ground black pepper
> 3-4 cups vegetable shortening for frying

Pan Gravy

> 3 tablespoons all-purpose flour
> ½ teaspoon dried thyme leaves
> 1 teaspoon lemon juice
> Salt
> Ground black pepper

1. Place chicken pieces in a gallon-size zipper-lock plastic bag. Mix buttermilk with 1 tablespoon salt and ½ teaspoon pepper. Pour buttermilk mixture over chicken, seal, then refrigerate for at least 2 hours and up to 24 hours.

2. Broth for Pan Gravy: Heat oil in a large saucepan or Dutch oven over medium-high heat. Add chicken back and other parts and onion; sauté until chicken loses its raw color, about 5 minutes. Reduce heat to low; cook until chicken releases all of its juices, about 20 minutes. Add 1 quart water and salt to taste; bring to a boil, reduce heat to low, then simmer until broth is flavorful, about 20 minutes. Strain into a 1-quart liquid measuring cup. (You will need 1½ cups for gravy; reserve remaining broth for another use.) Set aside.

3. To Fry Chicken: Measure 2 cups flour, 2 teaspoons salt and ½ teaspoon pepper into a large doubled brown paper bag; shake to combine. Lift half of chicken pieces from buttermilk, drop into flour mixture and shake thoroughly to coat completely with flour. Remove chicken from bag, shaking excess flour from each piece. Place pieces on a large wire rack set over a jelly roll pan until you are ready to fry. Coat remaining chicken pieces in the same manner. (Discard buttermilk.)

4. Meanwhile, spoon enough shortening to measure ½ inch deep in a 12-inch skillet; heat to 350°F. Drop chicken pieces, skin side down, into hot oil, cover (I use a cookie sheet) and cook for 5 minutes. Lift chicken pieces with tongs to make sure they are frying evenly; rearrange if some are browning faster than others. Cover again and continue cooking until pieces are evenly browned, about 5 minutes longer. Turn chicken over with tongs and cook, uncovered, until chicken is browned all over, 10 to 12 minutes longer. Remove chicken from skillet with tongs and place on wire rack set over jelly roll pan. Strain hot fat into a heat-safe container.

5. Pan Gravy: Pour browned bits from strainer and 3 tablespoons fat back into skillet. Whisk in 3 tablespoons flour and cook over medium-high heat, whisking constantly, until flour mixture turns golden brown, 2 to 3 minutes. Whisk in thyme, then 1½ cups broth. Bring to a simmer, and simmer until thickened, 2 to 3 minutes longer. Season with lemon juice and salt and pepper to taste. Serve immediately over mashed potatoes with fried chicken.

One-Pot Chicken Pot Pie

ALMOST EVERYBODY loves a good chicken pot pie, though, not surprisingly, few seem to have the time or energy to make one. Before the pie even makes it to the oven, the cook must poach a chicken, take the meat off the bone and cut it up, strain the broth, prepare and blanch vegetables, make a sauce and mix and roll out biscuit or pie dough.

Given the labor-intensive nature of pot pie, my goal was to develop a recipe that would be delicious but could be made as quickly as possible. Pot pie, after all, is supper food. The many recipes I reviewed showed me that I wasn't the first to try to simplify this dish. Canned vegetables, soups, biscuits and other processed convenience foods made for short ingredient lists and recipe instructions, but these time-savers obviously compromised flavor. Because I was looking to beat the clock, though, I was open to reasonable shortcuts. Ingredients like boneless, skinless chicken breasts, frozen puff pastry and frozen green peas were welcome possibilities.

Besides the time factor, I wanted to find my way around two other common problems with this dish. First, the vegetables tend to overcook. A filling chock-full of bright, fresh vegetables going into the oven looks completely different after 40 minutes of high-heat baking under a blanket of dough. Carrots become mushy and dull, while brilliant peas and fresh herbs fade to drab. I wanted to preserve the vegetables' natural colors. Other pot pies I made were too juicy. Before baking, the filling was thick and creamy. When cut into after baking, however, the pie looked like chicken soup in a crust. Although I wanted the pie moist and saucy, I also wanted it to be thick enough to eat with a fork—in short, a pot pie with great texture, great flavor and great color that could be made in good time.

Cooking the Chicken

Even though I knew boneless skinless chicken breasts and canned chicken broth were a quick and convenient substitute, I wanted to try traditional methods of cooking the chicken to make sure the pie's flavor wasn't compromised too dramatically.

Given the choice, I'd choose to eat roast chicken over boiled chicken most any day, but I wondered whether the flavor of roasted chicken meat would be noticeable in a pie filled with vegetables and rich sauce. In addition to making pies with roast chicken and poached chicken (poached in broth and a combination of broth and wine), I steamed and roasted whole chickens as well as braised chicken parts.

Poaching Preferred

I started with poaching—the most traditional cooking method. I simmered chicken quarters until just done. The breast/wings were fully cooked in 30 minutes, the leg/thigh sections needed about 10 minutes more. Of the two poaching liquids, I preferred the chicken poached in wine and broth. The wine infused the meat and made for a richer, more full-flavored sauce. Because the poaching broth is used to make the roux-based sauce that vegetables and chicken bake in, I made sauces with both broths. Once again, the wine-flavored sauce was my favorite.

What was good for the chicken and sauce, however, was not ultimately good for the vegetables. To my disappointment, the acidity of the wine-broth sauce caused the green peas and fresh herbs to lose their bright green color in the oven. Vegetables baked in the broth-only sauce kept their vivid color, though the bland sauce needed perking up—a problem I'd have to deal with further down the road.

The steamed chicken was time-consuming, requiring about an hour to cook through. I tried adding pie vegetables during the cooking process and steaming them alongside the chicken, but they cooked before the chicken and were difficult to fish out. On the whole, the process was more awkward than poaching, and although the chicken juices flavored the steaming liquid, the resulting broth wasn't sufficiently strong for the sauce.

Like the steamed chicken, the roasted chicken required an hour in the oven and had to be cooled before its meat could be removed. If I thought roast chicken really made a better pie, I would have reduced cooking time by roasting chicken parts instead of the whole bird, but by the time I took off the skin and mixed the meat in with sauce and vegetables, the roasted flavor was lost. On the other hand, the pan juices, which I deglazed with canned broth, gave the sauce an unmistakably roasted flavor, which tasted good, if a little odd for pot pie.

Much like the roasted chicken, the braised chicken lost its delicious flavor once the browned skin was removed. Also the sauce made from the braising liquid tasted too pronounced, distracting me from the meat, vegetables and crust.

The only result I was really pleased with at this point was the chicken parts poached in broth, which I was now ready to test against faster-cooking boneless, skinless chicken breasts.

Boneless Breasts: The Best

Because boneless, skinless breasts do cook so quickly, I could also sauté them. Before comparing breasts to other poached parts, I tried cooking the breasts three different ways. I cut raw breast meat into bite-size pieces and sautéed them; I sautéed whole breasts, shredding the breast meat once it was cool enough to handle; and I poached whole breasts in canned broth, also shredding the cooked meat. The poached chicken breasts were my favorite. The soft, tender, irregularly shaped pieces not only mixed well with the vegetables but attracted the sauce. The surfaces of the sautéed chicken pieces, on the other hand, were too slick to trap the sauce. For simplicity's sake, I had hoped be able to use the sautéed whole breasts. Unfortunately, sautéing caused the outer layer of meat to turn crusty, a texture I did not like in the pie.

My only concern with the poached boneless, skinless breasts was the quality of the broth. Though both the breasts and the other parts had been poached in canned broth, I thought the long-simmered poaching liquid made with chicken parts would be significantly better. But I was wrong. In comparing pies, I found no difference in quality and was able to shave a half hour off the cooking time (10 minutes to cook the breasts versus 40 minutes to cook the other parts). Those who like either dark or a mix of dark and white meat can use boneless, skinless chicken thighs as well.

How to Keep the Vegetables from Overcooking

I made pies with vegetables prepared three different ways to determine whether I could preserve their texture and color and, most importantly, their flavor. The first pot pie contained carrots and celery that I had parboiled until tender-crisp in the chicken-poaching liquid. I made the second pie with raw celery and carrots, and the third with sautéed celery and carrots. (For each pie, I first sautéed the onions and added the green peas frozen.) After comparing the vegetables in each of the pies, I found that the ones sautéed before baking held their color and flavor best, the parboiled carrots less so. The raw vegetables were not fully cooked at the end of baking time and gave off too much liquid, diluting both the flavor and thickness of the sauce.

Of course, the other aspect of keeping the vegetables fresh is getting the pie out of the oven as quickly as possible. To keep the pie from becoming overly rich and complicated, I had originally ruled out double-crust pies; the vegetables became my third reason for doing so. In order to get a bottom crust fully cooked, the pie would have to bake for at least 45 minutes, at which point the peas and carrots would be lifeless.

Milk: What a Surprise

Poached boneless skinless chicken breasts and sautéed vegetables gave me the quick, colorful pie I wanted. I now took on the sauce. Chicken pot pie sauce is traditionally roux-based, thinned with chicken broth (*sauce velouté*) and often enriched with cream (*sauce suprême*). The proportions of broth and cream vary from recipe to recipe, but almost without exception, pot pie sauce is made with butter, flour, chicken broth and milk or cream.

Because of the dish's inherent richness, I wanted to see how little cream I could get away with using. I tried three different pot pie fillings, enriching one 2-cup portion of sauce with ¼ cup cream, another with ¼ cup half-and-half, and the last one with 1 cup milk. Going into the oven, all the fillings had the right consistency and creaminess. Coming out was a different story. Vegetable and meat juices diluted both the cream and half-and-half sauces, while

the larger quantity of milk kept the creamy look and taste. Fortunately, I didn't have to try increasing the cream because I preferred the milk-enriched sauce.

To prevent it from becoming too liquid, I simply added more flour. A sauce that looks a little thick before baking will become the perfect consistency, thinned out by the chicken and vegetable juices that are released during baking.

I had worked out the right consistency, but because I had been forced to abandon the wine for the vegetables' sake, the pie tasted a little bland. Lemon juice, a flavor heightener I had seen in a number of recipes, had the same dulling effect on the vegetables as did the wine. I shared this cooking dilemma with my friend and colleague Stephen Schmidt, who suggested I might stir in a few tablespoons of dry sherry. Because sherry is more intensely flavored and less acidic, it gave me the dimension I was looking for without compromising the peas and carrots.

In addition to the more familiar pie pastry and biscuits, mashed potatoes, puff pastry or phyllo dough can also top all the pot pies that follow.

Simple Chicken Pot Pie

SERVES 6 TO 8

THIS POT PIE is especially quick when you top it with store-bought puff pastry, which you can cut into circles and set over the filling like biscuits or leave in one piece like pastry dough. If you are crunched for time, you can cut the puff pastry into 3-inch circles and bake, following package instructions, while preparing the filling. Simmer the filling on top of the stove a little bit longer to cook the vegetables fully. Skip the baking step and serve a portion of creamed chicken in a soup plate topped with a disk of baked puff pastry.

> Rich, Flaky Pie Dough (page 111) or Fluffy Buttermilk
> Biscuits (page 110) or see Topping Options (page 107)

1½ pounds boneless, skinless chicken breasts and/or thighs

2 cups homemade chicken broth or 1 can (16 ounces) low-sodium canned broth

1½ tablespoons vegetable oil

1 medium-large onion, chopped

3 medium carrots, peeled and cut crosswise ¼ inch thick

2 small celery ribs, cut crosswise ¼ inch thick

Salt

Ground black pepper

4 tablespoons butter

½ cup all-purpose flour

1½ cups milk

½ teaspoon dried thyme leaves

3 tablespoons dry sherry

¾ cup frozen green peas, thawed

3 tablespoons minced fresh parsley leaves

1. Make pie dough or biscuits and refrigerate until ready to use. If using commercial puff pastry or phyllo dough, follow package instructions for thawing.

2. Adjust oven rack to low-center position; heat oven to 400°F. Put chicken and broth in a Dutch oven over medium heat. Cover and bring to simmer; simmer until chicken is just done, 8 to 10 minutes. Transfer meat to a large bowl; transfer broth to another bowl.

3. Increase heat to medium-high; heat oil in Dutch oven. Add onion, carrots and celery and sauté until just tender, about 5 minutes. Season to taste with salt and pepper. Meanwhile, shred chicken into bite-size pieces. Transfer cooked vegetables to bowl with chicken; set aside.

4. Heat butter over medium heat in Dutch oven. When foaming subsides, add flour; cook for about 1 minute. Whisk in reserved chicken broth, milk, any accumulated chicken juices and thyme. Bring to a simmer, reduce heat to low and continue to simmer, stirring, until sauce fully thickens, about 1 minute. Season to taste with salt and pepper; stir in sherry.

5. Pour sauce over chicken-vegetable mixture; stir to combine. Stir in peas and parsley, and adjust seasonings. Pour mixture into a 13-by-9-inch pan or any shallow baking dish of similar size or into six 12-ounce ovenproof ramekins or bowls. Top as desired. Bake until pastry is golden brown and filling is bubbly, about 30 minutes for large pies, 20 to 25 minutes for smaller pies. Serve immediately.

TOPPING OPTIONS

IN ADDITION TO THE PASTRY TOPPINGS on pages 110-111, puff pastry, either commercial or homemade, can blanket the chicken filling. Or you can top the pie with four or five phyllo sheets that have been thawed according to package directions, trimmed to pan size and brushed with butter. If you want, you can top the pot pie with leftover mashed potatoes.

Chicken Pot Pie
with Leeks, Asparagus and Tarragon

SERVES 6 TO 8

To ensure that the asparagus does not overcook, bake this pot pie in individual baking dishes rather than one large dish.

1½	pounds boneless, skinless chicken breasts and/or thighs
2	cups homemade chicken broth or 1 can (16 ounces) low-sodium chicken broth
2½	tablespoons vegetable oil
1	medium leek, trimmed and thoroughly washed
2	medium carrots, peeled and cut crosswise ¼ inch thick
2	small celery ribs, cut crosswise ¼ inch thick
	Salt
	Ground black pepper
8	medium asparagus spears, trimmed and cut into 1-inch lengths
4	tablespoons butter
½	cup all-purpose flour
1½	cups milk
½	teaspoon dried thyme leaves
2	tablespoons dry sherry
1	tablespoon minced fresh tarragon leaves or 1 teaspoon dried tarragon

1. Follow recipe for Simple Chicken Pot Pie (page 106), substituting leek for onion in step 2 and sautéing in 1½ tablespoons oil.

2. After removing leek, carrots and celery from Dutch oven, add remaining 1 tablespoon oil. Add asparagus spears and sauté until bright green and starting to soften, 3 to 4 minutes. Mix asparagus with remaining vegetables and continue as directed, omitting peas and substituting tarragon leaves for parsley.

Chicken Pot Pie
with Mushrooms and Peas

SERVES 6 TO 8

FOR A TOUCH OF COLOR, sauté half a diced red pepper along with the carrots, celery and onion.

1½ pounds boneless, skinless chicken breasts and/or thighs
2 cups homemade chicken broth or 1 can (16 ounces) low-sodium chicken broth
2½ tablespoons vegetable oil
1 medium-large onion, chopped
2 medium carrots, peeled and cut crosswise ¼ inch thick
2 small celery ribs, cut crosswise ¼ inch thick
½ pound mushrooms (domestic or wild), thinly sliced
   Salt
   Ground black pepper
4 tablespoons butter
½ cup all-purpose flour
1½ cups milk
½ teaspoon dried thyme leaves
3 tablespoons dry sherry
¾ cup frozen green peas, thawed
3 tablespoons minced fresh parsley leaves

1. Follow steps 1 and 2 of recipe for Simple Chicken Pot Pie (page 106).

2. After sautéing onion, celery and carrots in 1½ tablespoons oil in step 3, remove from pot. Sauté mushrooms in remaining 1 tablespoon oil until liquid evaporates and mushrooms start to soften, 3 to 5 minutes. Continue as directed.

Fluffy Buttermilk Biscuits

MAKES ENOUGH TO COVER ONE 13-BY-9-INCH PAN
OR SIX 12-OUNCE OVENPROOF BAKING DISHES

THIS BISCUIT RECIPE was developed by the cookbook author Stephen Schmidt. These biscuits are made tender with a mix of cake and all-purpose flour and are my favorite topping for chicken pot pie.

1	cup all-purpose flour
1	cup plain cake flour
2	teaspoons baking powder
¼	teaspoon baking soda
1	teaspoon sugar
½	teaspoon salt
8	tablespoons (1 stick) unsalted butter, chilled, quartered lengthwise and cut crosswise into ¼-inch pieces
¾	cup cold buttermilk, plus 1-2 tablespoons more, if needed

1. Pulse flours, baking powder, baking soda, sugar and salt in a food processor fitted with a steel blade. Add butter pieces; pulse until mixture resembles coarse meal with a few slightly larger butter lumps.

2. Transfer mixture to a medium bowl. Add buttermilk and stir with a fork until dough gathers into moist clumps. Transfer dough to a floured work surface and form into a rough ball; roll dough ½ inch thick. Using a 2½-inch pastry cutter, stamp out 8 rounds of dough. If making individual pies, cut dough slightly smaller than circumference of each dish. (Dough rounds can be refrigerated on a lightly floured baking sheet covered with plastic wrap for up to 2 hours.)

3. Arrange dough rounds over warm filling and bake as directed in step 5 of recipe for Simple Chicken Pot Pie.

Rich, Flaky Pie Dough

MAKES ENOUGH TO COVER ONE 13-BY-9-INCH PAN
OR SIX 12-OUNCE OVENPROOF BAKING DISHES

THIS PASTRY DOUGH was developed by the *Cook's Illustrated* publisher, my friend Christopher Kimball. If you like a bottom crust in your pot pie, you can mimic that texture by tucking overhanging dough down into the side of the pan rather than fluting it.

> 1½ cups all-purpose flour
> ½ teaspoon salt
> 8 tablespoons (1 stick) unsalted butter, chilled and cut into ¼-inch pieces
> 4 tablespoons all-vegetable shortening, chilled

1. Mix flour and salt in a food processor fitted with a steel blade. Scatter butter pieces over flour mixture, tossing to coat butter with a little flour. Cut butter into flour with five 1-second pulses. Add shortening; continue cutting in until flour is pale yellow and resembles coarse cornmeal with some pea-size butter bits, about four more 1-second pulses. Turn out mixture into a medium bowl.

2. Sprinkle 3 tablespoons ice water over mixture. Using a rubber spatula, fold water into flour mixture. Then press down on dough mixture with broad side of spatula until dough sticks together, adding up to 1 tablespoon more water if dough will not come together. Gather dough into hands, shape into a ball, then flatten into a 4-inch-wide disk. Wrap in plastic and refrigerate for 30 minutes while preparing pie filling.

3. Roll dough on a floured surface to an approximate 15-by-11-inch rectangle, about ⅛ inch thick. If making individual pies, roll dough ⅛ inch thick and cut 6 dough rounds about 1 inch larger than pan circumference. Lay dough over pot pie filling, trimming to ½ inch larger than pan lip. Tuck overhanging dough back under itself so folded edge is flush with lip. Flute edges all around. Alternatively, don't trim dough, but simply tuck overhanging edges down into pan sides. Cut at least four 1-inch vent holes in large pot pie or one 1-inch vent hole in smaller pies. Bake as directed in step 5 of recipe for Simple Chicken Pot Pie.

A Better Burger

YOU DON'T NEED TO BE reminded of the billions served. We eat a lot of hamburgers, even though most of them satisfy hunger, not pleasure. That's unfortunate because making an exceptional hamburger isn't hard or time-consuming. While fast-food chains have good reasons for not offering hand-formed, 100-percent ground-chuck burgers, home cooks do not.

The perfect hamburger can be ready for a bun in under 15 minutes, assuming it's been seasoned, formed and cooked properly. The biggest difficulty for many cooks, though, may be finding the right beef.

Chuck It

I started my hamburger investigation by determining which cut or cuts of beef cook into the best burger. I made patties from chuck, round, rump, sirloin and hanging tenderloin—all ground to order with 20 percent fat. (Although I would look at fat percentages more closely later, I needed a standard for these early tests. Since the percentages of fat in ground beef range from 7 to 30 percent, 20 percent was a good mid-

point from which to make adjustments.) After a side-by-side taste test, I quickly concluded that most cuts of ground beef are pleasant but bland when compared to the robustly flavored ground chuck. Even pricier ground sirloin cooked up into a particularly boring burger.

Because retail ground-beef labeling is deceptive (page 113), I suggest buying a chuck roast and having the butcher grind it for you or, even better, grind it yourself. The butcher at my local grocery store was willing to grind to order, but she cautioned that butchers at larger grocery store chains might not be so amenable. Some meat, she added, always gets lost in the grinder, so count on losing a small amount (2 to 3 percent).

For cooks who decide to grind their beef at home, was there a simple way to do it, I wondered? Assembling a meat grinder (assuming the cook even had one) demanded far too much time and cleanup for a dish meant to be so simple. To see if there was an easier way, I tried chopping by hand and grinding the meat in a food processor. The hand-chopping method was just as time-consuming and messier than the traditional grinder. The meat must be thinly sliced,

WHERE'S THE CHUCK?

DOES GROCERY-STORE ground chuck compare to ground-to-order chuck? After talking with butchers, buyers and those at the beef board, I doubt it. Just because it's labeled ground chuck doesn't necessarily mean it is. According to Susan Parenti, assistant director of the National Livestock and Meat Board, only beef's fat percentage is checked and enforced at the retail level. If a package of beef is labeled 90 percent lean, then it must contain no more than 10 percent fat, give or take a point. Retail stores are required to test each batch of ground beef, make the necessary adjustments and keep a log of the results. Local inspectors routinely pull ground beef from a store's meat case for a fat check. If the tested meat is not within 1 percent of the package sticker, the store is fined.

Whether a package labeled ground chuck is, in fact, 100 percent ground chuck is a different story. I surveyed a number of grocery-store meat department managers who claimed that what was written on the label did match what was in the package. For instance, a package labeled "ground chuck," would indeed contain only chuck trimmings. The same was true for sirloin and round. Only a package of "ground beef" would contain mixed beef trimmings.

I got a little closer to the truth interviewing a respected butcher in the Chicago area who spoke candidly. Of the several grocery stores and butcher shops he had worked at over the years, he had never known a store to segregate meat trimmings. Susan Parenti explained that only meat ground at federally inspected plants is guaranteed to be true to its label. To most retailers, specific cuts of ground beef are more often indications of fat percentages: Ground sirloin is usually 90 to 92 percent lean. Round ranges from 85 to 90 percent lean. Chuck varies from 20 to 22 percent lean. And ground beef, by law, cannot have more than 30 percent fat (70 percent lean).

then cut into cubes, before you go at it with two chef's knives. The fat doesn't evenly distribute, meat flies everywhere and unless your knives are razor sharp, it's difficult to chop through the meat. What's worse, you can't efficiently chop enough for more than two burgers at a time. In the end, the hand-chopped burger looked like chopped steak.

The food processor ground the meat surprisingly well. I thought the steel blade would raggedly chew the meat, but to my surprise, the meat was evenly chopped and fluffy. The key is to make sure the roast is cold, that it is cut into small chunks and that it is processed in small batches (see page 116).

For those who buy a chuck roast for grinding, I found the average chuck roast to be about 80 percent lean. Marlis Belensky, test kitchen director at the National Livestock and Meat Board, recommends leaner cuts of chuck from the shoulder or arm for grinding. "The closer you move to the rib," she warns, "the fattier the roast." Cuts like blade roast are probably too fatty for grinding.

Up to this point, all of the beef had been ground with approximately 20 percent fat. A quick test of burgers with less and more fat helped me to decide that the 20-percent figure, give or take a few percentage points, is good for burgers. Any higher and the fat is left in the pan; any lower and the beef's juicy, moist texture begins to be compromised.

Less Seasoning Is Best

When to salt (and pepper) the meat may seem like an unimportant detail, but when making a dish as simple as a hamburger, little things matter. I tried seasoning the meat at four different times during the process. My first burger was seasoned before the meat was shaped, the second burger was seasoned right before cooking, the third after each side was seared and the fourth after the burger had been fully cooked.

The burger that had been seasoned before shaping tasted best. All the surface-seasoned burgers were the same, offering a hit of salt right up front and then going bland. It was clear that the seasonings had not penetrated most of the burger.

Though I liked seasoning the meat before shaping, I wondered how salt would affect it if the formed patties were refrigerated before cooking. Although I was afraid that salt would cause the patties to leach out their liquid or cause the meat to toughen, even the patties that were left in the refrigerator for a couple of days did not release any moisture, nor did I notice any textural or taste difference in them once they were cooked.

I tried other seasonings and culinary tricks. Most were distracting; a few were intriguing. Minced onions and bread crumbs made the burger taste like meat loaf, while garlic made it taste like a meatball begging for red sauce. One recipe suggested mixing a bit of milk into the meat. As I suspected, it did nothing for the flavor, and the natural sugar in the milk caused the patty to burn during cooking. Another recipe suggested adding beef broth to old meat to mask off flavors. Perhaps my trial meat was too far gone, but I don't think anything could mask the flavor of stale beef. Some recipes promised a juicier burger by adding ice water to the meat, but the juiciness had its price: the meat, in both raw and cooked form, was mushy. A similar tip—ice chips placed in the center of the patty—certainly kept the burger rare, but left a hole in its place. I never did get the point of the ice trick, because a rare burger can be achieved simply with less cooking time.

Perfecting the Patty

For those who like their burgers well done, poking a small hole in the center of the patty before cooking helps the burger center to get done before the edges dry out. And for those who love cheese, I recommend grating it into the raw beef as opposed to melting it on top. Because the cheese is more evenly distributed, a small amount goes much further.

Many hamburger recipes warn against overpacking and overhandling the patty, and I decided to defy those instructions by thoroughly working a portion of ground beef before cooking it. The well-done burger exterior was indeed dense, like a meat pâté, while the less well-done interior was compact and pasty.

In fact, it's pretty hard to overhandle a beef patty, especially if you're trying not to. Once the meat has been divided into portions, tossing it from one hand to another helps bring it together into a ball without overworking it. Pressing the formed ball of meat into a patty with my fingertips not only prevented overworking it, but it also gave good surface texture.

To my taste, a 4-ounce burger is a little skimpy. A 5-ounce portion of meat patted into a nice size patty—a scant 4 inches in diameter and just shy of 1 inch thick—is just the right size for a bun.

No cooking method surpasses grilling, but I was awfully fond of the thick-crusted burgers that I produced in a well-seasoned cast-iron skillet. I didn't even need any fat or salt in the pan to keep the burgers from sticking. Like a good loaf of bread, the perfect burger should display a crisp, flavorful crust that protects a moist, tender interior. Both grilling and pan-broiling deliver this ideal. Traditional broiling could not offer the contrast in texture I was looking for.

Whether you are grilling or pan-broiling, I make two suggestions. Make sure the pan or grill rack is hot before adding the meat. If not, the hamburger will not develop that crucial crusty exterior. Avoid the temptation to flip the burger continually during cooking.

Check the chart on page 118, setting a timer if you like. When the buzzer goes off, turn the burger. When the buzzer goes off again, pull it from the heat.

GRINDING HAMBURGER AT HOME

START WITH MEAT that is refrigerator-cold. (If you have time, freezing the meat for a half hour is even better.) For a 2-pound roast, cut the meat into 1-inch chunks and divide the chunks into four ½-pound portions. Place one portion in a food processor fitted with a steel blade. Pulse cubes until meat is ground, 15 to 20 1-second pulses, and repeat with the remaining portions of beef.

Better Burgers

SERVES 4

BECAUSE BURGERS require a hot fire, you'll need a lot of coals (5 pounds). So that you don't waste good hot coals, plan to grill a vegetable side dish. Or, because the coals are spread on only one side of the grill for the burgers, why not grill-roast a chicken or beef or pork roast for another meal? Simply place the roast on the side of the grill opposite the coals, cover and grill-roast. Because the roast is not cooking over direct heat, you can forget about it, at least while eating your burger. You can also pan-broil these burgers in a cast-iron skillet or a stovetop grill pan. If you have one, a spatter screen, placed over the pan-broiled burgers during cooking, does prevent a greasy mess.

> 1¼ **pounds 100% ground chuck**
> ¾ **teaspoon salt**
> ¼ **teaspoon ground black pepper**
> 4 **hamburger buns**
>   **Hamburger toppings**

1. Place ground chuck in a large bowl and break up with fingers to increase surface area for seasoning. Sprinkle salt and pepper over meat and toss lightly with hands to distribute seasoning. Divide meat into 4 equal portions (5 ounces each). With cupped hands, toss portion of meat back and forth to form a loose ball. Pat lightly to flatten to a 1-inch-thick burger, 3½ to 4 inches across, using your fingertips to create a pocked, textured surface. Repeat with remaining meat.

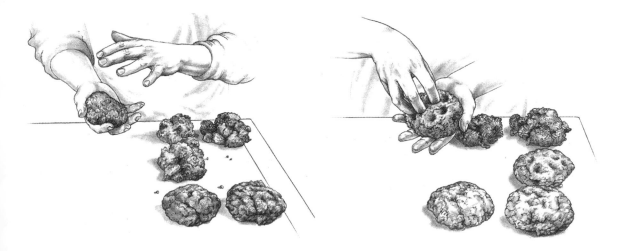

2. If you plan to grill burgers, heat enough coals to make a hot fire (at least 5 pounds). When coals are hot and covered with white ash, spread them over half of grill. Replace grill rack and lid; heat until grill rack is very hot, about 5 minutes. Place burgers on grill rack over hot coals, cover and grill on one side (see below for exact cooking time). Turn burgers and grill to desired doneness. If you are pan-broiling, heat a 12-inch cast-iron skillet over medium-high heat until very hot, at least 5 minutes. When pan is hot (drops of water flicked into the pan evaporate immediately), add patties and cook one side. Turn burgers and cook to desired doneness. Serve immediately with buns and desired toppings.

PERFECT TIMING FOR BURGERS

To cook a 5-ounce burger, about 1 inch thick, to your preferred doneness, use medium-high heat and follow these times:

Rare	3 minutes per side
Medium-Rare	4 minutes per side
Medium-Well	5 minutes first side, 4 minutes second side
Well Done	5 minutes per side

Bacon-Cheddar Burgers

SERVES 4

BLUE CHEESE, which is also excellent with the bacon, can substitute for the cheddar, but reduce the cheese amount to ½ cup crumbled.

4	slices bacon
1¼	pounds 100% ground chuck
¾	cup grated cheddar cheese
¾	teaspoon salt
¼	teaspoon ground black pepper
4	hamburger buns
	Hamburger toppings

1. Fry bacon in a medium skillet over medium heat until crisp, 5 to 7 minutes. Drain on paper towels, halve each bacon slice and set aside.

2. Follow recipe for Better Burgers (page 117), adding cheese along with salt and pepper in step 1 and tossing lightly. Shape patties and continue with recipe.

3. Put cooked hamburgers on each of buns. Top each hamburger with half slices bacon and serve.

Swiss Cheese Burgers
with Sautéed Mushrooms

Serves 4

THESE BURGERS DEMAND a glass of red wine. Deglaze the pan of mushrooms with a little of it, then serve the remainder at table.

       2 tablespoons butter
      12 ounces mushrooms (domestic or wild), thickly sliced
       1 small garlic clove, minced
       1 teaspoon minced fresh thyme leaves or
             scant ½ teaspoon dried thyme
          Salt
          Ground black pepper
       ¼ cup dry full-bodied red wine
      1¼ pounds 100% ground chuck
       ¾ cup grated Swiss or Gruyère cheese
          Hamburger buns
          Hamburger toppings

1. Heat butter over medium-high heat in a large sauté pan. When foaming subsides, add mushrooms, garlic, thyme and salt and pepper to taste. Sauté until juices release and evaporate and mushrooms begin to brown, about 5 minutes. Add wine; continue to cook until liquid evaporates, about 2 minutes longer. Remove from heat and set aside.

2. Follow recipe for Better Burgers (page 117), adding cheese along with salt and pepper in step 1 and tossing lightly. Shape patties and continue with recipe.

3. Put cooked hamburgers on each of buns. Top each hamburger with a portion of mushrooms and serve.

Jack Cheese Burgers
with Tomato-Avocado Salsa

Serves 4

For an even simpler topping for this burger, just stir a couple of tablespoons of prepared salsa into the mashed avocado, then adjust the seasonings with fresh lime juice, salt and a drop or two of hot red pepper sauce.

> 1 small avocado, peeled and pitted
> 1 small ripe tomato, cut into small dice
> 1 tablespoon minced scallion
> 1 teaspoon minced jalapeño pepper
> 1½ teaspoons minced cilantro leaves
> 1 tablespoon juice from ½ small lime
> Salt
> Ground black pepper
> 1¼ pounds 100% ground chuck
> ¾ cup grated Monterey Jack cheese
> 4 hamburger buns

1. Mash avocado with a fork until chunky. Add tomato, scallion, jalapeño, cilantro, lime juice and salt and pepper to taste. Set aside.

2. Follow recipe for Better Burgers (page 117), adding cheese along with salt and pepper in step 1 and tossing lightly. Shape patties and cook as directed.

3. Put cooked hamburgers on each of buns. Top each hamburger with a portion of salsa and serve.

Blue Cheese Burgers
with Grilled Red Onion

SERVES 4

BECAUSE OF THE SLABS of red onion, these burgers are best cooked on the grill. If you have a grill pan, you can also cook the onions on the stovetop.

1	medium red onion, sliced ½ inch thick
	Vegetable oil for brushing onion
	Salt
	Ground black pepper
1¼	pounds 100% ground chuck
½	cup crumbled blue cheese
4	hamburger buns

1. Brush onion with oil and sprinkle with salt and pepper.

2. Follow recipe for Better Burgers (page 117), adding cheese along with salt and pepper in step 1 and tossing lightly. Shape patties and continue with recipe, grilling onions alongside hamburgers, turning onions once and cooking until firm and grill-marked on both sides, 6 to 8 minutes.

3. Put cooked hamburgers on each of buns. Top each with a grilled onion slab and serve immediately.

Hamburgers with Caramelized Onions

SERVES 4

THESE ONIONS NEED LONG, slow cooking to sweeten and soften properly, so prepare them before cooking the hamburgers. And because they are made in a skillet, the onions are best served with pan-broiled burgers.

  2 tablespoons butter
  2 medium-large onions, thinly sliced
  ½ teaspoon dried thyme leaves
  ½ teaspoon sugar
    Salt
    Ground black pepper
  1¼ pounds 100% ground chuck
  4 hamburger buns

1. Heat butter over medium-high heat in a medium skillet. When foaming subsides, add onions. Season with thyme, sugar and salt and pepper to taste. When onions soften and start to brown, about 10 minutes, reduce heat to low and continue to cook until soft and caramel brown, 5 to 10 minutes longer.

2. Follow recipe for Better Burgers (page 117), shaping patties and cooking as directed.

3. Put cooked hamburgers on each of buns. Top each burger with a portion of cooked onions and serve.

Memorable Meat Loaf

DURING THE LATE eighties, meat loaf experienced a revival, with feature articles and even entire books devoted to this single subject. Little wonder—after a decade of nouvelle experiments and celebrity chefs, the food public began to long for Mama's cooking, or "comfort food," as it became known. Mashed potatoes, pot pies, stews and hearty soups became new party staples, and meat loaf, in particular, seemed to epitomize this brief fad.

While the culinary trendsetters have moved on, meat loaf has remained with us, though in forms Mama would scarcely recognize. Some ingredient lists, in fact, look more like the work of a proud child or defiant adolescent. Canned pineapple, canned soup, cranberry sauce, raisins, prepared taco mix and even goat cheese have all found their way into published recipes.

But rather than fuss over the ideal flavorings for a perfect meat loaf, I focused instead on meatier issues. I narrowed my research and testing to red-meat loaves, as poultry and vegetarian loaves presented a different range of issues. What

meat or mix of meats, I wondered, deliver good texture and flavor? Which fillers are the most unobtrusive? Which liquids subtly moisten the mix? Should the loaf be cooked free-form or in a standard loaf pan, or are the new perforated pans designed specifically for meat loaves worth the money? What about recipes that suggested cooking meat loaf over a pan of water or in a water bath? Should meat loaf be topped with bacon, ketchup or both? Is it better to sauté the onions and garlic before adding them to the meat mix, or are they just as good in raw, grated form?

Finding the Right Mix of Meats

In order to determine which ground meat or meat mix makes the best loaf, I started with a basic meat loaf recipe, making miniature loaves with the following:

♦ Half beef chuck, half pork
♦ Half veal, half pork
♦ One-third each beef chuck, veal and pork
♦ Half beef chuck, one-fourth each pork and veal

- Three-fourths beef chuck, one-fourth ground bacon
- Half beef chuck, half ham
- Beef chuck
- Veal

Meat markets, I quickly realized, haven't been selling meat-loaf mix (a combination of beef, veal and pork, usually in equal proportions) all these years for nothing, for the best version was prepared from precisely these three. Straight ground veal was tender, mild and mushy, while the all-beef loaf was coarse, liver-flavored and tough. Though interesting, neither the beef-ham nor the beef-bacon loaf looked or tasted like classic meat loaf: both were firm and dense—more like a terrine than a meat loaf. I preferred the bacon's smoky flavor and crispy texture surrounding, the loaf, not in it.

Although both combinations of beef, pork and veal were good, I preferred the mix with the higher proportion of ground beef, which gave the loaf a distinct but not overly strong flavor. Nonassertive, milder-flavored pork adds another flavor dimension. The extra percentage of beef keeps the loaf firm, making it easier to cut, while the small quantity of veal makes it tender. For those who don't get around to special-ordering this mix, I recommend the standard meat loaf combination of equal parts of beef, pork and veal.

Fad Fillers Fail

After comparing meat loaves made with and without fillers, I realized that starch in a meat loaf offers more than economy. Loaves made without filler were coarse, dense and too much like hamburger, lacking the distinct texture of meat loaf. But which one to use? After all, practically every hot or cold cereal box offers a meat loaf recipe using that particular product.

Although I made several meat loaves, each with a different filler, there was no clear-cut winner. After tasting all the versions, I concluded that a good binder should provide texture but not flavor. Rice left its obvious imprint, flecking the meat white and producing a taste and texture that stood out from the meat. Quick-cooking tapioca is great for thickening pies, but it sucked every ounce of juice from the meat, leaving the loaf dry and gelatinous. Neither of the cereal-bound loaves scored well: Grape-Nuts freckled the loaf and gave a wheaty aftertaste, and the cornflakes loaf tasted odd. Like the rice binding, grated potato didn't mix well with the meat, standing out visually and texturally. Mashed pinto beans made the loaf taste as if it needed taco chips and salsa. The binders I preferred were cracker crumbs, quick-cooking oatmeal and fresh bread crumbs. Although within the range of acceptability, dried bread crumbs made a loaf that was dense and rubbery compared to my favorite fillers.

Just as I opted for less distinctly flavored fillers, I preferred sautéed—not raw—onions and garlic in the meat mix. Because a meat loaf bakes to an internal temperature of only 160 degrees, raw onions never fully cook, and the loaf tastes too strongly of them. Sautéing the vegetables is a five-minute detour well worth the effort.

Dairy Moistens Best

Meat loaves need some added liquid, for without it, the filler robs moisture from the meat, making the loaf dry. A majority of meat loaf recipes call for some form of dairy for the liquid. I tried half-and-half, milk, sour cream, yogurt, buttermilk, evaporated milk and evaporated skim milk and even cottage cheese. Half-and-half and sour cream both made the meat loaf too rich. The evaporated-milk-flavored loaves tasted fine but offered nothing that would require the special purchase of that ingredient. Regular milk, buttermilk and low-fat plain yogurt were my liquids of choice, the low-fat plain yogurt and buttermilk offering a complementary, subtle tang to the rich beef.

Tomato juice in the meat loaf simply tasted like hot tomato juice, while tomato sauce made the meat loaf taste like a meatball with sauce. I liked the flavor of ketchup mixed in with the meat, but ultimately decided that I preferred it baked on top rather than inside. For the same reason that raw onions aren't a suitable addition, beer and wine are not ideal meat moisteners. The meat doesn't cook long enough or to a high enough internal temperature to burn off the alcohol, leaving the meat with a distinctly raw alcohol taste. Beef broth neither disqualified nor distinguished itself.

Free-Form or in the Pan?

People who have definite opinions about meat loaf care a lot about how it is baked. There are two camps: those who want a browned crust and those who prefer their meat loaf moist and soft throughout. Although a loaf pan is the usual choice for cooking meat loaf, it causes the meat to stew rather than bake. And for those who prefer a meat loaf with a glazed top, the loaf pan will disappoint, for it makes the meat juices bubble up from the sides, diluting the glaze. Similarly, bacon placed on top of the meat loaf baked in a loaf pan curls and doesn't properly attach to the loaf; if tucked inside the pan, the bacon never crisps.

If you prefer a crustless, soft-sided meat loaf, invest in a pan with a perforated bottom and accompanying drip pan. The enclosed pan keeps the meat soft, while the perforated bottom allows the drippings to flow to the pan below.

While still not ideal for a crispy bacon top, it does maintain a glaze.

For a perfectly browned, well-glazed meat loaf, baking it free-form on a wire rack set over a shallow baking pan gives the best results. Both the top and sides of the loaf brown nicely, and the brown sugar-ketchup sauce I developed for basting (page 128) glazes the entire loaf, not just the top. You can wrap bacon around the whole loaf as well and, because its drippings also fall onto the pan below, it crisps up nicely. Arrange the slices crosswise and overlap them slightly, so they adhere better and slice more easily. Tuck only the tip of the bacon under the loaf so that as much of the strip as possible will become crisp during baking.

Even though I knew I preferred a free-form loaf, I wanted to find out if there were any benefits to cooking a meat loaf in a water bath, or *bain marie*. Setting a pan of meat loaf in a water bath accomplished nothing except to prevent browning. Nor was the free-form meat loaf improved by baking it over a pan of simmering water. I dismissed both methods as unnecessary.

Finally, a meat loaf baked to an internal 160 degrees is well done, cooked to a safe temperature, yet still juicy.

Bacon-Wrapped Meat Loaf with Brown Sugar-Ketchup Glaze

SERVES 6 TO 8

IF YOU LIKE, you can double the glaze and omit the bacon topping from the loaf. Brush on half the glaze before baking, and the other half during the last 15 minutes of baking time.

Brown Sugar-Ketchup Glaze

¼ cup ketchup or chili sauce

2 tablespoons light or dark brown sugar

2 teaspoons cider or white vinegar

Meat Loaf

2 teaspoons vegetable oil

1 medium onion, chopped

2 garlic cloves, minced

2 large eggs

1 teaspoon dried thyme leaves

1 teaspoon salt

½ teaspoon ground black pepper

2 teaspoons Dijon mustard

2 teaspoons Worcestershire sauce

¼ teaspoon hot red pepper sauce

½ cup milk, buttermilk or low-fat plain yogurt

2 pounds meat-loaf mix (50% ground chuck,
   25% ground veal, 25% ground pork)

⅔ cup crushed saltine crackers (about 16)
   or quick oatmeal or 1⅓ cups fresh bread crumbs

⅓ cup minced fresh parsley leaves

6 ounces thin-sliced bacon (8-9 slices)

1. Glaze: Mix all ingredients in a small bowl; set aside.

2. Meat Loaf: Preheat oven to 350°F. Heat oil in a medium skillet. Add onion and garlic, and sauté until softened, about 5 minutes; set aside to cool.

3. Mix eggs with thyme, salt, pepper, mustard, Worcestershire, pepper sauce and milk or yogurt. Add egg mixture to meat in a large bowl, along with crackers, oatmeal or bread crumbs, parsley and cooked onions and garlic; mix with a fork until evenly blended and meat mixture does not stick to bowl. (If mixture does stick, add additional milk, a couple tablespoons at a time, and continue stirring until mixture stops sticking.)

4. Turn meat mixture onto a work surface. With wet hands, pat mixture into a loaf approximately 9 by 5 inches.

5. To bake free-form: Cover a wire rack with foil; prick foil in several places with a fork. Place rack on a shallow roasting pan lined with foil for easy cleanup. Set formed loaf on rack. Brush loaf with all of glaze, then arrange bacon slices, crosswise, over loaf, overlapping them slightly and tucking them under loaf to prevent curling.

6. Bake loaf until bacon is crisp and loaf registers 160°F, about 1 hour. Cool for at least 20 minutes. Slice and serve.

To bake in a loaf pan: Omit bacon and *double* glaze. Turn meat mixture into a loaf pan with a perforated bottom, fitted with a drip pan. Use a fork to pull mixture away from pan sides. Brush mixture with half of glaze. Bake until glaze is set, about 45 minutes. Brush with remaining glaze and continue to bake until second coat has set and loaf registers 160°F, about 15 minutes longer.

Simple, Satisfying Beef Stew

FEW DISHES are as soul-satisfying as a hearty beef stew. A good one starts with carefully browned meat and vegetables like onions and garlic. The stewing liquid should taste boldly of beef, supported but not overpowered by a generous splash of a rich red wine. The stew's vegetables should be bright and flavorful, infused by the stew but retaining their individual tastes. What a gift to the cook that such a dish demands so little preparation and effort.

My goal in developing a recipe for perfect beef stew was to keep the cooking process simple without compromising the dish's complex flavor. I skipped over recipes that began with instructions for homemade beef broth, knowing that many home cooks barely have time to make stew, much less broth. At the other extreme, I ignored those recipes that simply dumped meat, vegetables and liquid into a pot to simmer for a couple of hours, for I was certain that the process of browning and caramelizing was important to the flavor.

I focused on the issues that mattered. What cut or cuts of meat respond best to stewing? How much and what kind of liquid should you use? When and with what do you thicken the stew? How should the stew be cooked—in the oven, on top of the stove or does it matter? And, finally, when is the best time to add the vegetables?

Chuck and Shank Win

From previous beef tastings, I knew that chuck and shank are some of the most flavorful cuts of beef. Not surprisingly, they scored high in my stew tests as well. Bottom round cooked up dry with a sawdustlike texture. Sirloin tip had a pleasant, almost gamy flavor, but, like the bottom round, it was fairly dry. My least favorite stewing meat was brisket. When braised and thinly sliced, it has a wonderful texture. But cut into chunks, it became stringy, coarse and spongy. And because brisket is a single muscle, the cut chunks were a uniform block shape, with no variation in texture or shape. Much like the brisket, top round was gelatinous and coarse—not ideal stewing meat. As predicted, chuck and shank won out. Chuck's texture is not coarse like brisket and top round, and it doesn't dry out like sirloin tip and bottom round. Because it is multimuscular, the chunks of chuck are pleasantly uneven, offering a more pleasing texture to both eye and palate. Because it is so gelatinous, shank becomes particularly soft and silky. It is a bone-in cut, so the meat must be removed from the bone before cooking, but the process is simple, and the bones can be reserved for soup making.

The Skinny on Thickeners

After determining the best cut of meat, I went on to explore how and when to thicken the stew. Most thickening methods turned out to be acceptable, with the exception of quick-cooking tapioca, which produced a slimy stew.

Dredging beef cubes in flour is another roundabout way of thickening. The floured beef is browned, then stewed, with some of the flour from the beef dissolving into the cooking liquid. Though the stew cooked in this way thickened up nicely, the beef cubes had a "smothered-steak" look: the coating, and not the meat itself, had browned. This coating often falls off during cooking to expose pale meat that is less flavorful because it has not received the benefit of browning.

I also tried two thickeners added at the end of cooking: a *beurre manié* (softened butter mixed with flour) as well as cornstarch mixed with water. Either method is acceptable, but the *beurre manié* lightened the stew's color, making

it look more like pale gravy than stew juices. The extra fat grams did not improve the flavor enough to justify it. For those who prefer to thicken at the end of cooking, cornstarch dissolved in water does the job without compromising the stew's dark, rich color.

An alternative thickening method is to puree the cooked vegetables once the stew is fully cooked, after the meat is pulled from the pot. Although some cooks may prefer this technique, I felt the vegetable flavor became too dominant. Hearty beef stew began to taste like mixed vegetable stew with beef chunks.

Ultimately, I opted for the easiest method, thickening the stew with flour at the beginning and stirring it into the sautéing onions and garlic just before adding the liquid. That way, all the work is done at the beginning. Once the liquid starts to simmer, you're home free.

The Liquid Test

To determine which liquid or combination of liquids makes the most flavorful stew, I tried the following:

♦ all water
♦ water with a few shank bones thrown in for extra flavor
♦ all wine
♦ low-sodium canned beef broth
♦ wine with various partners (low-sodium canned beef broth, low-sodium canned chicken broth and water).

None of my tasters preferred the stews made with only one liquid. Predictably, the all-wine stew was too strong, while the all-water stew was thin and flat. The one made with water and bones was greasier, and adding the bones didn't improve the flavor dramatically. The all-beef broth stews were acceptable, but lacked that flavor edge that comes with wine. Of the stews that were made with part wine, the chicken broth-flavored stew beat out the one made with water, as well as the one made with part beef broth.

The Right Wine

The wine you select for the stew pot really makes a difference. My first set of stews were made with a moderately priced but full-bodied Shiraz. Without giving it much thought, I made my next group with a young Beaujolais. As I tasted, I noticed that these stews weren't as rich and complex as those made with Shiraz. For a richer stew, select a moderately priced but full-bodied wine such as Cabernet Sauvignon, Côtes du Rhône, Zinfandel, Shiraz or Barolo.

The more liquid you add, the less intensely flavored your stew will be. For a pure beef flavor, use a minimum of liquid. About 1 cup of liquid per pound of meat is just right, providing enough to generously moisten a mound of mashed potatoes, polenta or rice.

Vegetables—First or Last?

In order to determine when to add the vegetables, I made three different stews, adding carrots, celery and onions to one at the beginning of cooking, and halfway through the cooking process to another. For my final stew, I cooked onions and garlic with the meat but steamed the carrots and celery separately and added them when the stew was fully cooked. The stew with vegetables put in at the beginning was thin and watery, for although the vegetables gave up their flavor, they also diluted the liquid, making the dish taste more like beef-vegetable soup. The stew with vegetables added halfway through was less watery, but the vegetables still diluted the beef flavor. The stew with cooked vegetables stirred in at the last minute was the winner, for it had a rich, uncompromised flavor with fresh, bright, full-flavored vegetables. Adding vegetables at the beginning, picking them out at the end and replacing them with fresh-cooked ones, as some recipes recommend, is fussy and unnecessary and interferes with the full beef flavor of the stew.

I focused on low-temperature cooking methods because I knew that high heat toughens and dries out meat. I cooked stews on the stovetop over low heat, with and without a flame-taming device, and in a 200-degree oven. The flame-tamer kept the meat from becoming tender within a reasonable amount of time, and the stew juices tasted as though the wine hadn't cooked off. Although either method is acceptable for cooking the stew, I prefer the consistent, enveloping heat of the oven over the inconsistent heat of the burner. The burner must be constantly adjusted, while stew in the oven cooks more evenly.

Regardless of where you cook your stew, it will pass from the tough to the tender stage fairly quickly. At the two-hour mark, the tested meat would often be chewy, while 15 minutes later, it would be tender. It's important to stop the cooking as soon as the meat is tender.

STEWING SENSE

♦ Chuck and shank make the best stew.

♦ If you want your meat to have the best flavor, don't dredge it in flour.

♦ Thicken the stew with flour at the beginning rather than at the end.

♦ Use a combination of broth and wine for a more flavorful, well-balanced sauce and choose a full-bodied wine.

♦ Cook the stew vegetables separately and add them right before serving.

♦ For more even, consistent cooking, cook stew in the oven rather than on top of the stove.

Hearty Beef Stew
with Green Peas and Carrots

SERVES 6 TO 8

THIS STEW should be made in a large soup kettle measuring at least 10 inches in diameter. If the kettle is any smaller, you may need to cook the meat in three batches. I like mashed potatoes with my stew. If you prefer potato chunks in your stew, boil them separately and add them to the pot with the carrots and peas.

3 pounds beef chuck, cut into 1½-inch cubes,
    or about 4½ pounds beef shank, meat removed
    from bone and cut into 1½-inch cubes
Salt
Ground black pepper
2-3 tablespoons vegetable oil
2 medium-large onions, chopped (2 cups)
3 garlic cloves, minced
3 tablespoons all-purpose flour
1 cup full-bodied red wine (Cabernet Sauvignon,
    Côtes du Rhône, Zinfandel, Shiraz or Barolo)
2 cups homemade chicken broth or low-sodium canned broth
2 bay leaves
1 teaspoon dried thyme leaves
4 large carrots, peeled and sliced ¼ inch thick
1 cup (6 ounces) frozen peas, thawed
¼ cup minced fresh parsley leaves

1. Preheat oven to 200°F. Place meat in a large bowl. Sprinkle with 1½ teaspoons salt and 1 teaspoon pepper; toss to coat. Heat 2 tablespoons oil over medium-high heat in a large nonreactive soup kettle; add meat to pan in two batches. Brown meat on all sides, about 5 minutes per batch, adding an additional 1 tablespoon oil if necessary. Transfer meat to a platter.

2. Add onions to pot; sauté until almost softened, 4 to 5 minutes. Reduce heat to medium and add garlic; continue to sauté for about 30 seconds longer. Stir in flour and cook until lightly colored, 1 to 2 minutes. Stir in wine, scraping up any browned bits that may have stuck to pan. Add chicken broth, bay leaves and thyme; bring to simmer. Add meat and return to a simmer. Cover and place in oven, and simmer until meat is just tender, 2½ to 3 hours. (Stew can be cooled at this point, covered and refrigerated up to 3 days.)

3. Before serving, bring 1 inch water to a boil in a steamer pot. Place carrots in steamer basket and lower into pot. Steam until just tender, about 6 minutes.

4. Add steamed carrots and uncooked peas to fully cooked stew; cover and let stand to blend flavors, about 5 minutes. Stir in parsley, adjust seasonings and serve.

Beef Stew with Bacon, Mushrooms and Pearl Onions

Serves 6 to 8

THIS BEEF *bourguignonne*-style stew is made with a higher proportion of red wine to broth.

3 pounds beef chuck, cut into 1½-inch cubes,
    or about 4½ pounds beef shank, meat removed
    from bone and cut into 1½-inch cubes
    Salt
    Ground black pepper
4 ounces sliced bacon, cut into small dice
2 medium-large onions, chopped (2 cups)
3 garlic cloves, minced
3 tablespoons all-purpose flour
1½ cups full-bodied red wine (Cabernet Sauvignon,
    Côtes du Rhône, Zinfandel, Shiraz or Barolo)
1½ cups homemade chicken broth or low-sodium canned broth
2 bay leaves
1 teaspoon dried thyme leaves
1 pound domestic mushrooms, quartered
1 cup (8 ounces) frozen pearl onions,
    cooked according to package directions
¼ cup minced fresh parsley leaves

1. Follow recipe for Hearty Beef Stew with Green Peas and Carrots (page 134), seasoning meat as directed in step 1. Omit oil and fry bacon over medium-high heat in soup kettle until brown and crisp. Drain, reserving bits and fat separately and substituting 2 to 3 tablespoons bacon fat for vegetable oil when browning meat. Proceed as directed in steps 1 and 2, returning bacon to pot with broth, bay leaves and thyme.

2. Heat 2 tablespoons of reserved bacon fat over medium-high heat in a large skillet until hot. Add mushrooms and sauté over high heat until browned, 5 to 7 minutes. Remove from pan and set aside. Add pearl onions to pan and sauté until lightly browned, 2 to 3 minutes; set aside. When meat is almost tender, 2 to 2½ hours, add mushrooms and onions to stew. Cover and return to oven, and cook until meat and pearl onions are tender, 20 to 30 minutes longer. Stir in parsley, adjust seasonings and serve.

Beef Stew with Tomatoes, Orange Zest and Olives

Serves 6 to 8

SOFT POLENTA is a perfect partner for this stew. For cooks who don't have time or energy to cook traditional polenta, the instant variety, available in many supermarkets and Italian specialty stores, is ready in about five minutes.

3 pounds beef chuck, cut into 1½-inch cubes,
  or about 4½ pounds beef shank, meat removed
  from bone and cut into 1½-inch cubes
  Salt
  Ground black pepper
2-3 tablespoons vegetable oil
2 medium-large onions, chopped (2 cups)
3 garlic cloves, minced
3 tablespoons all-purpose flour
1 cup chopped canned tomatoes with juice
1 cup homemade chicken broth or low-sodium canned broth
1 cup full-bodied red wine (Cabernet Sauvignon,
  Côtes du Rhône, Zinfandel, Shiraz or Barolo)
2 strips orange zest
1 teaspoon herbes de Provence
1 cup black olives, such as kalamata
¼ cup minced fresh parsley leaves

1. Follow steps 1 and 2 of recipe for Hearty Beef Stew with Green Peas and Carrots (page 134), adding tomatoes, chicken broth, wine and orange zest in step 2. Substitute herbes de Provence for thyme and simmer in oven as directed.

2. Stir olives into fully cooked stew. Cover and let stand for 5 minutes. Stir in parsley, adjust seasonings and serve.

Beef Stew with Root Vegetables

SERVES 6 TO 8

CHOCK-FULL OF POTATOES, carrots, turnips and onions, this hearty stew is made complete with large hunk of good bread.

3 pounds beef chuck, cut into 1½-inch cubes,
   or about 4½ pounds beef shank, meat removed
   from bone and cut into 1½-inch cubes
   Salt
   Ground black pepper
2-3 tablespoons vegetable oil
2 medium-large onions, chopped (2 cups)
3 garlic cloves, minced
3 tablespoons all-purpose flour
1 cup full-bodied red wine (Cabernet Sauvignon,
   Côtes du Rhône, Zinfandel, Shiraz or Barolo)
2 cups homemade chicken broth or low-sodium canned broth
2 bay leaves
1 teaspoon dried thyme leaves
6 small new potatoes, peeled and halved
6 boiling onions, peeled and left whole
3 small white turnips, peeled and quartered
3 large carrots, peeled and sliced ¼ inch thick
¼ cup minced fresh parsley leaves

1. Follow steps 1 and 2 of recipe for Hearty Beef Stew with Green Peas and Carrots (page 134).

2. In step 3, steam potatoes, boiling onions and turnips with carrots until tender, 10 to 15 minutes. Add to fully cooked stew and continue as directed.

Beef Stew with Tomatoes, Cinnamon and Cloves

SERVES 6 TO 8

Serve this stew with steamed couscous. Like instant polenta, couscous cooks very quickly.

3   pounds beef chuck, cut into 1½-inch cubes,
      or about 4½ pounds beef shank, meat removed
      from bone and cut into 1½-inch cubes
    Salt
    Ground black pepper
3-4 tablespoons vegetable oil
2   medium-large onions, chopped (2 cups)
3   garlic cloves, minced
3   tablespoons all-purpose flour
1   tablespoon tomato paste
1   cup full-bodied red wine (Cabernet Sauvignon,
      Côtes du Rhône, Zinfandel, Shiraz or Barolo)
1   cup chopped canned tomatoes
1   cup homemade chicken broth or low-sodium canned broth
1   teaspoon ground cinnamon
⅛ teaspoon ground cloves
2   bay leaves
1   teaspoon dried thyme leaves
1   cup (8 ounces) frozen pearl onions,
      cooked according to package directions
⅓ cup dried currants
¼ cup minced fresh parsley leaves

1. Follow steps 1 and 2 of recipe for Hearty Beef Stew with Green Peas and Carrots (page 134), browning meat in 2 to 3 tablespoons oil, and stirring in tomato paste after flour has colored in step 2. Add tomatoes with wine and chicken broth, and cinnamon and cloves with bay leaves and thyme.

2. Heat remaining 1 tablespoon oil in a medium skillet, add pearl onions and sauté until lightly browned, 2 to 3 minutes. When meat is almost tender, add pearl onions and currants. Cover, return to oven and cook until meat and pearl onions are tender, 20 to 30 minutes longer. Stir in parsley, adjust seasonings and serve.

III

Special Dinners

Perfect Roast Turkey

EVEN THOUGH AMERICANS are eating more turkey these days, most cooks reserve the ritual of roasting the whole bird for the holidays. After roasting more than 40 turkeys, I think I know why. A whole bird may look like a picture on the platter, but cooked the way most cookbooks and butchers advise, it never tastes as good as it looks.

Is it possible to roast a turkey perfectly? Experience has taught me that succulent, juicy breast meat comes with a price—shocking pink legs and thighs. I want each section cooked to perfection. Everyone knows you can abuse the dark meat: it's almost impossible to dry out. The trick is the breast. Because it is exposed, it parches, while the legs and thighs take their time creeping toward doneness. Most techniques try to remedy this problem; few are successful.

I found literally hundreds of recipes for roast turkey but decided to focus on a dozen or so fairly different ones—ranging from traditional to idiosyncratic—though no one technique had the edge as I began testing. In addition to finding an acceptable roasting method, I wanted to determine the ideal internal temperature—one that was safe as well as satisfying. Is basting a ritual done more for the sake of tradition than the turkey, or is it important? Stuffing is another issue—it's good, but does it keep the bird in the oven too long? Should the stuffing be cooked inside the cavity or separately? Does roasting celery, carrots and onions alongside the bird make noticeably better gravy? Is it really worth searching for a needle to truss up the turkey? It was only after I had roasted all those turkeys that I finally got the answers to those questions . . . as well as ones I hadn't known to ask.

The Turkey Roastathon

Working with 10-to-12-pound fresh turkeys, I began roasting. I determined fairly quickly that all turkeys roasted traditionally, breast side up, produced breast meat that was always 10 degrees ahead of the leg/thigh meat. That is, the breast meat cooked to perfection at 160 degrees, while the legs and thighs lost their last shades of pink at about 170 degrees. Just when the legs and thighs were getting done, the breast was a dry 180 degrees. Roasting both cuts to perfection seemed impossible. Tenting the breast with heavy-duty foil was the only technique that narrowed the big temperature gap between breast and thigh, bringing them 4 degrees closer, but the results were far from ideal.

I started off with the method promoted by most of the turkey producers and processors, the National Turkey Federation and the USDA: the traditional method of roasting the bird in an open pan in a moderate (325-degree) oven. I tested this technique twice—once basting the turkey and once without basting. The basted turkey displayed beautifully tanned skin compared to the pale skin of the unbasted bird. Both birds were cooked to 170 degrees in the leg/thigh (10 degrees lower than recommended), while each of the breasts registered a parched 180.

Roasting Detours

I tried braising the bird at 425 degrees in airtight heavy-duty foil for an hour as another recipe recommended. Then I removed the foil and roasted the turkey at a slightly lower temperature for another hour. As with all the breast-up methods, the white meat cooked 10 degrees higher than the dark meat, but the turkey appeared juicier than birds cooked with dry heat. The turkey's unattractive appearance, however, was a definite drawback. Its spotty brown skin looked sticky, thin and translucent. Because the turkey did not roast, there were no caramelized browned pan drippings, and the gravy made from this turkey tasted like a mild cream of chicken soup.

A similar technique—roasting the turkey in a large, chemical-free brown paper grocery bag—produced a bird that got a high score for its gorgeous brown skin but only average marks for taste and texture, for it was dry and bland. As with the foil method, the turkey was initially roasted at a moderate temperature (325 degrees), then turned up to 425 degrees and freed from its wrapping during the last half hour so that it browned.

According to another recipe, a flour-butter paste rubbed onto the turkey skin before roasting would form a crust, sealing in the juices and allowing the turkey to roast to perfection. This turkey was roasted at an intense 450 degrees for the first 40 minutes. At this temperature, the bird starts to looks more like a burn victim—bubbled, blistered, crisp—than a smart-looking edible fowl. Reducing the temperature and basting the turkey frequently produced disappointing results. The turkey's skin was swelled and soggy, holding the juices in at the surface. The breast meat was dry and chalky, the skin inedible, leaving a flavorless, pasty feeling in the mouth.

HOW MUCH DOES A 12-POUND TURKEY REALLY WEIGH?

AFTER I REMOVED the packaging and giblets and drained each turkey, I was surprised to find variations of up to 1½ pounds from the weight noted on the sticker. (Often, the tail pieces had been removed during the processing and added to the giblets.) For example, an 11¾-pound turkey weighed as little as 10¼ pounds its second time at the scale. It's best to figure serving amounts and cooking times on the basis of net, not gross, weight, because gross weight includes the giblets, packaging and excess liquid. If you calculate the cooking time for a 12-pound turkey when it's actually closer to 10, your bird could be ready 40 to 50 minutes before you've planned to serve it. Weigh it after you've removed the giblets and rinsed it. If you don't own a scale, know that your bird will be at least a pound lighter than its stated weight.

A number of recipes called for placing butter-soaked cheesecloth over the breast for most of the roasting time, with occasional basting. During the last minutes of cooking, the cheesecloth was removed so the skin could brown. Although this technique produced a magazine-cover turkey, the cheesecloth and basting did nothing to lower the temperature of the breast meat, and neither the white nor the dark meat was spectacular. This turkey's beauty was only skin-deep, and this recipe joined numerous others in the reject pile.

Injecting butter, salt and pepper into the turkey was another of my attempts to keep it juicy and make it flavorful—a sort of homemade Butterball. During roasting, the skin ballooned and crisped at first, only to deflate and wrinkle once out of the oven. Much of the injected butter seemed to end up in the cavity and at injection sites and did not infuse the entire bird as I had hoped. Even though the meat surrounding the pockets was seasoned nicely, the overall results were inconsistent, and the technique felt contrived.

Foil:
Moderately Successful

Loosely tenting the breast and upper portions of the legs with heavy-duty foil rather than completely enclosing it is moderately successful. The foil helps deflect the heat, reducing the difference in temperature between the white and dark meat from 10 to 6 degrees. The bird is roasted at a consistent 325-degree temperature, and during the last 45 minutes of roasting, the foil comes off, allowing enough time for the bird to color a beautiful brown. If you're partial to the simplicity of this open-pan roasting method, I recommend the foil shield; it ran a close second to the final preferred method.

Turkey Dissection

First, though, I tried Julia Child's clever technique of roasting breast and legs/thighs separately. Despite my worry that dismembering the turkey by cutting out the backbone and separating the whole legs from the breast would be difficult, the whole process took less than 10 minutes. I was also impressed with how quickly the turkey parts roasted—less than one hour in a hot oven (400 degrees). Cooking more quickly than the white meat, the legs were fully done in 45 minutes, and the breast followed with a temperature of 160 to 165 degrees about 10 minutes later. I secured the legs to the breast with skewers and put the reassembled bird on a serving platter with lots of herbs for garnish to see if it looked believable: almost, but not quite. Nevertheless, this turkey does have two advantages—a small bird roasts in less than one hour, and each portion can be tailor-roasted to perfection.

On the theory that the cavity takes longest to cook, I tried roasting a turkey with its backbone removed. Although this technique brought the temperature variation between the breast and leg down a few degrees and produced juicy breast and leg meat, not surprisingly, the bird looked fat, stubby and unnatural. After my two attempts at turkey dissection, I decided that although these methods were perfectly acceptable at other times during the year, the holiday turkey should be spared the knife until it comes to the table.

A friend of mine roasts his turkey whole, carves the breast at table and sends the legs back to the oven to finish cooking. Guests enjoy white meat the first time around and feast on dark meat for seconds. As a person who enjoys both cuts, I could easily savor white first and dark later. But a quick poll revealed that many people prefer one or the other, and with this technique dark-meat lovers would have to wait for their dinner.

Brining Makes a Big Difference

Among all these apparent failures, some real winners emerged. Three turkeys, though none perfect, caught my attention. I knew I was on to something when I tasted Maria Eugenia Cerqueirra Da Mota's roast turkey in Jean Anderson's *Food of Portugal* (William Morrow,

1986). The turkey is placed in a cool place such as a winter basement and soaked for up to 24 hours in water seasoned with a full 2 pounds of salt. I refrigerated the first turkey for the duration of the brining time. What emerged from the salt water the following day was a beautiful, clean, milky white turkey—both skin and cavity. I roasted the bird following the recipe instructions, breast side up in a 400-degree oven until done. Except for some parched marks along the breast bone and leg tops, this nicely browned turkey showed well. The texture of the breast seemed different from any other. It was firm yet juicy. It tasted fully seasoned compared to other turkeys, which required a bite of skin with the meat to achieve the same effect. There were two drawbacks, however. The meat might be a bit too salty for some (although it was perfect for me), and the pan drippings were inedibly saline (a full quart of unsalted broth did little to dilute the intensity).

I brined several more turkeys and discovered that four to six hours produces pleasantly seasoned turkeys and pan juices that are not too salty for gravy. Much like koshering, brining draws out the blood, giving the bird a clean, fresh flavor. At the same time, the salt water permeates the bird, making each bite, rather than just the skin, taste seasoned.

NOT ALL SALTS ARE ALIKE

I HAD LONG THOUGHT there was a tremendous difference in salts, particularly kosher and table salt. To confirm this suspicion, I dissolved 1 tablespoon of kosher salt in 1 quart of water and 1 tablespoon of ordinary table salt in another quart of water. The water seasoned with kosher salt was pleasant, while the table-salt-seasoned water was as intense as the stuff you gargle for sore throats

This makes perfect sense to David Strietlmeier, technical representative for Morton Salt in Chicago, Illinois. According to Strietlmeier, kosher salt and table salt are manufactured by different processes and as a result weigh differently by volume. To complicate matters further, the two brands of kosher salt in this country—Diamond and Morton—are produced by different methods.

Common table salt is formed by placing a water-sodium chloride mixture, or saturated brine, into a vacuum crystal-lizer. This solution is boiled down and simultaneously agitated, resulting in the formation of individual salt crystal cubes.

Kosher salt, on the other hand, is made by one of two methods. Diamond is manufactured like table salt, with the saturated brine being placed in a vacuum crystallizer. This solution is boiled but allowed to settle so that the crystals knit together at their corners to form four-sided pyramid shapes, hollow inside. Morton, though, is made by compaction, a process in which four or five table salt crystals are compressed together into a flat platelet. Diamond is lighter and fluffier, nearly 50 percent greater in volume by weight than table salt, while Morton is about 25 percent greater. If substituting Diamond kosher salt for table salt, use 1½ teaspoons kosher salt for every teaspoon of table salt. If using Morton, use 1¼ teaspoons kosher salt for every teaspoon of table salt.

Fresh Versus Frozen

Until I conducted a side-by-side taste test, I had always believed that fresh turkeys were superior to frozen ones. After seeing the flavor and textural improvements brining made, I wondered if brining would make a frozen turkey taste as good as a fresh one. Selecting two 15-pound turkeys—one fresh, one frozen—I brined the two birds and roasted them, following the instructions for larger turkeys.

Before brining and cooking, the frozen turkey was easy to pick out. It looked dull, dark and limp compared to its fresh counterpart. During the soaking phase, the frozen turkey's brining liquid was much pinker than the fresh-turkey brine, an indication that the frozen turkey contained more blood. The pink color, however, was a good sign that the brine was drawing out the excess blood. And after its salty bath, the frozen turkey looked much improved in color, though still a bit limp.

After roasting, differences between the two turkeys were less apparent. Both looked equally brown and appetizing. After sampling platters of dark and light meat from both turkeys, only a few tasters picked the fresh as the clear winner. Most could not tell the difference.

With my brining experiments successfully concluded, I focused again on perfecting the roasting technique. My most successful attempt at achieving at least equal temperatures in the leg and the breast came when I tried James Beard's method of roasting the turkey on a V-rack—available at most cookware stores—first breast side down, then on each of its sides, and finally breast side up. Beyond simply holding the turkey in place, the rack, which is found in most cookware stores, elevates it, protecting the breast in particular from the hot surface of the roasting pan. Using the rack and rotating the turkey, I finally brought the breast temperature down to (and frequently below) the leg's temperature range.

For Best Results, Rotate

I set out to fine-tune this rotation roasting method because my turkeys were smaller than Beard's. Larger turkeys spend enough time in a 350-degree oven to brown nicely, but some of the smaller turkeys were getting done in as little as one and a half hours, leaving them blond-breasted, yet fully cooked. Clearly, I needed higher heat.

Reviewing my notes thus far, I noticed that the basted birds were usually the beauties. This finding supported the food scientist Harold McGee's observations. According to McGee, the oven transforms the protein and sugar found in the pan juices and the butter into "a dark, richly flavored essence," which does make the bird brown evenly. A combination of higher heat (400 degrees) along with basting gave me what I wanted. In an effort to streamline the procedure, I tried to skip roasting the bird on each side, and instead simply turned it breast side down, then breast side up. But in order for small turkeys to brown evenly all over, the two extra turns are necessary if beauty indeed is as important as taste.

Cooking a Bigger Bird

Up to this point, for purposes of convenience, I had been using the smallest turkeys I could find. Would the high oven temperatures and multiple turns work for larger turkeys as well? Pressing on, I began to roast 18-to-20-pounders. Rotating these larger turkeys to cook on their sides was just asking for trouble. Even if it were possible, most ovens aren't big enough for a really large turkey to sit wing side up.

Because of the turkeys' large size, temperatures of 350 and 400 degrees tended to overcook the exteriors by the time the interior was done. Ultimately, I found that roasting large turkeys at 250 degrees and turning them only once—from breast side down to breast side up—ensures the most even cooking. To brown the skin, increase the oven temperature to 400 degrees during the final minutes of roasting. Turning a large, hot turkey is not difficult with the help of another person. While one person holds the V-rack steady, the other

turns the bird. With a large wad of paper towels in each hand, grab the turkey at the neck and the tail and quickly flip it breast side up (see the illustration on page 156).

A Better Stuffing

To determine whether stuffing keeps poultry in the oven longer, I roasted two birds of similar weights—one stuffed, the other one not. After one hour, the unstuffed cavity registered 160 degrees, while the stuffed cavity was only 133 degrees. Unless your Thanksgiving isn't complete without the stuffing inside the turkey, don't put it there. You'll be forced to roast the bird beyond doneness just to get the cavity to a safe temperature.

Baking the stuffing separately also cuts down on the number of things you have to do at the last minute because you don't need to dig it out of the turkey cavity while you assemble all the other side dishes. But the main reason I don't stuff my birds is because I actually prefer stuffing that's been cooked in a baking dish, for it has contrasting crisp and moist textures that I love.

If you do decide to cook your stuffing in the bird, and you want to use one of the recipes on pages 157-160, reduce the amount of broth to about ⅓ cup.

Aromatic vegetables and herbs placed inside the cavity do good things for the turkey. Though the differences are subtle, a turkey whose cavity is filled is more flavorful than an unfilled bird, especially the inner leg and thigh meat.

When roasted alongside the turkey as well as being placed in the cavity, the same vegetable-herb combination works wonders on the pan juices. Tasted next to the juices from the caramelized vegetables, plain pan juices taste flat and one-dimensional. It's easy for these vegetables to dry up fairly quickly, however, so check the turkey often, adding water as needed to keep the pan moistened. Once the gravy is made, toss out the vegetables in the cavity and the pan, for they have given up all their flavor.

Trussing without Tears

An elaborate truss is time-consuming—especially for those who attempt it only annually on what is perhaps the busiest cooking day of the year. Besides, some cooks think that trussing constricts the bird, making it take longer to get done. For these special occasions, however, some form of trussing is nec-essary to keep the turkey from sagging in the oven and looking unkempt at the table. My goal was to keep the procedure as simple as possible. I first tried tying the legs together. The result: a turkey with limp crossed legs. My final attempt, a simple two-step truss (see page 153) works so perfectly that I've used it ever since.

Talking Turkey

For a beautiful holiday bird with a juicy breast, well-seasoned meat and delicious pan gravy, brine your bird and truss it before roasting. Place a few vegetables in the cavity and a few in the roasting pan to add flavor to the meat and gravy. Roast small turkeys (up to 14 pounds) at 400 degrees. For larger birds, a long, slow roast at 250 degrees with a final blast of 400-degree heat to brown them works best. Rotating the bird helps it roast evenly and ensures that your guests will talk about your turkey with admiration for weeks to come.

TO TRUSS A TURKEY

1. Bring the legs together and tie a 48-inch piece of kitchen twine around them to hold them in place.

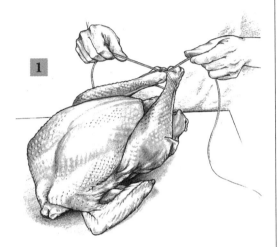

2. Bring each end of twine around to the neck end past the thigh and the lower breast. Tie as tightly as possible at the neck end. This simple truss will hold the legs and wings in place.

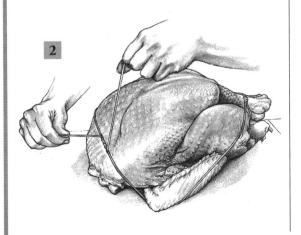

TO TEST A TURKEY FOR DONENESS

1. To check breast meat, stick the probe of an instant-read thermometer **parallel and deep** into the breast at its thickest point. If the thermometer registers between 160° and 165°F, the meat is perfectly cooked.

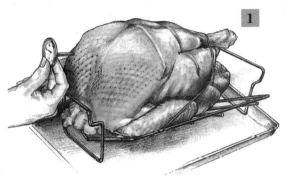

2. To check leg/thigh meat, stick the probe of an instant-read thermometer into the leg pit so it touches the bone of the leg/thigh joint. If the thermometer registers about 170° to 175°F, the bird is done.

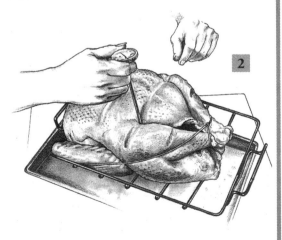

Oven-Roasted Turkey with Giblet Pan Sauce

FOR A 10-TO-12-POUND TURKEY
SERVES 10 TO 12

YOU CAN DOUBLE the salt and soak for four hours, if you are in a hurry.

1 turkey (12-14 pounds gross weight), giblets
and tail removed and all giblets, except liver,
cut into 1-inch pieces; turkey rinsed thoroughly
2 cups kosher salt or 1½ cups table salt
2 teaspoons vegetable oil
3 medium onions, coarsely chopped
1½ medium carrots, coarsely chopped
1½ celery stalks, coarsely chopped
6 thyme sprigs
1 bay leaf
3 tablespoons butter, melted, plus extra for basting
1 cup white wine
3 tablespoons cornstarch

1. Place turkey in a pot or clean bucket large enough to hold it. Add salt and 2 gallons cold water to cover, rubbing salt into bird and stirring water until salt dissolves. Set in a cool spot for 10 to 12 hours. Remove turkey from salt water and rinse cavity and skin under cool running water for several minutes until all traces of salt are gone.

2. While turkey soaks, heat oil in a large sauté pan over medium-high heat. Add giblets, except liver, and 1 onion; sauté until giblets lose their raw color, about 5 minutes. Reduce heat to low, cover and cook until giblets release their liquid, about 20 minutes. Add one-third of carrots and celery. Add 5 cups water along with 2 sprigs thyme and bay leaf. Bring to a boil, then reduce heat to low and simmer, uncovered, for about 30 minutes to make a flavorful broth. Add liver during last 5 minutes of cooking. Strain broth, setting aside neck, tail and giblets, including liver. Cool to room temperature and refrigerate until ready to use; you should have about 4 cups. Remove meat from neck and tail, cut giblets and liver into medium dice and refrigerate meat and giblets separately.

3. Preheat oven to 400°F. Toss half of remaining onions, carrots and celery and 2 sprigs thyme with 1 tablespoon butter and place in turkey cavity. Bring turkey legs together and truss (see illustration, page 153).

4. Scatter remaining vegetables and thyme in a shallow roasting pan; pour 1 cup water over vegetables. Set a V-rack adjusted to its widest setting in pan. Brush entire breast side of turkey with 1 tablespoon butter, then place turkey, breast side down, on rack. Brush back side of turkey with 2 tablespoons butter.

5. Roast for 45 minutes. Remove pan from oven, close oven door and baste turkey with butter. With a wad of paper toweling in each hand, turn turkey leg/thigh side up (see illustration, page 156). If water has evaporated, add ½ cup more to pan. Return turkey to oven and roast for 20 minutes. Remove from oven, baste and use paper toweling to turn turkey so other leg/thigh side faces up. Roast for 20 minutes more. Remove turkey from the oven for the final time, baste and turn it breast side up. Roast until a meat thermometer stuck in leg pit (see illustration, page 153) registers 170° to 175°F—30 to 45 minutes more. Breast should be 160° to 165°F. Transfer turkey to a platter; let rest for 20 to 30 minutes.

6. Meanwhile, skim fat from roasting pan, then place it over 2 burners set on medium heat. Add wine and, using a wooden spoon, stir to loosen brown bits. Strain contents of roasting pan through a fine strainer into a large saucepan. Add reserved giblet broth (reserving ½ cup) and giblets; bring to a boil. Mix cornstarch into ½ cup cold reserved broth and gradually stir into pan juices. Bring to a boil, reduce heat to low and simmer until sauce thickens slightly. Carve turkey; pass gravy separately at table.

♦ For an 18-to-22-pound turkey

Serves 18 to 20

1. Follow recipe for Oven-Roasted Turkey with Giblet Pan Sauce (page 154) through step 4, but use an 18-to-20-pound turkey and preheat oven to 250°F.

2. Roast turkey, breast side down, for 3 hours, basting back side every hour or so, and adding small quantities of water if pan vegetables look dry. Remove pan from oven, close oven door and baste turkey with butter. With a wad of paper toweling in each hand, turn turkey breast side up. Continue to roast for 1 hour, basting once or twice. With turkey still in oven, increase oven temperature to 400°F, and roast until skin has browned and a meat thermometer stuck in leg pit (see illustration, page 153) registers 170° to 175°F, about 1 hour more. Breast should be 160° to 165°F. Transfer turkey to platter and let rest for 20 to 30 minutes.

3. Follow step 6 to make gravy and serve.

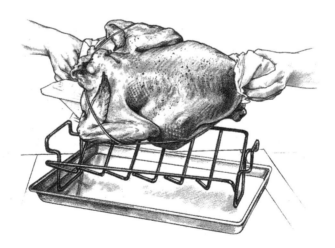

With a large wad of paper toweling in one hand, turn
the turkey either wing side or breast side up, depending
on the size of the bird.

Simple Herbed Bread Stuffing

M A K E S A B O U T 10 C U P S, S E R V I N G 12 T O 16

MAKE THE BREAD CRUMBS for the turkey in advance. Place cut bread in a single layer on two large jelly roll pans and allow them to dry out at room temperature for at least two hours and preferably overnight, then bake in a 400°F oven, stirring frequently, until light brown and toasty, 12 to 15 minutes.

If you like, add a pint of strained oysters and substitute the oyster liquid for the chicken broth.

4 tablespoons (½ stick) butter

2 medium onions, cut into medium dice

2 medium celery stalks, cut into small dice

1 pound sliced firm white sandwich, French, Italian or sourdough bread, cut into ½-inch cubes (10-12 cups), dried out and toasted (see above)

¼ cup minced fresh parsley leaves

1 teaspoon rubbed sage or 1 tablespoon minced fresh sage leaves

1 teaspoon dried thyme leaves or 1 tablespoon minced fresh thyme

¾ teaspoon salt

½ teaspoon ground black pepper

1 cup homemade chicken broth or low-sodium canned broth

2 large eggs (optional, for a firmer texture)

1. Adjust oven rack to lower-middle position and preheat oven to 350°F. Heat butter in a large skillet over medium heat. Add onions and celery and sauté until fully cooked, 8 to 10 minutes.

2. Transfer to a large bowl; add bread cubes and remaining ingredients, including eggs, if using. Toss to combine and adjust seasonings.

3. Turn into a 3-quart buttered casserole and bake until top forms a crust and dressing has heated through, 30 to 40 minutes.

♦ Bread Stuffing with Prunes and Toasted Walnuts

MAKES ABOUT 12 CUPS, SERVING 12 TO 18

Follow recipe for Simple Herbed Bread Stuffing (page 157), adding ¾ cup toasted walnuts and ¾ cup diced prunes when tossing bread with the seasonings.

♦ Bread Stuffing with Sausage and Apples

MAKES ABOUT 14 CUPS, SERVING 16 TO 20

1. Fry 1 pound bulk sausage over medium-high heat in a large skillet, stirring frequently and breaking into bite-size pieces with a slotted spoon, until fully cooked, 8 to 10 minutes. Drain, leaving 2 tablespoons drippings in pan. Peel and core 3 large apples, such as Granny Smiths. Cut into medium dice. Sauté apples in drippings until tender, about 5 minutes.

2. Follow steps 1 and 2 of recipe for Simple Herbed Bread Stuffing (page 157). Toss sausage and apples with bread and seasonings. Continue as directed.

Simple Corn Bread Dressing

MAKES ABOUT 10 CUPS, SERVING 12 TO 16

CUT OR CRUMBLED CORN BREAD and cubed bread should be placed in a single layer on two large jelly roll pans and allowed to dry out at room temperature for at least two hours, and preferably overnight, then baked in a 400°F oven and stirred frequently until light brown and toasty, 12 to 15 minutes.

4 tablespoons (½ stick) butter

2 medium onions, cut into medium dice

2 medium celery stalks, cut into small dice

Southern-Style Corn Bread (page 277), recipe doubled and baked in a 13-by-9-inch pan, cooled, cut into ½-inch cubes, and dried and toasted (see above)

4 cups sliced firm white sandwich, French, Italian or sourdough bread, cut into ½-inch cubes, dried and toasted

¼ cup minced fresh parsley leaves

1 teaspoon rubbed sage or 1 tablespoon minced fresh sage leaves

1 teaspoon dried thyme leaves or 1 tablespoon minced fresh thyme

¾ teaspoon salt

½ teaspoon ground black pepper

1 cup homemade chicken broth or low-sodium canned broth

2 large eggs (optional, for a firmer texture)

1. Adjust oven rack to lower-middle position and preheat oven to 350°F. Heat butter in a large skillet over medium heat. Add onions and celery and sauté until fully cooked, 8 to 10 minutes. Transfer to a large bowl; add corn bread, bread cubes and remaining ingredients, including eggs, if using. Toss to combine and adjust seasonings.

2. Turn into a 3-quart buttered casserole and bake until top forms a crust and dressing has heated through, 30 to 40 minutes.

♦ Corn Bread Stuffing with Dried Cranberries and Toasted Pecans

MAKES ABOUT 12 CUPS, SERVING 12 TO 18

Follow recipe for Simple Corn Bread Dressing (page 159), adding ¾ cup toasted pecans and ¾ cup dried cranberries when tossing corn bread with seasonings.

A Grilling Sensation

Roasting a turkey on the grill frees up the oven for all the holiday side dishes that stack up waiting for the bird to get done. In addition, this method is a nice change from the usual routine: the skin turns a smashing mahogany color, and the smoke subtly permeates the meat, which tastes perfectly roasted, not barbecued.

In *The Grilling Encyclopedia* (Atlantic Monthly Press, 1992), A. Cort Sinnes shares a fascinating recipe for turkey on the grill, named Pandora's Turkey because the grill's lid must remain closed for two and a half to three hours until the 5 pounds of ignited charcoal have died out. Following Sinnes's instructions, I arranged hot coals on opposite sides of the grill, set the turkey in a roasting pan on the grill rack and closed the lid. My grill has a built-in thermometer, so I was able to track the inside temperature. For the first one and a half hours, the heat never fell below 450 degrees.

And because I was using a slightly smaller bird than suggested, I had definitely overcooked it—180-degree thigh meat and 190-degree breast meat. The unprotected breast and leg tops were pretty dry from the intense heat. Despite the overcooking, this technique had potential.

A combination of brining and charcoal roasting produced a flavor that most found superior, and I was driven to perfect it. I tried tenting the breast with foil, but found that the grill heat was so high that tenting proved ineffective. By turning the turkey just once, I achieved a bird with a nice bronze back but a lily white, juicy breast, even after long cooking. Sinnes is correct: the fire dies if the grill lid is removed, and the turning costs precious heat. To counter this loss, I added a burst of hot coals at the midpoint turn, with the result that the turkey browned nicely and was perfectly cooked without any more fanfare.

Grill-Roasted Turkey with Giblet Pan Sauce

SERVES 10 TO 12

A GRILLED TURKEY has a delicate, smoky flavor, which is perfect for the holiday table. Before beginning, make sure your grill lid is tall enough to accommodate a turkey. In order to provide enough heat to fully cook the turkey, you will need to add additional charcoal about halfway through grilling, heated in either a chimney or a separate grill.

1 turkey (12-14 pounds gross weight), giblets
   and tail removed and all giblets, except liver,
   cut into 1-inch pieces; turkey rinsed thoroughly

2 cups kosher salt or 1½ cups table salt

2 teaspoons vegetable oil

3 medium onions, coarsely chopped

1½ medium carrots, coarsely chopped

1½ celery stalks, coarsely chopped

6 thyme sprigs

1 bay leaf

2 tablespoons butter, melted, plus extra for basting

1 cup white wine

3 tablespoons cornstarch

1. Follow recipe for Oven-Roasted Turkey with Giblet Pan Sauce (page 154) through step 3 but do not preheat oven.

2. Heat 5 pounds of charcoal. If using a chimney starter, remove grill rack and pour half of coals into two piles on opposite sides of grill. If you heat coals in grill rather than in chimney starter, use long-handled tongs to separate coals into two piles on opposite sides of grill. Return grill rack to position.

3. Scatter remaining vegetables and thyme in a 15-by-10-inch roasting pan (a disposable one, if you like). Pour 1 cup water over vegetables. Set a V-rack adjusted to widest setting in the pan. Cover pan, fitting foil around V-rack, to keep pan juices from evaporating. Position turkey breast side down on V-rack.

4. Grill-roast turkey, positioning pan between piles of coals, with lid closed, for 1 hour. After about 40 minutes, heat another 1½ pounds charcoal (½ chimney-full), either in a chimney or a separate grill. Remove turkey from grill, remove grill rack, stir up coals and add half of new hot coals to each pile; replace lid. Baste back side of turkey with butter. With a wad of paper toweling in each hand, turn turkey breast side up (see illustration, page 156) and baste. Check pan drippings and add ½ cup more water if vegetables are starting to burn. Return pan to grill, replace lid quickly and roast until a meat thermometer stuck in leg pit (see page 153) registers 170° to 175°F, 1 to 1¼ hours more. Breast should be 160° to 165°F. Transfer turkey to a platter; let rest for 20 to 30 minutes.

5. Follow step 6 to make gravy and serve.

Cornish Hens for Company

CORNISH HENS are perfect party birds. They're inexpensive, simple to prepare, easy to stuff and beautiful. As an extra benefit, your guests carve them, so you won't have to.

Cooking Cornish hens to perfection, however, is not an easy task. As with all poultry, if roasted breast side up, the breast will overcook before the legs and thighs are done. As with turkey, you can solve this problem by using a V-rack (available at most cookware shops), which allows you to rotate the bird with ease during roasting. But since the V-rack holds only a couple of birds at a time, this method won't work when a crowd is coming for dinner.

My goal was stuffing and roasting at least six grocery store-quality Cornish hens so that they looked good, tasted great and weren't overcooked—all without smoking up the kitchen.

Briny Baths for Little Birds

After roasting the first few of these birds, I wondered if they tasted good enough for me to bother writing about them. My experience with brining turkeys (see page 148) made me suspect that these lackluster hens might benefit from a few hours in a salt-water bath. My hunch was right. Just two hours in salt water transformed these mediocre-tasting birds into something I would proudly serve to guests.

Get 'Em Up

Unless you have a commercial oven and pans, roasting more than six hens at a time makes them cook and brown unevenly. Also, deep roasting pans shield the birds from the oven heat, and too snug a fit in the pan further prevents browning. My first move was to get the birds out of the roasting pan by setting them on a wire rack over it. My second step in the right direction was to space the birds as far apart as possible so they could brown.

From my initial test, I determined that rotating the birds was crucial for moist and juicy breast meat. Though browner in color, the breast meat of unturned birds was drier and coarser than those that had been rotated. But because Cornish hens are in the oven for a relatively short time and because I was cooking so many of them, I turned them only once.

Roasting the birds on a rack allowed me to place them breast side down. Although the birds were still too lightly colored, they browned fairly well. However, dripping fat caused the roasting pan to smoke, particularly at high temperatures. I liked the rack-roasted birds, so I decided to put the smoking problem on hold.

Temperature Variables

I roasted Cornish hens at temperatures ranging from 350 to 500 degrees. Birds roasted at 450 degrees and up smoked too much and still didn't brown as well as I had hoped. These higher oven temperatures also seemed to cause the birds' skin to bubble more than it did at lower temperatures.

Roasting the birds at lower oven temperatures solved the smoking problem, but the resulting skin was too pale. Increasing the temperature at the end of cooking gave the best results, because the rendered skin browned much more quickly. I finally settled on 400 degrees, cranking up the oven to 450 degrees during the last few minutes of roasting. This temperature is high enough to encourage browning, while low enough to keep the oven from smoking dramatically. Adding water to the roasting pan once the fat starts to render and juices start to flow further ensures a smokeless kitchen at both 400 and 450 degrees. Another plus: once the birds are roasted, the juices can be scraped into a saucepan without deglazing the roasting pan over two burners.

Browned to Perfection

Big bubbles occur when juices build up under the skin, causing it to separate from the meat. Ballooning can happen at any roasting temperature. The bubbles are unsightly and prevent the waterlogged skin from browning. Carefully pricking the breast and leg skin, but not the meat, with the tip of a small paring knife before roasting creates small openings from which the juices and rendered fat can flow.

Even roasted at a relatively high 400 to 450 degrees, the birds still lacked that gorgeous mahogany skin color. Turkeys have three to four hours of oven time to develop beautiful skin; Cornish hens must brown in 40 minutes. Because of their artificial flavor, I didn't want to use commercial browning liquids, but the idea got me thinking in the right direction. To test glazes, I roasted six birds, brushing half with balsamic vinegar mixed with a little olive oil, and half with jam thinned with some soy sauce right before they were turned, and once again after the oven was increased to 450 degrees. All the glazed birds colored more beautifully than the unglazed ones. The high oven heat caramelizes the sugar in the glazes, producing a pleasantly spotty brown, barbecued look.

The Right Stuff

My final challenge was roasting stuffed Cornish hens without overcooking them. From previous testing, I knew that bringing a stuffed cavity to a salmonella-safe temperature of 160 degrees means keeping the bird in the oven longer than is right for the meat. Two things help. Starting the birds breast side down keeps the breast meat from overcooking. And heating the stuffing before spooning it into the birds' cavities—a trick I picked up from my cooking colleague Stephen Schmidt—also reduces oven time. By stuffing the birds with microwave-hot stuffing, I was able to roast birds that registered 172 to 174 degrees in the breast and 176 to 178 degrees in the leg/thigh by the time the stuffing reached 160 degrees. Even though I thought that the breast meat might be dry at this temperature (160 to 165 degrees is ideal), it was tender and juicy. Tying the hens' legs was the only thing necessary to improve their looks and secure the stuffing.

Casual Butterflied Cornish Hens

SERVES 2 TO 4

FOR WEEKNIGHTS, removing the back of a Cornish hen and flattening it solves nearly all the problems of roasting a whole one. Butterflied birds are an even thickness, so they don't require turning to roast evenly, and if they are not brown enough at the end of cooking, you can put them briefly under the broiler. Removing the back also reduces cooking time (25 minutes compared to 45 minutes for whole, stuffed birds), making these birds perfect for weeknight cooking.

Birds weighing more than 1½ pounds can serve two people for weeknight dining. During the week, you'll probably have no time to brine; if you do, it's worth it. But it's easy to lift the skin of these butterflied birds and season the meat directly with salt, pepper and herbs.

> 2 Cornish hens (1½-1¾ pounds), butterflied
>   and flattened according to directions on page 83
>   Salt
>   Ground black pepper
>   Dried herbs, such as thyme, basil or tarragon, for sprinkling
> 2 teaspoons butter, softened

1. Adjust oven rack to lower-middle position and preheat oven to 500°F.

2. Gently loosen skin around leg/thigh and along breast bone to expose meat (see illustration, page 85). Generously sprinkle meat with salt, pepper and herb of choice; leave skin in place. Snip skin in 4 or 5 places to prevent bubbling. Rub skin with softened butter. Place hens on a large roasting pan.

3. Roast until hens are golden brown and juices run clear, 20 to 25 minutes. Remove from pan, cut down along each breast bone with a chef's knife or kitchen shears if each bird is to be split between 2 people. Drizzle pan juices over each portion and serve.

Roast Stuffed Cornish Hens

SERVES 6

To prevent the birds from smoking, pour water into the roasting pan after 25 minutes once the birds are turned. The water addition makes instant *jus*, eliminating the need to deglaze the pan over two burners. Pour the chicken juice from the pan to a measuring cup for drizzling over the hen. For a slightly enriched flavor, however, pour the chicken juice into a small saucepan and simmer it with a little vermouth or white wine.

A 1½-pound Cornish hen is perfect for two people (it yields about 12 ounces of cooked meat and skin), but for individual presentation, seek out the smaller hens or look for poussins. Though a little more expensive, these baby chickens usually weigh about a pound and are perfect for one person.

> 2 cups kosher salt or 1½ cups table salt
> 6 Cornish hens (each less than 1½ pounds if possible), giblets removed; hens rinsed well
> 1 recipe stuffing, heated (see pages 170-174)
> 6 tablespoons balsamic vinegar mixed with 3 tablespoons olive oil, or 6 tablespoons seedless raspberry jam mixed with 2 tablespoons balsamic vinegar
> ¼ cup dry vermouth or white wine

1. Pour 5 quarts water into a small clean bucket or a large bowl. Add salt; stir until dissolved. Add Cornish hens to salt water, arranging them breast side down and legs up to ensure that meaty portions are covered with salt water. Refrigerate for 2 hours. Remove hens from water, rinse thoroughly, pat dry and prick skin with a paring knife, particularly on breast and legs, to keep skin from bubbling during roasting.

2. Preheat oven to 400°F. Spoon about ½ cup hot stuffing into cavity of each hen and tie legs together with a 6-inch piece of kitchen twine (see figure 1). Arrange birds breast side down with wings facing out on a large (at least 19-by-13-inch) wire rack, set over a large (at least 17-by-11-inch) roasting or jelly roll pan, leaving as much space as possible between birds (see figure 2). Roast until backs are golden brown, about 25 minutes. Remove pan from oven, brush backs with balsamic mixture and turn hens breast side up with wings facing out. Brush breast and legs with additional glaze (see figure 3). Once roasting pan is returned to oven, pour 1 cup water into pan and continue to roast until a meat thermometer inserted into the stuffed cavity registers about 150°F, 15 to 20 minutes more.

3. Increase temperature to 450°F, carefully remove pan from oven, brush birds with glaze again, adding ½ cup water to pan once it is back in oven. Roast until birds are brown and cavity is 160°F, 5 to 10 minutes more, depending on size of birds. Brush birds with remaining glaze as you remove them from oven. Let rest for 10 minutes.

4. Meanwhile, pour hen juices from roasting pan into a small saucepan set over medium-high heat. Add vermouth or white wine and simmer until flavors blend, 2 to 3 minutes. Drizzle a little sauce over each hen and serve, passing remaining sauce separately at table.

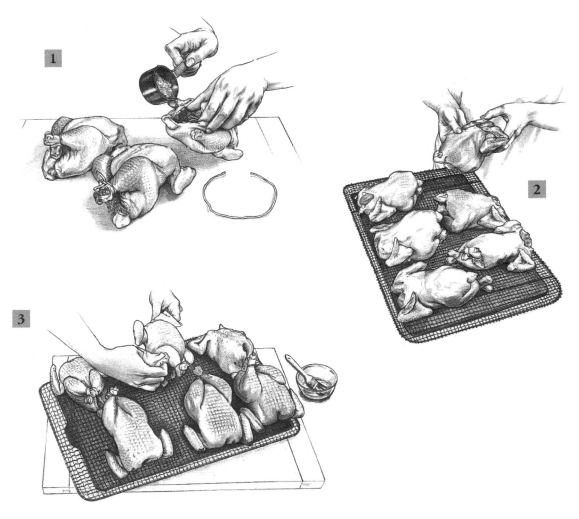

Wild Rice Stuffing with Carrots, Mushrooms and Thyme

Makes about 3 cups, enough to stuff 6 Cornish hens

PLAIN WILD RICE does not hold together sufficiently well to make a good stuffing. Instead, I prefer to use the packaged wild-rice blend, which also contains some brown rice.

1	ounce dried porcini mushrooms, soaked in 1 cup hot water for 20 minutes until softened
1¼	cups homemade chicken broth or low-sodium canned broth, or more if necessary
1	cup wild-rice blend
2	tablespoons butter
1	small onion, finely chopped
1	small carrot, finely diced (¼ cup)
½	small celery rib, finely diced (¼ cup)
4	ounces shiitake mushrooms, stemmed and thinly sliced
2	teaspoons minced fresh thyme leaves
2	tablespoons minced fresh parsley leaves
	Salt
	Ground black pepper

1. Squeeze porcini mushrooms dry and coarsely chop them, reserving approximately ¾ cup mushroom liquid. If liquid is gritty, strain it through a paper-towel-lined fine-mesh strainer.

2. Add enough chicken broth to mushroom liquid to equal 2 cups. Bring to a boil in a medium saucepan, add rice and return to a boil. Reduce heat to low, cover and simmer until rice is fully cooked, 40 to 45 minutes. Turn out rice into a medium microwave-safe bowl and fluff with a fork.

3. Meanwhile, heat butter in a medium skillet over medium heat. Add onion, carrot and celery and sauté until softened, 3 to 4 minutes. Add shiitake mushrooms and sauté until tender and liquid evaporates, 2 to 3 minutes. Add porcini mushrooms and thyme and cook, stirring until well coated and blended with other ingredients, 1 to 2 minutes more. Add mushroom mixture to rice; toss to combine. Add parsley and season to taste with salt and pepper.

4. To reheat stuffing in microwave-safe bowl, cover with plastic wrap and heat in microwave on high power until very hot, 2 to 4 minutes. (Alternatively, place in a medium saucepan, add 1 to 2 tablespoons water and reheat on stovetop.) Spoon hot stuffing into Cornish hens.

Couscous Stuffing with Currants, Apricots and Pistachios

Makes about 3 cups, enough to stuff 6 Cornish hens

Toasted slivered almonds can be substituted for the pistachio nuts.

2 tablespoons butter

1 small onion, minced

2 medium garlic cloves, minced

¼ teaspoon ground cinnamon

⅛ teaspoon ground ginger

⅛ teaspoon turmeric

1 cup plain couscous

1⅓ cups homemade chicken broth or low-sodium canned broth

¼ cup finely chopped dried apricots

3 tablespoons dried currants

¼ cup shelled pistachio nuts, chopped

2 tablespoons minced fresh parsley leaves

Salt

Ground black pepper

1. Heat butter over medium heat in a medium saucepan. Add onion, garlic, cinnamon, ginger and turmeric, and sauté until onion softens, 3 to 4 minutes. Add couscous; stir until well coated with spices and butter, 1 to 2 minutes. Add chicken broth, bring to a simmer, remove from heat, cover and let stand until couscous has absorbed all water, about 5 minutes.

2. Fluff couscous with a fork, then stir in dried fruit, nuts and parsley. Season to taste with salt and pepper.

3. To reheat stuffing, place in a microwave-safe bowl, cover with plastic wrap and heat in microwave on high power until very hot, 2 to 4 minutes. (Alternatively, place in a saucepan, add 1 to 2 tablespoons water and reheat on stovetop.) Spoon hot stuffing into Cornish hens.

Wild Rice Stuffing
with Cranberries and Toasted Pecans

MAKES ABOUT 3 CUPS,
ENOUGH TO STUFF 6 CORNISH HENS

I LOVE THE INTENSE BRIGHT FLAVORS of dried cranberries and cherries. Either fruit can be used in this stuffing. Toast the nuts in a 300°F oven for about 10 minutes, until fragrant.

- 2 cups homemade chicken broth or low-sodium canned broth
- 1 cup packaged wild-rice blend
- 2 tablespoons butter
- 1 small onion, finely chopped
- ½ small celery stalk, finely diced (¼ cup)
- ¼ cup pecans, toasted
- ¼ cup dried cranberries
- 2 tablespoons minced fresh parsley leaves
- 2 teaspoons minced fresh thyme leaves

1. Bring chicken broth to a boil in a medium saucepan. Add rice; return to a boil. Reduce heat to low, cover and simmer until rice is fully cooked, 40 to 45 minutes. Turn out rice into a medium microwave-safe bowl and fluff with a fork.

2. Meanwhile, heat butter in a medium skillet. Add onion and celery, and sauté until softened, 3 to 4 minutes. Add to rice. Stir in pecans, cranberries, parsley and thyme; toss to coat.

3. To reheat stuffing in microwave-safe bowl, cover with plastic wrap and heat in microwave on high power until very hot, 2 to 4 minutes. (Alternatively, place in a medium saucepan, add 1 to 2 tablespoons water and reheat on stovetop.) Spoon hot stuffing into Cornish hens.

Orzo Stuffing with Red Pepper, Liver and Fresh Herbs

MAKES ABOUT 3 CUPS, ENOUGH TO STUFF 6 CORNISH HENS

UNLIKE THE OTHER suggested stuffings, which have a distinct fall or winter feel, this one, with its bell peppers, scallions and fresh herbs, is just right for spring and early summer.

    1   cup uncooked orzo
    2   tablespoons butter
    6   Cornish hen livers
    ¼   small red bell pepper, finely diced (about ¼ cup)
    3   medium scallions, thinly sliced (about ½ cup)
    2   tablespoons minced fresh parsley leaves
    2   tablespoons minced fresh basil leaves
        Salt
        Ground black pepper

1. Bring 2 quarts water to a boil in a large soup kettle. Add orzo and boil over medium-high heat until al dente, 9 to 11 minutes. Drain, then cool orzo under cold running water to prevent further cooking. Turn into a medium microwave-safe bowl; set aside.

2. Meanwhile, heat 1 tablespoon butter in a medium skillet over medium-high heat. Add chicken livers and sauté until just cooked, about 5 minutes. Remove livers from pan and cut into small dice when they are cool enough to handle. Add to cooked orzo. Heat remaining 1 tablespoon butter in same skillet. Add red pepper and sauté over medium-high heat until almost softened, about 2 minutes. Add scallions and continue to sauté until softened, 2 to 3 minutes more. Add vegetables to pasta, add parsley and basil and toss to coat. Season to taste with salt and ground black pepper.

3. To reheat stuffing in microwave-safe bowl, cover with plastic wrap and heat in microwave on high power until very hot, 2 to 4 minutes. (Alternatively, place in a medium saucepan, add 1 to 2 tablespoons water and reheat on stovetop.) Spoon hot stuffing into Cornish hens.

Perfect Prime Rib

PRIME RIB is a little like roast turkey. You cook one a year, usually for an important occasion, often for a crowd. You stick with the standard 350 degrees, for although you know there are other techniques that may deliver a better roast, they're not worth the risk. You don't want to be remembered as the cook who carved slices from a raw standing rib, or the host who delayed dinner for hours waiting for the roast.

Last Christmas I became the cook who gambled the $40 standing rib roast and holiday dinner memories. I ordered a prime rib roast from the butcher, with instructions taped to it that read, "Roast in a 500-degree oven for 35 minutes (five minutes per pound). Turn oven heat off and let roast stand for exactly one hour. Do not open oven door once heat has been turned off." My butcher promised that this method would produce a memorable medium-rare roast, and though the instructions sounded odd, I couldn't resist giving them a shot. A few of my guests liked their meat closer to well done than rare, so I increased the oven time to six minutes per pound.

I recognized this technique's drawbacks fairly quickly. The oven was unusable for the final hour and a half or so before dinner—a potential problem for single-oven owners. Smoking fat triggered the kitchen smoke alarm after 30 minutes, so cooks with larger roasts would have to disengage it, turn on the fan and brace themselves for a hazy kitchen. Despite these obstacles, the prime rib emerged from the oven a rich, dark brown. It carved into unevenly cooked portions: two medium-well slices, two medium slices, two medium-rare slices and a couple of fairly rare center slices. While I at least broke even, the odds were good that I could do better.

Prime Temperature

Besides using general criteria like juicy and tender, I wasn't exactly sure how to define perfect prime rib when I started testing, so I had no preconceived ideas about what techniques or methods would deliver a superior roast. In addition to the normal cookbook research, I decided to interview a few of the thousands of professional chefs who cook prime rib every day. Between what I discovered in books and what I learned from these chefs, I came up with about a dozen fairly different approaches. Although a number of minor issues came up—whether the roast needed to be tied, whether it should be roasted on a rack—two big questions demanded my attention. At what temperature should prime rib be roasted? And does prime rib need special treatment beyond a little salt and pepper?

I started with oven temperatures. Suggestions ranged from a bold 425 degrees to a tepid 200 degrees. Most, though, fell somewhere in between. Other recipes recommended searing the meat at an initial high temperature (450 to 500 degrees), then reducing the oven to a more moderate temperature (350 degrees). To test the full range of alternatives, I roasted prime ribs at the following temperatures:

Roast 1—500°F for 5 minutes per pound, then left in the turned-off oven for 2 hours (a variation on the first method I tried)

Roast 2—500°F, immediately reduced to 350°F as the roast was placed in the oven

Roast 3—425°F for the entire cooking time

Roast 4—450°F for ½ hour and 350°F until done

Roast 5—350°F for the entire cooking time, with the roast placed on a rack over a pan of water

Roast 6—325°F for the entire cooking time

Roast 7—250°F for the entire cooking time

Roast 8—200°F for the entire cooking time

Roast 1, which had been left in the turned-off oven for two hours, was barely warm at carving and cold before I could finish eating it. All the prime ribs roasted at oven temperatures exceeding 300 degrees were pretty much the same. Each slice of carved beef was well done around the exterior, medium toward the center and a beautiful medium-rare pink at the center. The only advantage to cooking the roast over a pan of water was that it prevented fat from spitting onto the oven walls. But because I prefer beef roasted at lower temperatures, sputtering fat isn't a problem.

Love at First Bite, Not at First Sight

It's ironic that I ended up preferring the prime rib roasted at 200 degrees because it certainly wasn't love at first sight. About halfway through this roast's cooking time, I wrote in my notes, "Though the meat looks virtually raw, the internal temperature registers a surprising 110 degrees, and very little of its fat has rendered." But I changed my mind quickly as soon as I carved the first slice. This roast was as beautiful on the inside as it

Dry-Aged Versus Wet-Aged Beef

Like good wine, beef benefits from aging. This process allows the beef time to develop flavor and become more tender. All retail beef in this country is aged by one of two methods—dry-aging or wet-aging.

Dry-aged beef starts with a freshly slaughtered animal, which is hung in a cool, dry space, where it loses water and develops flavor. Because hanging quarters of beef take up refrigerator space and time and because the meat loses weight from dehydration and trimming to remove the dried exterior, it costs more, and for that reason many butchers no longer dry-age beef.

Most beef today is vacuum-packed in plastic at the processing plant and allowed to wet-age between the plant and the retailer. Wet-aged beef loses virtually no weight and comes butchered, packaged, aged and ready to sell.

To see if dry-aged beef is worth seeking out, I ordered a roast of each type from a restaurant supplier in Manhattan. Like a good, young red wine, the wet-aged beef tasted pleasant and fresh on its own. When compared to the dry-aged beef, though, its flavors were less concentrated, and the meat seemed washed out. The dry-aged beef engaged the mouth. It was stronger, richer and gamier-tasting, with a pleasant tang. The dry-aged and wet-aged beef were equally tender, but the dry-aged beef had an added buttery texture and tasted more mellow.

Dry-aged beef can be mail-ordered, or you may find a local butcher that's willing to age it for you. Because of the price, however, you may want to age it yourself, which simply involves making room in the refrigerator and remembering to purchase the roast a week or so early. To dry-age prime rib, pat the roast dry and place it on a wire rack set over a paper-towel-lined cake pan or plate. Set it in the refrigerator and let it age until ready to roast, up to seven days. *Before attempting to age meat, make sure your refrigerator registers lower than 40 degrees.* Before roasting, shave off the exterior meat that has completely dehydrated. (Between the trimming and dehydration, count on the roast losing a pound or so for a week's aging.)

was anemic on the outside. Unlike the roasts cooked at higher temperatures, this one was rosy pink from the surface to the center. Of all the roasts I cooked, it seemed the juiciest and most tender. This was prime rib at its best.

Besides being evenly cooked, the prime rib roasted in a 200-degree oven has another benefit: its internal temperature increases only a degree or two during its resting period. A roast cooked to 128 degrees, for example, rose to only 130 degrees after a 45-minute rest.

With the roasts cooked at higher temperatures, on the other hand, internal temperatures increased much more dramatically out of the oven. As a matter of fact, I noticed a direct correlation between oven temperature and the roast's temperature increase after cooking. Prime ribs roasted at more moderate temperatures (325 to 350 degrees) increased, on average, 14 degrees during resting. For example, a roast pulled from the oven at a rare 126 degrees moved up to a solid medium (140 degrees) by the end of its resting period. The prime rib roasted at 425 degrees increased a whopping 24 degrees (from 119 to 143) during its rest. Those roasted at a lower 250 degrees crept only up only 5 degrees before carving. I liked being able to pull the roast from the oven at my preferred temperature, rather than trying to speculate how many degrees the temperature would jump as it rested.

In addition to its stable internal temperature, the prime rib roasted at 200 degrees also loses less weight than those roasted at higher temperatures. A 6¾-pound roast cooked in a 200-degree oven weighed just over 6¼ pounds when it came out of the oven, a loss of less than 8 ounces. Roasts cooked in a 325-degree oven lost just over a pound, while the roast cooked at 350 degrees lost 1½ pounds. The prime rib cooked at 425 degrees lost a shocking 2 pounds. Part of the weight loss is fat, but a good portion is juice. These tests confirmed my observation that the beef roasted at 200 degrees was indeed juicier than those roasted at the higher temperatures.

I decided to check the safety of this low-heat method before becoming too sold on it. After conversations with a number of food scientists across the country, I determined that low-temperature roasting is as safe as higher-temperature roasting. Though the odds of finding bacteria inside a prime rib are virtually zero, the only way to guarantee a bacteria-free slab is to roast it to an internal temperature of a well-done 160 degrees, regardless of cooking method.

For Once, Salt Doesn't Make It Better

Because I knew firsthand salt's ability to improve certain foods and because I saw so many roast beef recipes promoting salt crusts and doughs, I felt certain salt would play a role in the perfect prime rib. Following some recipes and adapting others, I tested several methods.

♦ Following the recipe on the back of the Morton's kosher salt box, I coated a prime rib with a 3-pound box of salt and roasted it.

♦ Adapting a recipe from Patricia Wells's *Simply French* (William Morrow, 1991), I made a salt dough consisting of 3 cups kosher salt, 1 tablespoon each dried rosemary and thyme; 3 large egg whites; 1 cup cold water and 3 cups all-purpose flour. After searing the roast on top of the stove, I encased it in the rolled dough and roasted it.

♦ Following the recommendations of a chef, I covered a prime rib with ½ cup coarse sea salt and refrigerated it for 24 hours, then roasted it.

♦ Remembering my success with poultry brining, I placed a rib roast in a salt brine of 1 pound (4 cups) kosher salt and 1 gallon water and soaked it for 9 hours.

None of the rib roasts was improved by the salting techniques. In fact, most of them were clearly inferior. Although the prime rib roasted in kosher salt was nicely browned under the thick coating of salt, the salt did not penetrate past the surface. This roast was as juicy as the others, but the meat texture was firmer—not an advantage as far as I was concerned.

The prime rib encased in salt dough

cooked quickly. In fact, when I checked it at two hours (the minimum cooking time for most of the roasts), the roast registered 140 degrees, and by the time I was ready to carve, it had already moved up to 160 degrees. I found no reason to roast a prime rib this way. Whatever I saved in oven time was offset by the effort of rolling out the dough and blanketing the roast with it.

The roast covered with coarse sea salt and refrigerated was inedibly salty, while the interior was completely unaffected. The real loser was the brined roast. Brining turned my fine-textured, tender prime cut into an ordinary, coarse and firm-textured, cheaper cut of beef. My $5.29 per pound roast tasted more like brisket.

Tying Things Up

I was back to my slow-roasted prime rib. The sole factor that bothered me about it was its raw-looking, unrendered fatty exterior. This was easily remedied by searing the meat on top of the stove before slow-roasting it.

Unless the roast is tied, the outer layer of meat pulls away from the rib-eye muscle, with unattractive results. Separated from the main roast, this outer flap of meat also tends to overcook. To solve this problem, tie the roast at both ends and in the middle with the twine running parallel to the bone (see page 181) before you slow-roast it.

Perfect Prime Rib

SERVES 6 TO 8

THERE ARE TWO DISTINCT CUTS on a rib roast. The first cut (ribs one to three) is closer to the loin end and is the more desirable of the two. It contains the large, single rib-eye muscle and is less fatty. The second cut (ribs four to seven) is closer to the chuck end and has a smaller rib-eye muscle and is more multi-muscled and fatty. Although some butchers charge extra for the first cut, others do not. Ask for the first cut. Even if you don't purchase your roast a week ahead of time, just a day or two of aging in the refrigerator will make it taste better. The longer the uncooked roast sits at room temperature, the higher its internal temperature and the shorter its roasting time. For this reason, I let the prime rib stand at room temperature several hours before roasting.

Although this size roast averages about 30 minutes per pound, larger roasts do not need proportionately longer cooking times.

> 1 3-rib standing rib roast (7 pounds), the first cut,
>   aged if possible (see page 177), set at room temperature
>   for up to 3 hours, and tied (see figure 1)
> Salt
> Ground black pepper

1. Adjust oven rack to low position and preheat oven to 200°F. Heat a large roasting pan over 2 burners set at medium-high heat. Place roast in hot pan and sear on all sides until nicely browned and about ½ cup of fat has rendered, 6 to 8 minutes.

2. Remove roast from pan. Set a wire rack in pan; set roast on rack. Generously season meat with salt and pepper.

3. Place roast in oven and roast until a meat thermometer registers 130°F for medium-rare, about 3½ hours. If roast is done sooner than you expect, simply turn oven as low as possible (preferably 150° to 170°F) and let stand until ready to serve.

4. Transfer roast to a cutting board, with rib bones perpendicular to board. Using a carving fork to hold roast in place, cut along rib bones to sever meat from bones as shown in figure 2. Set roast cut side down and carve meat across grain into ¾-to-1-inch-thick slices. Serve immediately.

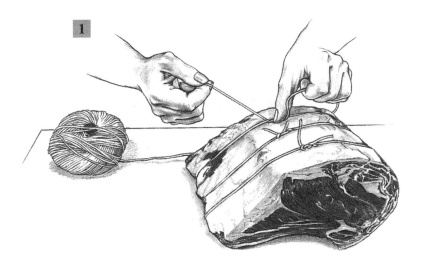

1. To keep the outer muscle from overcooking and separating from the roast, tie the roast at both ends and in the middle, with the twine running parallel to the bone. Remove the twine before carving.

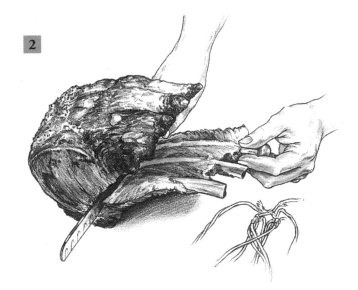

2. To facilitate carving, cut the rib bones away from the roast before serving.

THE SIMPLE JOYS OF BEEF TENDERLOIN

FOR A FESTIVE SIT-DOWN DINNER, prime rib is hard to beat. For a larger party, however, beef tenderloin is the cut I choose. Its sleek, boneless shape makes for quick roasting, easy carving and carefree serving, while its fork-tender texture is more diner-friendly. And while I would never think of serving tepid or cold prime rib, beef tenderloin, to me, is at its best at room temperature or even chilled.

Located near the rib, beef tenderloin is long and cylindrical, tapering from the larger butt end into a thin tip. Because of its tapered shape, the whole tenderloin roasts a bit unevenly, making it an ideal cut for large parties where guests' tastes may range from rare to well done. You can buy just the butt, or thicker end of the roast, or the entire tenderloin, and both are available "peeled" (trimmed of all fat) or "unpeeled" (virtually untrimmed). Having roasted both peeled and unpeeled roasts, I prefer tenderloins with at least a little fat on them. For this reason, I buy untrimmed roasts and trim them a bit myself.

Expect to pay about $50 for a whole beef tenderloin. This price isn't as high as you may first think: when it is thinly sliced and served warm, room temperature or cold, this cut can serve up to 25 people.

After roasting several beef tenderloins, I found that, unlike standing rib roast, tenderloin responds best to a relatively high roasting temperature (425 degrees). Although all roasts should rest 15 to 20 minutes after cooking, I found that tenderloin improves dramatically if left uncarved even longer. If cut too soon, its slices are a bit flabby. A slightly longer rest, however, will allow the meat to firm up appealingly. The sauces on pages 186-187 work well with room-temperature or even cold beef tenderloin.

Simple Roast Beef Tenderloin

SERVES 12 TO 20

MUCH LIKE PRIME RIB, beef tenderloin benefits from a few days of aging in the refrigerator. If you have time, prepare the roast as described below, then sprinkle it with a couple of tablespoons of kosher salt. Place the roast on a wire rack set over a paper-towel-lined roasting pan or a jelly roll pan and let age for up to five days (see page 177). Continue with roasting instructions, peppering but not salting the roast. Serve with one or more of the sauces that follow. Parsley Sauce with Cornichons and Capers (page 186) is especially nice with this simply flavored roast.

1   beef tenderloin (about 7 pounds unpeeled or about
      5 pounds peeled), trimmed of most excess fat,
      thin tip end turned under, roast tied crosswise
      at 1-inch intervals and aged if possible (see above)
2   tablespoons olive oil
1   tablespoon kosher salt
2   tablespoons coarsely ground black pepper

1. Adjust oven rack to upper-middle position and preheat oven to 425°F. Set meat on a sheet of plastic wrap and rub all over with oil. Sprinkle salt and pepper onto meat, lifting plastic wrap up and around meat to press on excess.

2. Roast tenderloin on a wire rack set on a shallow roasting pan until a meat thermometer inserted into the thickest part registers about 125°F for medium-rare to medium meat, about 45 minutes. Let roast stand at room temperature until temperature falls to between 90° and 100°F for warm room-temperature meat. (Tenderloin can be cooled to room temperature, wrapped in plastic wrap and refrigerated.)

3. Cut meat into ¼-to-½-inch-thick slices. Arrange on a serving platter and serve with one or more of the sauces on pages 186-187.

THE CADILLAC OF
MEAT THERMOMETERS

So that you can monitor a roast's internal temperature at all times, I recommend investing in a Poldar Thermo-Timer. Attached to a digital-read thermometer is a two-foot-long metal wire with a probe at the other end. The wire is so thin that the oven door can remain closed while the thermometer remains outside the oven. This setup allows the cook to check the roast's temperature without pulling the meat in and out of the oven. All the cooks to whom I've recommended this gadget say they don't know how they lived without it. Although I've seen it for less, the Poldar Thermo-Timer retails for about $35.

◆ Peppercorn-Coated Roast Beef Tenderloin

THE MIX OF STRONG and mild peppercorns makes this roast peppery, but not harsh. Be sure to crush the peppers in a mortar and pestle or with a heavy-bottomed saucepan or skillet. Do not use a coffee or spice grinder, which will grind the softer green and pink peppercorns to a powder before the harder black and white peppercorns begin to break up.

Follow step 1 of recipe for Simple Roast Beef Tenderloin (page 183), substituting 6 tablespoons mixed peppercorns (black, white, pink and green), coarsely crushed, for pepper. Continue as directed.

◆ Chile-Rubbed Roast Beef Tenderloin

IF YOU CANNOT FIND CHIPOTLE and ancho chile powders, you can very easily make your own by roasting two dried chipotle chiles and two dried ancho chiles in a 350°F oven until they puff, about 5 minutes. Cool the peppers slightly, then stem, seed and break them into small pieces. Working with one kind of pepper at a time, grind each to a powder in a spice grinder or coffee grinder that you have designated for grinding spices.

1. Mix 2½ tablespoons chipotle chile powder and 1 tablespoon ancho or pasilla chile powder with 1½ teaspoons cumin and ½ teaspoon dried oregano.

2. Follow step 1 of recipe for Simple Roast Beef Tenderloin (page 183), pressing chile powder onto tenderloin with salt and pepper. Continue as directed.

Parsley Sauce
with Cornichons and Capers

MAKES ABOUT 1 CUP

SUBSTITUTE MINCED BABY DILL PICKLES if cornichons are unavailable.

¾   cup minced fresh parsley leaves
12 cornichons, minced (6 tablespoons),
      plus 1 teaspoon cornichon juice
¼   cup capers, drained and coarsely chopped
 2   medium scallions, minced
      Pinch salt
¼   teaspoon ground black pepper
½   cup extra-virgin olive oil

Mix all ingredients in a medium bowl and serve at room temperature with tenderloin.

Mustard-Green Peppercorn Sauce

MAKES ABOUT 1½ CUPS

THIS COOL YET PIQUANT SAUCE goes well with a peppercorn-coated fillet. You can find green peppercorns in brine in the gourmet section of many grocery stores or in specialty food shops. If you can't find them, just omit them from the recipe.

1   cup Dijon mustard
½   cup crème fraîche or sour cream
1   tablespoon green peppercorns in brine, minced

Mix all ingredients in a medium bowl. Cover and refrigerate until ready to serve.

Poblano Cream with Roasted Jalapeños

ALTHOUGH VERY GOOD with Simple Roast Beef Tenderloin (page 183) or the peppercorn-coated version, this sauce is a perfect match for the chile-rubbed roast. For instructions on how to make chile powder, see page 185.

3 medium jalapeños, roasted, stemmed, seeded and minced

4 teaspoons minced fresh cilantro leaves

¼ teaspoon poblano chile powder (see above)

1 cup sour cream

Mix all ingredients in a medium bowl. Cover and refrigerate until ready to serve.

Holiday Pork Roast

CROWN ROAST is the king of pork roasts. It consists of two center cut loins trussed together to form a ring. The "frenched" rib bones around the perimeter and stuffing in the shallow cavity make it the crowning glory of many festive celebrations.

So I set out to perfect my roasting technique of this cut. After several attempts, I found that no matter what the oven temperature (200 to 400 degrees) or the pork's internal temperature (145 to 160 degrees), crown roast never tastes as impressive as it looks. As I ate one of the chops, I realized that the only satisfying part was the meat and fat around the rib bone. Even roasted to a low 145 degrees, this lean cut is at once juicy and dry, much like the texture of white tuna packed in water.

The problem is compounded by the roast's shape. Because the ribs form the outside of the crown, only the bones brown. Turned inward and covered with stuffing, the loin steams rather than roasts, with no possibility of browning.

To find out how to fix my crown roast of pork, I decided to interview those who know pork best—the producers, the processors, the professors and the promoters—to see if they could offer me any advice. As I described the crown roast's deficiencies, I expected an industry sales pitch touting the benefits of the modern ultralean pork. But almost without exception, each person readily acknowledged its problems.

Lean and Mean

Before World War II, hogs were raised as much for their fat as for their meat—a pig with four to five inches of exterior fat (equivalent to about 60 pounds of lard) at slaughter was the norm. After the war, vegetable fats in the form of oils, shortening and margarine became popular, and very quickly lard was viewed as a liability rather than an asset. The trend toward healthier diets in recent decades also helped force the industry to put pork on a diet. Now many processors penalize producers whose pigs have more than a mere 8/10 inch of exterior fat.

Much of this fat reduction is a result of genetic engineering. Industry's success at eliminating the pig's surface fat, however, has resulted in the loss of its intramuscular fat as well. Known as marbling, this fat traps and retains juices during cooking and gives the meat flavor and body. Slaughtering pigs young, before they start to fatten, makes for tasteless, characterless meat. Fattier cuts of pork like fresh hams, picnics and shoulder are less affected by the new breeding programs than are naturally leaner cuts such as the loin and tenderloin, which have been dramatically affected. To compensate for the flavor loss and dry texture, processors have begun to "marinate" these cuts at the plant, infusing them with salt, citric acid, water and flavorings such as teriyaki or peppercorns.

Let the Circle Be Broken: Rack Supplants Crown

Given this genetically engineered problem, I set out to give this loin cut all the flavor I possibly could. I headed back to the kitchen after a detour to my local butcher, who suggested I roast the two frenched loin roasts separately, much like rack of lamb, rather than sew them together to form a crown. This arrangement allows the loins to cook independently of each other, ensuring that the meat browns rather than steams. Getting the roast out of a circle and separating it into two parts did make it brown better, just as the butcher promised. At the table, the presentation is just as impressive with the frenched loins crossed, honor guard-style.

It matters which end of the loin the

roast comes from. The whole loin is about two feet long and cylindrical. It is made up of three sections: the rib end near the shoulder; the center loin; and the loin end, close to the rump. Of the three sections, the rib is the fattiest and most flavorful. Located close to the shoulder, this part of the loin is multimuscular, with much-needed fat separating the muscles.

Bones also add flavor to meat. In order to make the loins bend into a crown roast, the chine bone must be removed, further robbing the meat of flavor. Shaping the loin into a rack, however, does not require complete removal of the chine bone and allows the loin to roast on the bone, so it can take on more flavor.

A Flavorful Solution

To improve the roast's flavor even further, I decided to mimic the pork industry's meat-marinating technique. Using a gadget I found at my local cooking shop called the Zap Flavor Injector (see page 195), I marinated roasts with three different mixtures. Dying each solution blue so that I could track it in the meat, I made one of salt and water; one of salt, sugar and water; and a final mixture of salt, water and oil. I roasted these three roasts along with one seasoned on the surface only.

The results were amazing. The injected flavorings permeated the roasts, gravitating to the center, making the loin muscle much more flavorful and juicy than in the surface-seasoned roast. In addition, the roast with added oil tasted more tender. This instant marinating step takes about 10 minutes, and the results are worth the effort. For those who choose not to perform the extra step, simply selecting the right roast and cooking it at the suggested oven temperature in the recipe will certainly produce a good-looking, respectable-tasting roast.

Because I knew that beef's flavor could be improved with aging (see page 177), I bought a second pork roast, coating each rack with 2 tablespoons of kosher salt, and set it on a wire rack over a paper-towel-lined plate to age for one week. After thoroughly brushing off all the remaining salt and removing thin slices of dried-out pork from each end of the roast, I cooked this rack. Its flavor and texture were even better than those of the injected one. Even though it was a little too salty, it tasted like real pork, with a smooth, buttery texture. Reducing the salt the second time around gave me an even better roast.

For those who buy their rack of pork the afternoon before they want to serve it, I recommend the injection method. For those who think as much as three or four days ahead, salting and refrigerating the roast produce big flavor.

Is It Safe?

Even though I had not been pleased with the taste and texture of the crown roasts, I did learn one thing during my initial testing. The best roasts were those that were slow-roasted, with the temperature increased at the end to brown the meat and create pan drippings. Slow-roasting allows the roast to cook more evenly, ensuring that the outside does not overcook and lose precious juices. I prefer meat roasted at 200 degrees, but because many ovens are not properly calibrated, I recommend roasting the loin at 250 degrees. Once it reaches an internal temperature of 120 degrees, increase the oven temperature to 425 degrees to brown the meat.

The right internal temperature is key to any good roast pork loin. For years, the standard for pork was 180 degrees—an appropriate temperature for pre–World War II pork, but hardly right for today's young lean meat. The Pork Council currently promotes 160 degrees as the new standard, but I found loins roasted to this temperature too dry. After much testing, I settled on an internal temperature of 145 degrees, which will rise 3 or 4 degrees more during the roast's resting period. At this temperature, the roast is still very juicy and has just lost the last of its pink color.

This temperature is perfectly safe. The industry's 160-degree recommendation builds in a safety factor for cooks who may be armed with potentially inaccurate meat thermometers and/or who lack expertise in taking meat temperatures. It is also intended to take into account an unevenly thawed roast with cold spots. Furthermore, because pigs are fed a controlled grain-based diet these days, trichinosis is virtually nonexistent. According to David Meisinger, assistant vice president of pork quality for the National Pork Producers Council, the very few reported incidents result from privately raised pigs and rustic pro-duction conditions. Even so, trichinosis is killed at 140 degrees.

Because the inside of the roast is bacteria-free, it is only the cut surfaces of the roast that might be contaminated. But as long as the outside reaches 140 degrees within four hours, the roast is safe.

I look forward to the day when they figure out how to marble pork again without the surface fat. Until then, I'm sticking close to the shoulder, hoarding the bones, infusing the meat with a little fat and flavor and roasting it slow and low.

TO PREPARE A RACK OF PORK FOR ROASTING

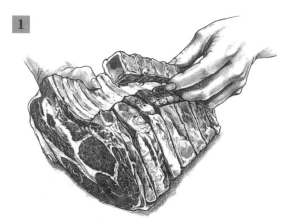

1. So that the frenched bones will cross at presentation, have the butcher remove the tip of the chine bone.

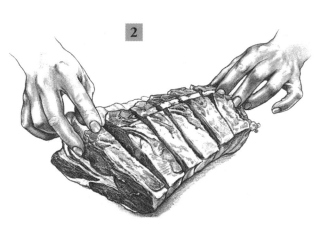

2. So that chops can easily be carved from the roast, ask the butcher to cut the chine bone between each rib.

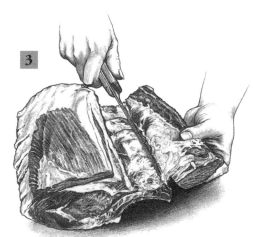

3. To expose the rib bones, have the butcher remove the thin flap of meat on each rib roast.

4. So that the ribs on each roast will cross, remove the meat from between each rib.

5. For a more refined presentation, "french" the exposed rib bones by removing the excess meat and fat.

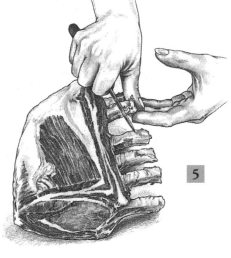

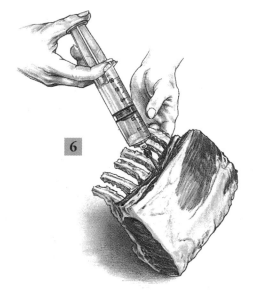

6. If marinating the roast, inject flavorings all over, particularly at each loin end and between each rib bone.

Roast Cured Rack of Pork
with Garlic-Thyme Rub

Serves 6 to 8

Dry-curing requires only that you make space in the refrigerator and purchase the meat three to five days before serving it. If you don't have time, try the optional marinade (see page 196). Or if you're in a real rush you can skip both, knowing that choosing the right roast and cooking it according to the suggested method will deliver better-than-average results. Because I prefer the pork to roast on as much bone as possible for maximum flavor, I recommend having the butcher remove only the tip of the chine bone. To facilitate carving, the butcher should then cut through the remaining chine bone between each rib.

2 pork loin roasts (5-6 ribs each) from rib end of loin,
    tip of chine bone removed, remaining chine cut between
    each rib, rib bones frenched (see figure 5, page 193)

2 tablespoons kosher salt or 1½ tablespoons table salt

Garlic-Thyme Rub

3 medium garlic cloves, minced (about 1 tablespoon)

2 teaspoons ground black pepper

2 teaspoons dried thyme leaves

2 tablespoons olive oil

Vegetables

1 small carrot, cut into 1-inch chunks

1 small onion, coarsely chopped

1 tablespoon olive oil

3 tablespoons Madeira

1. Rub each loin roast with a portion of salt. Place on a wire rack set over a paper-towel-lined jelly roll pan and refrigerate, uncovered, for 5 days. Before roasting meat, shave off very thin exterior layer of hardened, dehydrated meat on each end of each loin.

2. Garlic-Thyme Rub: Adjust oven rack to lower-middle position and preheat oven to 250°F. Mix garlic, pepper, thyme and olive oil to make a thick paste. Rub each loin with a portion of paste.

3. Vegetables: Toss carrot and onion with olive oil and place in a large roasting pan.

4. Place a large roasting rack over pan and set loins on rack. Roast until internal temperature of loins is 120° to 125°F, about 1½ hours. Increase oven temperature to 425°F and continue to roast until meat registers 145°F, about 30 minutes more, adding 1 cup water to roasting pan once pan drippings turn brown and just start to smoke. (Internal temperature will continue to rise after loins are removed from oven.)

5. Transfer each loin to a serving platter, arranging ribs so they cross. Cover loosely with foil while making sauce. Strain pan drippings into a measuring cup, pressing on vegetables to release liquid, and skim fat. Add additional water, if necessary, to equal 1 cup. Transfer to a small saucepan, add Madeira and simmer to blend flavors, about 5 minutes. Carve roast, cutting between each rib, and pass *jus* separately at table.

ZAP IT!

THE ZAP FLAVOR INJECTOR, a culinary syringe, is available nationwide at most stores that carry cooking gadgets and sells for about $5.95. A sturdier model is available by mail. For $11.95, the Cajun Cook (1-800-434-2809) offers an injection kit that includes a 1- and 2-ounce infusion tube as well as the syringe.

Roast Marinated Rack of Pork

SERVES 6 TO 8

NEXT TO CURING, the next best way to improve flavor in a pork roast is to inject it with this simple marinade. For a hint of sweetness in the meat, you can dissolve 1 tablespoon brown sugar, along with the salt, in the marinade.

> 2 pork loin roasts (5-6 ribs each) from rib end of loin, tip of chine bone removed, remaining chine cut between each rib, rib bones frenched (see figure 5, page 193)

Marinade

> 2 teaspoons table salt or 1 tablespoon kosher salt
> ¼ cup flavorless oil, such as canola or corn

Garlic-Thyme Rub

> ½ teaspoon salt
> 3 medium garlic cloves, minced (about 1 tablespoon)
> 2 teaspoons ground black pepper
> 2 teaspoons dried thyme leaves
> 2 tablespoons olive oil

Vegetables

> 1 small carrot, cut into 1-inch chunks
> 1 small onion, coarsely chopped
> 1 tablespoon olive oil

> 3 tablespoons Madeira

1. Marinade: Dissolve salt in ⅓ cup lukewarm water in a lidded container. Add oil and shake to emulsify. Fill syringe and inject each loin (see page 193), shaking injector occasionally to ensure that oil and water do not separate.

2. Garlic-Thyme Rub: Rub ¼ teaspoon salt over each rack. Follow step 2 of recipe for Roast Cured Rack of Pork with Garlic-Thyme Rub (page 194). Continue as directed.

Pale, Soft and to Be Avoided

Ever cook up a pork roast or chop that was especially tasteless and dry? It's what's known in the industry as PSE pork, which stands for "pale, soft and exudative," meaning that the meat doesn't hold its liquid during cooking. Although no one is sure how much of this meat makes it to the retail level, 15 to 20 percent of all pork at slaughter is PSE.

PSE pork is the result of a dramatic drop in the level of enzymes after slaughter. Part of the problem is genetic, and high on researchers' wish lists is breeding this tendency out of future pigs. The other cause of this enzyme drop is the pig's state of mind at slaughter. The levels of enzymes in pigs herded to slaughter straight from the delivery truck tend to drop lower than in pigs that are rested for a day.

To avoid PSE pork, select roasts and chops that are reddish pink (the redder the better, but remember that redder pork will spoil more quickly), firm and moist but not watery.

How to Select, Cook and Serve a Lobster

OUR CHURCH youth group hosts a lobster feast each May, at which we sell more than a thousand lobsters. One night in a kitchen with a crew of inexperienced cooks, and you find out pretty quickly that most people are not at all comfortable handling or cooking lobster. Even though all it takes is a pot of steaming water and 10 minutes of time, most of us don't cook lobsters often enough to get good at it. For one thing, lobsters are expensive. They often vary in quality, cooking up succulent and delicious one time, shriveled and watery the next. They also have the discomforting distinction of being just about the only food we cook live. And that, I think, is what bothers us the most.

Boiled lobster is the only cooking option at our church dinner, but I suspected steaming was a better method when cooking fewer lobsters. Although our fast-paced operation also demands a close-your-eyes-and-throw-them-in-the-pot approach, I wanted to investigate whether there was a more merciful means of slaughter.

Some lobster claws rip open as easily as an aluminum flip-top can, while others require shop tools to crack. The claw meat is wimpy and limp in some, and full and packed in others. Some lobsters are watery. Is this inconsistency in quality the result of improper handling, improper cooking or Mother Nature?

How to Select a Lobster

After talking to U.S. and Canadian research scientists, renowned food authorities, chefs of all varieties, fishmongers, restaurateurs, industry types, seafood experts, university professors, lobstermen, cookbook authors, caterers that specialize in lobster bakes and a couple of Maine home cooks, I've come to believe that lobster is like a pineapple: you can squeeze it, you can eye it, but you'll never know if it's great until you cut it open.

Lobster quality, as it turns out, is dependent on the season. Just like crabs, lobsters molt, or shed, their shells for bigger ones each year. Unlike crabs, however, newly molted lobsters are not usually identified as soft-shells.

The Meaning of Molting

Most of the lobsters we eat during the summer and fall are in some phase of molting. During late spring, the cold ocean waters begin to warm, and the lobsters start to form preshell tissue beneath their shells. According to Susan Waddy, a research scientist and lobster-molting expert at the Department of Fisheries and Oceans in New Brunswick, Canada, lobsters start to molt as early as June off the shores of New Jersey and in July or August in the colder Maine and Canadian waters. In the process of molting, the lobster pulls its claws out through its old shell. This is possible because the crustacean becomes dehydrated, which causes the claw meat to shrink.

Once the lobster casts off its old shell, it emerges with nothing but a soft, wrinkled covering. Within 15 minutes, it inflates itself with water, increasing its length by 15 percent and its weight by 50 percent. This extra water expands the soft covering, allowing the lobster room to grow long after the new shell starts to harden. The newly molted lobster immediately eats its old shell, which provides it with the calcium it needs for the new one.

For the next three or four months, according to Waddy, the lobster continues its calcium-rich diet, and its shell further hardens. Lobsters caught and impounded during this postmolt phase, she adds, are slow to develop hardened shells. Because they are fed very little in the holding areas and not at all in the tanks, they don't get the calcium they need for shell development, which may explain why many lobsters I bought in January were still soft-shelled.

The Best Season for Lobster

Lobsters are prime only when their shells are fully hardened. If you can find hard-shells, enjoy them. Before buying one, however, squeeze its body for shell hardness (see illustration, page 200).

During the winter months, lobsters are expensive. Weather conditions keep the lobstermen from checking their traps as often, and cold water slows the lobster's metabolism so that it loses interest in food, making it hard to catch. Lobster can cost as little as $3.99 per pound on a Labor Day weekend in my area, but in December, the price goes up to $9 a pound.

Spring lobsters are among the best, as they have been developing meat since the previous year's molting. They are more reasonably priced as well because they are more plentiful. Warmer water stimulates the lobster's appetite, and better weather makes it possible for the lobstermen to bait and check their traps frequently. As a rule of thumb, hard-shell lobsters are a good price from about Mother's Day through the Fourth of July.

IF YOU BUY A SOFT-SHELL

SOME PEOPLE don't like soft-shell lobsters, while others reserve them for chowder, salad or lobster rolls, and still others prefer them over hard-shells. In the summer, soft-shells are usually cheap and plentiful. If you buy them, here's what you need to know:

♦ They are much more perishable than hard-shells. Wrapped in wet newspaper, frisky hard-shell lobsters are usually just as feisty the following day. Soft-shells, on the other hand, slow way down after a night in the refrigerator, and I'm never surprised to find one dead.

♦ For claw meat fans, soft-shells will surely disappoint. Their claws are small, underdeveloped and spongy

♦ Because the newly molted lobster is full of water and not fully developed, it contains less meat than a hard-shell lobster of the same size. The meat from a 1½-pound soft-shell lobster is equal to that of a 1-to-1¼-pound hard-shell. If serving soft-shell lobsters, you may consider buying larger ones (1½-to-1¾-pounders for each person) or, if the price is really good, two small lobsters per person.

♦ Soft-shell lobsters are much easier to eat than hard-shells because they don't require special equipment. The claws readily snap open by hand, and because the tail meat is not filled out, it easily slips out of its shell.

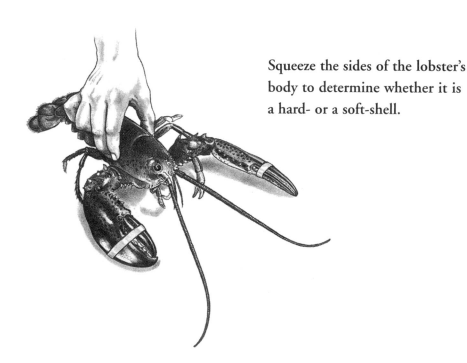

Squeeze the sides of the lobster's body to determine whether it is a hard- or a soft-shell.

How to Cook a Lobster

Once I determined that lobster quality was mostly dependent on its molt cycle, figuring out how to cook it was almost anticlimactic. Except for the size of the water puddle on the plate, I couldn't detect much difference between boiled and steamed lobsters. As I had suspected, boiling works best when you are cooking lobsters in quantity, but for a single batch, steaming on a rack or in a steamer basket is more efficient and less messy and keeps the lobster from becoming waterlogged. (If you happen to be near the ocean, you can collect seaweed to make a natural rack.) Neither beer nor wine in the steamer improved the lobster's flavor.

Once in the pot, lobsters are very easy to cook, and the timing is about the same whether you are steaming or boiling. Unlike more temperamental or delicate foods, they have a relatively wide window of doneness. Cooking them a couple of minutes beyond the chart times (see page 206) does not affect meat quality. After over- and undercooking many lobsters, I have found that it's better to cook them a little too long than not long enough. The tail meat of an undercooked lobster is very chewy, and the eggs of an undercooked female are an unappetizing murky green rather than the brilliant red of those that are fully cooked. If lobsters are significantly overcooked, however, the tail meat will be mushy. After the lobsters are done, I remove the lid from the pot, turn off the heat and let them sit in the pot a few minutes longer before serving.

As for dry-heat cooking methods, I found the steady, even heat of the oven preferable to broiling. To keep the tail from curling during roasting, run a skewer through it (see figure 7, page 209).

How to Kill a Lobster

I don't like killing anything, lobsters included, but the occasional act reminds me of what someone spares me every time I eat a boneless, skinless chicken breast or a piece of filleted salmon.

Lobsters are particularly troublesome. Like slaughtered chickens, they continue to move long after everyone assures you they are dead. I once observed the swimmerets on a lobster tail moving 18 hours after I had severed the body from the tail.

There is much debate over how much or little pain a lobster feels once it hits the pot. Some experts say a lobster cannot survive in temperatures over 80 degrees, so death is instant in a pot of steaming or boiling water. Others say the lobster should be frozen and its brain removed before cooking.

Judging from experience, I prefer freezing the lobster before cooking it. After 10 minutes in the freezer, the lobster is numbed. At that point, you can steam it or split it for roasting.

Tail Spin

After tasting tails from more than three dozen lobsters, I began to take note of their texture. Regardless of how I cooked them—roasted, broiled, steamed or boiled—most of the tails were, at least to some degree, rubbery and chewy.

I was confident I could solve this problem by some adjustment in the cooking method. I reasoned that if tough cuts like pork shoulder and beef brisket can be made tender by long, slow heat, so could lobster. If that didn't work, I suspected that just as scallops and shrimp can be saved from toughness by quick, high heat, so could lobster. A few phone calls, I thought, and I would have this lobster thing in the trap.

I thought wrong. What started as mild curiosity turned into an obsessive six-month search. I knew of one study that suggested the superiority of catfish cooked after they have passed through rigor mortis. In this experiment, the Washington State seafood expert John Rowly cooked two catfish fillets—one fresh-killed, the other iced for three days. Counterintuitively, the three-day-old fish fillet had a better texture and flavor than the freshly killed fish.

Might this phenomenon apply, I wondered, to lobster as well? Would killing the lobster and then letting it rest on ice before cooking ensure a tender tail?

Because no one seemed to know if lobsters actually go through rigor mortis,

I wasn't sure how long to let them rest. (I also knew it shouldn't be too long; bottom-feeding lobsters carry plenty of bacteria.) To play it safe, I killed six lobsters, refrigerated them, and cooked one every hour after their death, comparing each to one that was steamed live.

The results were varied, but generally the dead lobster meat looked dull compared to the bright, fresh-looking tail meat of the live-cooked ones. Many of the dead lobsters also tasted "off," and most of them were mushy. I subsequently learned that at death, lobsters release gastric enzymes from the stomach sac that cause the meat to deteriorate. Although the meat was less tough, the attendant compromise in texture was undesirable.

If the stomach sac releases destructive gastric enzymes, I decided to see what would happen if I took it out. Although this procedure may sound a bit excessive, the stomach sac is routinely removed when the lobster is split before broiling or baking. Located right behind the eyes, the sac is easily removed from a chilled lobster with kitchen shears. Removing the sac also meant I was removing the brain, an organ many scientists believe should come out before cooking, for humane reasons. This little operation, I reasoned, might save the tail meat from destructive gastric juices and guarantee that the lobster would be feeling no pain.

Some scientists also suggested there might be gastric juices in the tomalley as well, so I prepared three different lobsters, all purchased at the same time from the same store. I killed one lobster, then completely severed the tail from its body, thus ensuring that the tail was completely isolated from the stomach sac and the tomalley. For lobster two, I removed the head sac and brain, making sure the bulk of gastric enzymes could not deteriorate the tail. I left lobster three whole, wrapping it in wet newspaper to keep it alive while the two dead lobsters rested on ice overnight. To my surprise, the following day, each cooked lobster was equally delicious and tender.

The results of this final test confirmed what my early research had suggested: the secret to good lobster has more to do with the initial selection than with the actual preparation and cooking.

Tall Tales and Tough Tails

♦ "Choose the right gender." While females often contain the treasured roe, their tails are no more tender than those of their male counterparts.

♦ "Select soft-shells over hard-shells." The tail of a soft-shell might be sweeter, but compared to a hard-shell, it's smaller and tougher.

♦ "Avoid chicken lobsters." Some speculate that 1-pound lobsters swim more, thus developing a tougher tail muscle. I found chicken lobsters that were tough, but also some that were tender.

♦ "Avoid large, older lobsters." Some say that after years of exercising its tail, older lobsters are tougher. I tasted both tough and tender old-geezer lobsters.

♦ "Freeze the lobster." On the theory that an adrenaline rush at death causes the tail to toughen, a few experts suggested freezing the lobster 10 minutes before cooking. Though freezing numbs the lobster, it doesn't prevent toughness.

♦ "Pet the lobster." Some cooks stroke the lobster's body to hypnotize it. But this premortem massage doesn't guarantee a tender, succulent tail.

♦ "Don't overcook the lobster." Many suggest cooking the lobster until the thickest part of the tail is barely opaque. But some of the toughest tails I encountered were cooked to this doneness.

♦ "Don't undercook the lobster." Mainers, in particular, laugh at recipes that recommend 8 minutes per pound. Most of them steam their 1¼-pounders at least 15 to 20 minutes. It didn't take too many lobsters, however, to convince me that this was too long.

♦ "Let the lobster rest." A California chef told me that after cooking 60 lobsters, he discovered that a five-minute rest after cooking delivered a more tender tail. After testing, I let this idea rest in peace.

♦ "Start the lobster in cold water, then gradually bring it to a simmer." Some believe this method also kills the lobster humanely. My experience ran contrary. The lobster cooked this way was tough. And it continued to move even when the eyes had turned white from the heat.

♦ "Use a chopstick to kill the lobster." One person was certain that the Chinese had the secret. A chopstick run up the tail and through the body guaranteed instant death and a tender tail. After trying this method, I decided I couldn't ask anyone to kill a lobster this way. The tail looked torn and mutilated.

♦ "Steam the lobster over very low heat." This method did not work, and the slow, low heat caused the lobster to retain its body liquids. The tomalley, which many people enjoy, turned from a soft liver-like texture to soup.

Steamed Whole Lobsters

Serves 4

FREEZING THE LOBSTERS before cooking definitely makes them less frisky going into the pot. Leaving them in the freezer too long, however, causes their appendages to snap off more easily.

4 lobsters, frozen for 10 minutes
8 tablespoons butter, melted (optional)
Lemon wedges

Bring about 1 inch water to a boil over high heat in a large soup kettle set up with a wire rack, pasta insert or a seaweed bed. Add lobsters, cover and return to a boil. Reduce heat to medium-high and steam until lobsters are bright orange-red (see below for approximate cooking times). Serve immediately with warm butter, if desired, and lemon wedges.

APPROXIMATE STEAMING OR BOILING TIMES AND MEAT YIELDS

Lobster Size	Cooking Time (Minutes)	Meat Yield (Ounces)
1 pound, soft-shell	8-9	about 3
1 pound, hard-shell	10-11	4-4½
1¼ pounds, soft-shell	11-12	3½-4
1¼ pounds, hard-shell	13-14	5½-6
1½ pounds, soft-shell	13-14	5½-6
1½ pounds, hard-shell	15-16	7½-8
1¾-2 pounds, soft-shell	17-18	6¼-6½
1¾-2 pounds, hard-shell	about 19	8½-9

Classic Lobster Salad

SERVES 4

LOBSTER CHOWDERS and salads are the perfect way to take advantage of the less expensive soft-shell lobsters. Out of the shell and chopped, their small bodies and shrunken claws are not noticeable.

4   steamed whole lobsters, 1¼-1½ pounds each
     (see previous page), meat removed from shells
     and cut into small bite-size pieces
     (about 3 cups meat)
½   cup mayonnaise
3   tablespoons minced celery
1   tablespoon minced fresh parsley leaves
1   tablespoon snipped fresh chives
1   teaspoon grated zest and ½ teaspoon juice
     from 1 small lemon

Mix all ingredients in a medium bowl. Cover and refrigerate until well chilled.

To Prepare a Lobster for Roasting

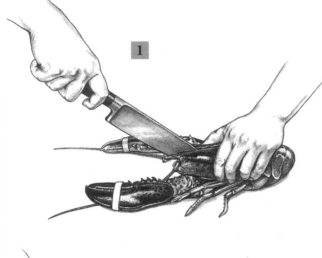

1. With the blade of a chef's knife facing the head end, kill the lobster by plunging the knife into the body where the shell forms a T. Move the blade toward the head.

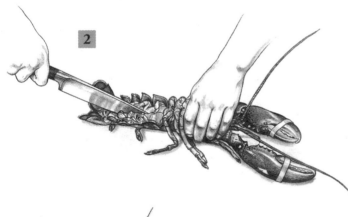

2. Turn the lobster back side down. Holding the upper body with one hand and with the knife blade facing the tail end, cut through the body. Move your hand down to the lower body and continue cutting through the tail, making sure not to cut all the way through the shell.

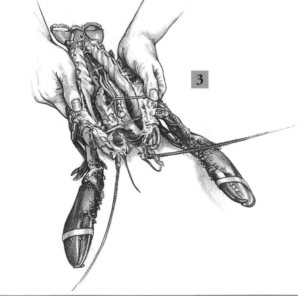

3. Holding half of the tail in each hand, crack but do not break the back shell to butterfly the lobster.

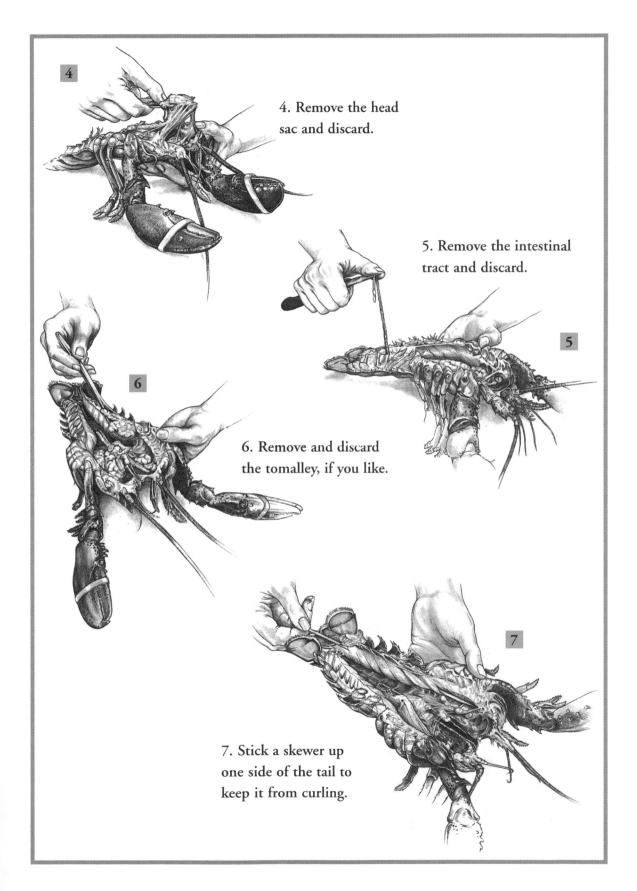

4

4. Remove the head sac and discard.

5. Remove the intestinal tract and discard.

5

6

6. Remove and discard the tomalley, if you like.

7

7. Stick a skewer up one side of the tail to keep it from curling.

Oven-Roasted Lobster with Herbed Bread Crumbs

Serves 4

ROASTING THE LOBSTERS at a high temperature rather than broiling them ensures more even cooking. To keep the tails from curling in the oven, don't forget to run long skewers through them before roasting.

4 tablespoons (½ stick) butter

½ cup dried bread crumbs

2 tablespoons minced fresh parsley leaves or 1 tablespoon minced fresh tarragon leaves or snipped chives

4 lobsters, prepared according to illustrations on pages 208-209

Salt

Ground white pepper

Lemon wedges

1. Adjust oven rack to upper-middle position and preheat oven to 450°F. Heat 1 tablespoon butter in a small skillet over medium heat. When foaming subsides, add bread crumbs and cook, stirring constantly, until toasted and golden brown, 3 to 4 minutes. Stir in herbs and set aside.

2. Arrange lobsters crosswise on two 17-by-11-inch foil-lined jelly roll pans, alternating tail and claw ends. Melt remaining 3 tablespoons butter and brush over body and tail of each lobster; season with salt and white pepper to taste. Sprinkle bread crumb mixture evenly over body and tail meat.

3. Roast lobsters until tail meat is opaque and bread crumbs are crisp, 12 to 15 minutes. Serve immediately with lemon wedges.

Lobster and Corn Chowder

Makes about 2 quarts, serving 6

WHENEVER YOU STEAM LOBSTERS, keep the steaming liquid. Refrigerate or freeze it and use it as a base for lobster or other seafood chowders.

2 lobsters (1¼-1½ pounds each)

2 tablespoons butter

1 medium-large onion, cut into medium dice

3 tablespoons all-purpose flour

½ cup dry white wine

2 medium boiling potatoes, cut into medium dice

4 ears corn, kernels cut from cob (or 2 cups frozen, thawed)

⅛ teaspoon cayenne

¼ teaspoon dried thyme

1 cup heavy cream

2 tablespoons minced fresh parsley

Salt

Ground black or white pepper

1. Bring 1 quart water to a boil in a large soup kettle fitted with a steamer basket. Add lobsters, cover and steam until lobsters are bright orange-red and fully cooked, about 10 minutes. Transfer lobsters to a large bowl; cool slightly. Working over a bowl to catch lobster liquid, remove meat from each claw and tail. Return all lobster shells and their liquid to steaming liquid; chop lobster meat into small bite-size pieces and set aside. Bring lobster broth and shells to a simmer and continue to simmer to further flavor broth, about 10 minutes. Pour broth through a fine strainer and set aside; discard shells. (You should have about 4½ cups broth; if not, add enough water to complete the measure.) Rinse and dry kettle; return to burner.

2. Heat butter in kettle over medium-high heat. Add onion and sauté until softened, about 5 minutes. Add flour and stir until lightly colored, about 1 minute. Gradually whisk in wine, then lobster broth. Add potatoes, corn, cayenne and thyme and simmer until potatoes are tender, about 10 minutes. Add lobster, cream, parsley and salt and pepper to taste; bring to a simmer. Remove from heat and serve.

IV

On the Side,
But Not Forgotten

The Cabbage Makes the Slaw

OR ME, no picnic, barbecue or fish fry is complete without a big bowl of coleslaw. And during the winter months, this wonderfully simple cabbage salad often takes the place of the usual tossed greens at our family dinner.

Despite its simplicity, two things have always bothered me about my coleslaw. If I make it ahead and refrigerate it, the dressing turns the consistency of milk and sinks to the bottom of the bowl. If I serve the salad right away, it tastes too sharp, regardless of which vinegar I use.

With those problems in mind, I began my coleslaw tests. I wanted to keep the cabbage from watering down the dressing; I wanted to make the salad piquant without tasting too sharp, and I also wanted to find out if there was an easy way to hand-shred cabbage.

Shred, Slice, Sliver or Grate?

I started with shredding. I knew the food processor would win on speed, but could it produce the long, thin, shaved cabbage I thought made good slaw? After shredding the cabbage with a knife,

on a box grater, with a mandoline-style gadget and in a food processor with a slicing blade, a steel blade and a shredding disk in turn, I determined that the slicing blade of the food processor was indeed the best tool for large batches.

On the other hand, the processor's steel blade and the shredding disk produced cabbage that was neither shredded nor chopped. The shredding disk turned out chewed-up, rough-looking pieces, while the steel blade gave inconsistent results—some pieces chopped fine, others too big. The cabbage from both methods looked bruised, and bruised cabbage, I quickly noticed, stank.

For small batches of a half cabbage or less, though, I preferred a shredding technique adapted from Phillip Schulz's method in *As American as Apple Pie* (Simon and Schuster, 1990). Rather than tediously hacking away at a hard, thick cabbage half or quarter, Schulz recommends coring the cabbage, separating the leaves, then stacking them and slicing them on the diagonal as thin as possible with a sharp chef's knife.

Although these short stacks of leaves were easier to handle than cabbage halves or quarters, I did find the process of separating the leaves from the cored cabbage fairly time-consuming. Instead, I quartered and cored the cabbage, then separated sections of leaves from each quarter into thin piles that lay flat when pressed. Using a chef's knife, I thinly sliced the piles of flattened leaves on the diagonal, as shown in figure 1, page 219. The resulting shreds were long and thin, perfect for coleslaw. For those who prefer chopped slaw, it is easy to separate the piles of leaves and simply roll them up to fit them through the feeder tube of a food processor. To chop by hand, cut the shreds into a fine dice. Then turn them crosswise and chop fine.

Icy Plunge or Salt and Dry?

While most recipes advocate immediately tossing the shredded cabbage with dressing, a few add an extra step: either soaking the cabbage in ice water for crisping and refreshing, or salting the cabbage—or in some cases tossing it with a mixture of salt, sugar and spice—to drain and wilt it.

The cabbage soaked in ice water was crisp, plump and fresh. If looks were all that mattered, the iced cabbage would have scored high next to the limp, salted cabbage in the neighboring colander. The soaked cabbage was as crisp as celery and as mild tasting as lettuce. (A whiff of the soaking water confirmed

that it did absorb some of the odor.) But its good looks were deceiving. Even though I drained the cabbage and dried it thoroughly, the dressing didn't adhere to it. In only minutes, the cabbage shreds started to lose their recently acquired water, and an even larger puddle of water diluted the creamy dressing. The stiff shreds were also strawlike, making them difficult to fork and even more difficult to get into the mouth without leaving a creamy trail.

The salted cabbage, by contrast, lost most of its liquid, leaving it wilted but pickle-crisp and better able to take on the dressing's flavors. Unlike the stiff icy shreds, this limp cabbage is also easier to eat. Day-old slaw made from the salted cabbage tastes fresh, with no milky pool at the bowl bottom to reveal its age.

The process does leave the cabbage a bit too salty, but a quick rinse in cold water removes the excess. If the slaw is to be served immediately, rinse it in ice water to bring the cabbage temperature down quickly. Coleslaw, at least the creamy style, needs to be eaten cold.

The Acid Test

I was now ready to tackle the dressing's acidity problem. I found a few creamy coleslaw recipes that tossed the cabbage with sour cream only, or a combination of mayonnaise and sour cream, leaving the vinegar out completely.

THE SCIENCE OF SALTING

VEGETABLES THAT SOAK in ice water become crisp, while salted and drained vegetables go limp. I didn't realize the same principle was at work in both instances until I consulted the Atlanta-based food scientist Shirley Corriher. "Vegetable cells are filled with liquid," states Corriher, "but the cell walls are semipermeable, allowing liquid to flow into and out of the cell. Depending on where the salt quantity is greater, that's where the water flows."

When soaked in ice water, cabbage shreds become stiffer and crisper because the cabbage cells contain more salt than the ice water. As the ice water is drawn into the cells, the shreds plump up. A scored radish that blossoms into a radish rose when it is soaked in ice water is an even more dramatic example of this principle.

When shredded cabbage is salted, on the other hand, the cell water is drawn out by the clinging salt. This same principle is true for other vegetables with high water content. You should salt and drain carrots, zucchini, yellow squash and cucumber before tossing them with dressings.

These versions, however, proved too mild for my taste. Other recipes called for using lemon juice rather than vinegar, and although this alternative was pleasantly tart, it lacked the depth that vinegar offered.

Recalling an article in *Cook's Illustrated* on quick pickle making, in which rice wine vinegar gave vegetables a pleasant, acidic flavor without the puckery aftereffects, I decided to give this low-acid vinegar a try. I drizzled a bit over the mayonnaise-tossed cabbage, and found its mild acidity perfect. Interestingly, though, this slaw proved too mild the following day. My conclusion: use rice wine vinegar for slaw to be eaten right away.

Although there are several styles of coleslaw, the two that follow are classics—one mild and creamy, the other sweet and sour. Adjust either recipe to your taste. If sour cream is a must, substitute some or all of it for the mayonnaise. Add green pepper or celery, red onions or apples. Try caraway seeds or fresh dill, radishes or nuts.

Creamy Coleslaw

SERVES 6 TO 8

IF THE SALAD is to be refrigerated overnight and served the next day, substitute cider vinegar for the rice vinegar. If you like caraway or celery seed in your coleslaw, you can add ¼ teaspoon of either with the mayonnaise and vinegar. If you have time to let the cabbage drain a little longer, you can sprinkle it to taste with salt and skip the rinsing step.

> 1½ pounds (about ½ medium head) red or
> green cabbage, finely shredded or chopped
> (9 cups; see illustrations)
> 1 large carrot, peeled and grated
> 1 tablespoon kosher salt or 2 teaspoons table salt
> ½ small onion, minced
> ½ cup mayonnaise
> 1 tablespoon rice wine vinegar
> Ground black pepper

1. Toss cabbage and carrot with salt in a colander set over a medium bowl. Let stand until cabbage wilts and releases much of its liquid, at least 1 hour and up to 4 hours.

2. Drain liquid from bowl. Rinse cabbage and carrot thoroughly in cold water (use ice water if serving slaw immediately). Press but do not squeeze cabbage to drain (a salad spinner does the job perfectly). Pat dry with paper towels. (Cabbage can be stored in a zipper-lock plastic bag and refrigerated overnight.)

3. Pour drained cabbage and carrot back into bowl. Add onion, mayonnaise and vinegar; toss to coat. Season with pepper to taste. Cover and refrigerate until ready to serve. (Coleslaw can be refrigerated overnight.)

SHREDDING CABBAGE

1. To shred cabbage by hand, quarter, then core, the cabbage. Separate the quarters into stacks of leaves that flatten when pressed lightly. Use a chef's knife to cut each stack diagonally into thin shreds.

2. To chop cabbage, turn the pile of shredded cabbage crosswise; cut the shreds into fine dice.

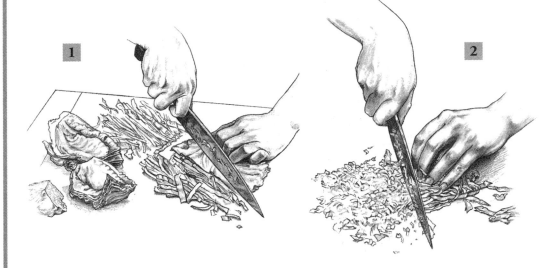

Sweet and Sour Coleslaw

SERVES 6 TO 8

As with CREAMY COLESLAW, you may want to substitute cider vinegar if making the slaw a day in advance.

1½ pounds (about ½ medium head) red or
    green cabbage, finely shredded or chopped
    (9 cups; see illustration, page 219)
1 large carrot, peeled and grated
½ cup sugar
2 teaspoons kosher salt or 1 teaspoon table salt
¼ teaspoon celery seed
6 tablespoons vegetable oil
¼ cup rice wine vinegar
    Ground black pepper

1. Toss cabbage and carrot with sugar, salt and celery seed in a colander set over a medium bowl. Let stand until cabbage wilts, at least 1 hour and up to 4 hours.

2. Pour draining liquid from bowl; rinse bowl and dry. Transfer wilted cabbage and carrot to bowl.

3. Add oil and vinegar; toss to coat. Season with pepper to taste. Cover and refrigerate until ready to serve. (Coleslaw can be refrigerated for up to 5 days.)

Curried Coleslaw
with Apples and Raisins

Serves 6

Toasted sliced almonds are the perfect nutty accent with the apple and raisins in this recipe; add ¼ cup, if you wish.

1½ pounds (about ½ medium head) red or
green cabbage, finely shredded or chopped
(9 cups; see illustration, page 219)

1 large carrot, peeled and grated

½ cup sugar

2 teaspoons kosher salt or 1 teaspoon table salt

¼ teaspoon celery seed

6 tablespoons vegetable oil

¼ cup rice wine vinegar

1 teaspoon curry powder

1 medium apple, peeled, cored and cut into small dice

¼ cup golden or dark raisins (optional)

Ground black pepper

Follow recipe for Sweet and Sour Coleslaw, adding curry powder, apple and raisins, if desired, with oil and vinegar in step 3.

Great Greens

GROWING UP in the Deep South, I ate all the regionally correct greens—turnips, collards and mustard. Kale, Swiss chard and beet greens were foreign flora, and spinach was served from a can. Some 30 years later, the greens section of most supermarkets across the country has changed dramatically. Regional preferences are not as obvious as they used to be: almost everyone now loves tangy greens like kale, mustard and chard, and nobody seems to eat spinach from a can anymore.

But just because we have a jungle of greens at our fingertips doesn't necessarily mean we know what to do with them. Too often, we make the mistake of lumping all greens together in our mind and preparing them the same way. We tend to use a single set of stemming, cutting and cooking instructions, regardless of the fact that some greens are delicate enough for salads, while others seem tough enough to have survived the Jurassic Age. After cleaning, stemming and cooking more than 100 pounds of greens, I realized that about all they had in common was their color.

Tougher, more assertive greens—mustard, turnip and collard, as well as kale and broccoli rabe—are strong-flavored, tough-textured and relatively dry. Because of these characteristics, they demand a particular cooking method.

Spinach, beet greens and Swiss chard are tender. Because their leaves are more delicate, they cook quickly. These greens are also succulent and therefore need no additional liquid during cooking. Because they are so mild, tender greens take well to lots of seasoning. Though many greens are available year-round, the assertive varieties are generally available from late fall to spring, while tender types come to market from spring through fall.

Cleaning Greens

There's no getting around it: cleaning greens is not easy. If they're not washed properly, though, you've wasted precious time and produce. At first I tried simply throwing gritty greens into a sink of clean water before stemming them, thinking that as much dirt should be removed as soon as possible. I soon realized that besides leaving me with prune fingers, working with wet, dirty greens was a damp, cold, messy business.

It's simpler to stem the greens when they are dry, which also does away with much of the dirt. Dropping the stemmed leaves into a sink of clean water allows most of the grit to fall naturally to the bottom. Usually one more rinse—removing the leaves, emptying and refilling the sink, then dropping and swishing the leaves—makes them skillet-ready.

Stemming Greens

Mature spinach and beet greens with tougher stems should be stemmed by holding each leaf between the thumb and index finger of one hand, while pulling back the stem with the other hand (see figure 1, page 224). Much like an asparagus stalk, the tough stem breaks off naturally at the tender point. Younger spinach and beet greens with stems almost as tender as the leaves need simply to be pinched or snipped where the stem meets the leaf (see figure 2, page 224). For ease of stemming, I prefer spinach sold in bunches to the bagged loose leaves because the whole clusters can be stemmed at one time. To do this, hold the bunch by the root, leaf end down, over a sink filled with clean water, then pinch each leaf from its stem, dropping leaves into the water as you accumulate a handful.

Swiss chard, collards, kale and mustard greens aren't usually as dirty as spinach and beet greens, and their larger (and therefore fewer) leaves are much eas-

ier to stem. Hold each leaf over a sink full of clean water and, using a sharp knife (I like to use a boning knife), slash down both sides of the stem (see figure 3, page 224). Let the leaves fall into the clean water, discard the stems, and repeat the process with the remaining leaves.

Turnip greens, with their multileaved stems, are easier to strip by hand (see figure 4), letting the stripped leaves drop into a sink of clean water.

It's simplest to rough-chop tough greens before blanching.

Cooking Tender Greens: Beet, Spinach and Chard

I put four different cooking methods to the test to determine the best and simplest way to cook tender greens: blanching, steaming, microwave cooking and wilting (cooking the damp greens in a large covered pan until limp). Although blanching produced the most brilliantly colored greens, it compromised both their taste and texture. Blanched greens were mushy and less flavorful than those cooked by any of the other methods. Steaming produced acceptable results but required setting up a steamer basket and heating water, unnecessary steps in that these tender, succulent greens did not need the added moisture. Tender beet greens, spinach and Swiss chard can be cooked in the microwave successfully, but I found no time savings with this method. The microwave cooks 1 pound

STEMMING GREENS

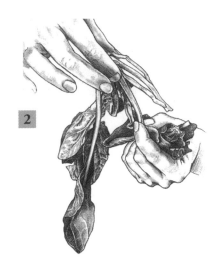

1. To stem mature spinach and beet greens, hold each leaf between the thumb and index finger of one hand, while pulling back the stem with the other hand.

2. To stem young spinach and beet greens, hold the bunch by the root, leaf end down, then pinch each leaf from its stem.

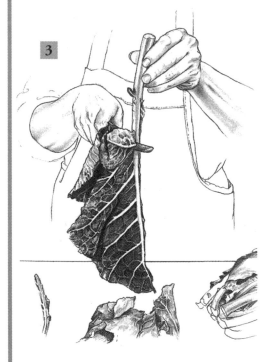

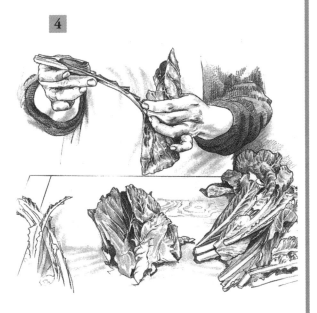

3. To stem Swiss chard, collards, kale and mustard greens, slash down both sides of the leaf with a sharp knife.

4. To stem turnip greens, strip the leaves off the stem with your hands.

in five minutes, the same amount of time required for wilting and steaming. But if you are so inclined, the microwave is an acceptable option.

Wilting is the simplest, most straightforward of the cooking methods. Simply toss the leaves, wet from washing, into a heated sauté pan and cover them, stirring occasionally, until the greens wilt in the steam produced by their own liquid. The greens are done in minutes and absorb almost all of their flavorful liquid once the lid is removed. Wilted greens can be shocked in cold water, squeezed of excess liquid and used in recipes calling for blanched greens.

When combined with sautéing, wilting becomes even more attractive because you can accomplish both cooking methods almost simultaneously in the same pan. Heat oil in the pan, with spices and aromatics if you like. Add the wet greens, cover and steam until wilted. Once they wilt, remove the lid and sauté the greens over high heat until the liquid evaporates. You may add other flavorings or enrichments at this point.

Cooking Kale, Turnips, Collards and Mustard

Kale, turnips, collards and mustards are too tough, bitter and dry to be cooked by wilting. Prepared this way, leaves at the bottom of the pan often scorch before cooking is complete. Steaming does not remove enough of their bitterness. The microwave scores even lower than steaming, accentuating rather than taming the tough greens' negative features. Conventional blanching, cooking them in large quantities of salted water, yields better results, though the greens give up too much flavor and lose their individual character once they are drained and rinsed.

For optimum results—good color, full flavor without bitterness and a tender texture—cook assertive greens in 1 quart of water per pound of greens until they are just tender, about seven minutes.

After this shallow-blanching, assertive greens can be cooked in five minutes following one of the recipes on pages 234-236.

INCREDIBLE SHRINKING GREENS

BECAUSE GREENS SHRINK so dramatically when cooked, it's sometimes hard to know how much to buy. Though based on averages (every bunch will fluctuate an ounce or so), this chart should help you make more accurate guesses.

10-ounce package of fresh (curly-leaf) prerinsed, prestemmed spinach =
- 8½ ounces leaves
- 8 cups lightly packed leaves
- Generous ⅔ cup wilted and lightly squeezed leaves

1-pound bundle of flat-leaf spinach =
- 9-10 ounces leaves
- 8-9 cups lightly packed leaves
- About 1 cup wilted and lightly squeezed leaves

10-ounce package of frozen spinach =
- Scant 1 cup lightly squeezed leaves

1 pound of beet greens =
- 8 ounces leaves
- 7-8 cups lightly packed leaves
- 1 cup wilted and lightly squeezed leaves

1 pound of collard greens =
- 9½ ounces stems plus 6½ ounces leaves
- 7 cups lightly packed raw leaves
- 1 cup cooked and lightly squeezed leaves

1 pound of Swiss chard =
- 9 ounces stems (cut into 1-inch pieces to equal 4 cups) plus 7 ounces leaves
- 6 cups lightly packed leaves
- 1 cup wilted and lightly squeezed greens
- 1½ cups sautéed stems

1 pound of kale =
- 9 ounces stems plus 7 ounces leaves
- 7 cups lightly packed raw leaves
- 1¼ cup cooked and lightly squeezed leaves

1 pound of mustard greens =
- 7½ ounces stems plus 8½ ounces leaves
- 7 cups lightly packed raw leaves
- Scant 1 cup cooked and lightly squeezed leaves

1 pound of turnip greens =
- 8 ounces stems plus 8 ounces leaves
- 7 cups lightly packed raw leaves
- Scant 1 cup cooked and lightly squeezed leaves

Wilted Sautéed Tender Greens

SERVES 4

To avoid oversalting, season the greens toward the end of sautéing when they have fully wilted.

2 medium garlic cloves, minced
3 tablespoons olive oil
2 pounds tender greens, such as spinach, beet greens
   or Swiss chard, cleaned and stemmed
   (water left clinging to leaves)
   Salt
   Ground black pepper
   Lemon wedges (optional)

1. Heat garlic with oil over medium-high heat in a large, nonreactive sauté pan or Dutch oven. When garlic sizzles and starts to turn golden, add wet greens to pan; cover and cook, stirring occasionally, until completely wilted but still bright green, 3 to 5 minutes.

2. Uncover, season to taste with salt and pepper and cook until most of liquid evaporates, about 2 minutes more. Serve immediately with lemon wedges, if desired.

Tender Greens with Bacon, Onions and Cider Vinegar

Serves 4

For a variation without bacon, heat 2 tablespoons of olive oil in its place.

3 ounces bacon, cut crosswise into thin strips
1 small onion, minced
2 medium garlic cloves, minced
¼ teaspoon hot red pepper flakes
2 pounds tender greens, such as spinach, beet greens
    or Swiss chard, cleaned and stemmed
    (water left clinging to leaves)
1 tablespoon cider vinegar
   Salt
   Ground black pepper

1. Fry bacon over medium-high heat in a large sauté pan or Dutch oven until crisp, remove with a slotted spoon and set aside. Remove or add fat to pan to equal 2 tablespoons. Add onion and sauté until partially softened, about 1 minute. Add garlic and pepper flakes and sauté until softened, 2 to 3 minutes.

2. Add wet greens, cover and cook, stirring occasionally, until completely wilted but still bright green, 3 to 5 minutes. Uncover and cook until most of liquid evaporates, about 2 minutes longer. Add vinegar and season with salt and pepper to taste. Sprinkle with reserved bacon and serve immediately.

Tender Greens with Nutmeg and Cream

SERVES 4

FOR CREAMED SPINACH LOVERS, this method simplifies the cooking and uses only one pot.

- 2 tablespoons butter
- 3 medium shallots, minced
- 2 pounds tender greens, such as spinach, beet greens or Swiss chard, cleaned and stemmed (water left clinging to leaves)
- ½ cup cream
- Salt
- Ground black pepper
- ¼ teaspoon ground nutmeg

Heat butter in a large sauté pan or Dutch oven. Add shallots and sauté over medium-high heat until softened, 2 to 3 minutes. Add wet greens, cover and cook, stirring occasionally, until completely wilted but still bright green, 3 to 5 minutes. Uncover and cook until most of liquid evaporates, about 2 minutes longer. Add cream and cook, uncovered, until thickened slightly, 2 to 3 minutes more. Stir in nutmeg, season to taste with salt and pepper and serve immediately.

Tender Greens with Indian Spices

SERVES 4

THESE HIGHLY SEASONED GREENS are the perfect accompaniment to simple sautéed chicken breasts or fish fillets. For extra flavor, sprinkle a little curry or cumin into the flour used for dredging the chicken or fish.

2 tablespoons vegetable oil
1 small onion, minced
2 medium garlic cloves, minced
1 teaspoon minced ginger
½ medium jalapeño pepper, minced
2 teaspoons curry powder
½ teaspoon ground cumin
2 pounds tender greens, such as spinach, beet greens or Swiss chard, cleaned and stemmed (water left clinging to leaves)
¼ cup cream
2 teaspoons light or dark brown sugar
Salt
Ground black pepper

1. Heat oil in a large sauté pan or Dutch oven. Add onion and cook over medium-high heat until partially softened, about 1 minute. Add garlic, ginger, jalapeño, curry powder and cumin and cook until onion softens and spices are fragrant, about 2 minutes more.

2. Add wet greens, cover and cook, stirring occasionally, until completely wilted but still bright green, 3 to 5 minutes. Uncover and cook until most of liquid evaporates, about 2 minutes longer. Add cream and brown sugar and cook, uncovered, until cream thickens, about 2 minutes more. Season with salt and pepper to taste and serve immediately.

Tender Greens with Tex-Mex Flavors

SERVES 4

SERVE WITH SAUTÉED chicken or fish, and season the flour used for dredging the chicken or fish with cumin to enhance and unify the flavors.

> 3 tablespoons vegetable oil
> 1 small onion, minced
> 2 medium garlic cloves, minced
> ½ jalapeño pepper, seeded and minced
> 1½ teaspoons ground cumin
> 2 large plum tomatoes, seeded and chopped
> 2 pounds tender greens, such as spinach, beet greens
>   or Swiss chard, cleaned and stemmed
>   (water left clinging to leaves)
> 2 tablespoons minced fresh cilantro leaves
>   Salt
>   Ground black pepper
>   Lime wedges (optional)

1. Heat oil in a large sauté pan or Dutch oven. Add onion and sauté over medium-high heat until partially softened, about 1 minute. Add garlic, jalapeño and cumin and cook until liquid evaporates, about 2 minutes more. Add tomatoes and cook until their juices release, about 1 minute.

2. Add wet greens, cover and cook, stirring occasionally, until completely wilted but still bright green, 3 to 5 minutes. Uncover and cook until most of liquid evaporates, about 2 minutes longer. Add cilantro and salt and pepper to taste. Serve immediately with lime wedges, if desired.

Tender Greens with Asian Flavors

SERVES 4

SERVE THESE GREENS with seared tuna, swordfish or pan-broiled steak.

2 teaspoons sesame seeds
2 teaspoons rice wine vinegar
2 teaspoons sugar
1½ tablespoons soy sauce
1 tablespoon sesame oil
2 medium garlic cloves, minced
½ teaspoon hot red pepper flakes
2 tablespoons vegetable oil
2 pounds tender greens, such as spinach,
    beet greens or Swiss chard, cleaned and
    stemmed (water left clinging to leaves)

1. In a small skillet over medium heat, toast sesame seeds until fragrant, 2 to 3 minutes; transfer to a small bowl and set aside.

2. Mix vinegar, sugar, soy sauce and sesame oil together in a small bowl; set aside.

3. Heat garlic and red pepper flakes with vegetable oil in a large sauté pan or Dutch oven over medium-high heat. When garlic sizzles and starts to turn golden, add wet greens, cover and cook, stirring occasionally, until completely wilted but still bright green, 3 to 5 minutes. Uncover and cook until most of liquid evaporates, about 2 minutes longer. When liquid has almost evaporated, add vinegar mixture and sauté until almost evaporated, about 1 minute more. Sprinkle sesame seeds over greens and serve immediately.

Tender Greens
with Raisins and Almonds

SERVES 4

THESE GREENS are the perfect partner with roast pork or pork chops.

3   tablespoons almonds
3   garlic cloves, minced
3   tablespoons olive oil
2   pounds tender greens, such as spinach, beet greens
    or Swiss chard, cleaned and stemmed
    (water left clinging to leaves)
⅓   cup golden raisins
½   teaspoon minced zest from 1 small lemon
    Salt
    Ground black pepper

1. In a small skillet over medium heat, toast almonds until fragrant, 3 to 4 minutes. Transfer to a small bowl; set aside.

2. Heat garlic with oil in a large sauté pan or Dutch oven over medium-high heat. When garlic sizzles and starts to turn golden, add wet greens and raisins, cover and cook, stirring occasionally, until greens are completely wilted but still bright green, about 5 minutes. Uncover and cook until most of liquid evaporates, about 2 minutes longer. Stir in zest, almonds and salt and pepper to taste and serve immediately.

Shallow-Blanched Greens

MAKES ABOUT 2 CUPS

YOU NEED ONLY ROUGH-CHOP the greens so that they fit into the pot more easily. Then chop them a second time after they have cooked.

1½ teaspoons salt
2 pounds assertive greens, such as kale, collards, mustard or turnip greens; stemmed, cleaned in 2-3 changes of clean water, and coarsely chopped

Bring 2 quarts water to a boil in a soup kettle or large, deep sauté pan. Add salt and greens; stir until wilted. Cover and cook until greens are just tender, about 7 minutes. Drain in a colander, rinse kettle with cold water to cool it down, then fill with cold water. Pour greens into cold water to stop cooking process. Gather a handful and squeeze water until only steady droplets fall from it. Repeat with remaining wet greens. Cut each handful of greens into medium dice. Proceed with one of the following recipes.

Quick-Cooked Greens with Garlic and Red Pepper Flakes

SERVES 4

CHICKEN BROTH, rather than traditional pork-flavored liquid, moistens and flavors the greens.

  2 large garlic cloves
¼ teaspoon hot red pepper flakes
  3 tablespoons olive oil
    Shallow-Blanched Greens
⅓-½ cup homemade chicken broth or low-sodium canned broth
    Salt
    Lemon wedges

In a large sauté pan, heat garlic and pepper flakes with oil over medium heat until garlic starts to sizzle. Add greens; sauté to coat with oil. Add ⅓ cup broth, cover and cook over medium-high heat, adding more broth during the cooking process if necessary, until greens are tender and juicy and most of broth is absorbed, about 5 minutes. Season with salt to taste. Serve with lemon wedges.

♦ Quick-Cooked Greens with Prosciutto

Follow recipe for Quick-Cooked Greens with Garlic and Red Pepper Flakes (page 235), adding 1 ounce thin-sliced prosciutto, cut crosswise into thin strips, after garlic sizzles. Continue as directed, stirring ¼ teaspoon lemon zest into greens right before serving.

♦ Quick-Cooked Greens with Black Olives and Lemon Zest

Follow recipe for Quick-Cooked Greens with Garlic and Red Pepper Flakes (page 235), adding ⅓ cup pitted coarsely chopped black olives (oil-cured or brine-soaked) after garlic sizzles. Continue as directed, stirring ¼ teaspoon lemon zest into greens right before serving.

♦ Quick-Cooked Greens with Red Bell Pepper

Follow recipe for Quick-Cooked Greens with Garlic and Red Pepper Flakes (page 235), sautéing ½ red bell pepper, cut into thin strips, in oil until softened, about 4 minutes, before cooking garlic. Continue as directed. Serve with lemon wedges.

♦ Quick-Cooked Greens with Bacon and Garlic

Follow recipe for Quick-Cooked Greens with Garlic and Red Pepper Flakes (page 235), frying 2 bacon slices, cut crosswise into thin strips, over medium-low heat until crisp, 4 to 5 minutes. Remove bacon bits with a slotted spoon and set aside. If necessary, add vegetable oil to drippings to equal 2 tablespoons, then cook garlic and continue as directed. Sprinkle greens with 2 teaspoons cider vinegar and bacon bits and serve.

Corn on the Cob: How to Buy It, Store It and Cook It

BECAUSE I DIDN'T grow up in corn country, I used to think people who wouldn't pick corn until the cooking water started to boil were a bit fanatical. And I couldn't imagine why farmstands practically gave away their day-old corn, while charging top dollar for fresh-picked. What I've since learned is that when you live in a place where good corn is available for only a month or two, you want to get it right.

My goal, then, was to test different methods for cooking corn on the cob—boiling, steaming, heating in the microwave and grilling—so that I got perfect results each time. I also wanted to see if one cooking method stood out as the best.

Just a Spoonful of Sugar

The most popular way of preparing corn, boiling, presented the most opportunities for testing. Should the corn be started in cold water or dropped into boiling water? Should the water be seasoned with sugar, salt or nothing at all? Should part of the water be replaced with milk?

James Beard's recipe for boiled corn instructs you to cover the ears with cold water and bring them to a boil. Once the water boils, you remove the pot from the heat and let the ears stand in the water for 5 minutes. For those who want to drop the corn into the pot and forget about it, this method produces fine results.

Although corn boiled in part milk and part water seems a bit more tender and tastes richer than corn boiled in plain water, the milk tends to mask the kernels' clear, sweet flavor. The big downside of boiling corn in milk, though, is the cleanup. After scrubbing the accidental milk overflow from the burner dish and scouring the pan's interior, I gave this method a thumbs-down. After all, one of the best parts of boiled corn is being able to hang up the pot as soon as you've drained it.

Corn kernels boiled in salted water are tougher than those boiled in unsalted water. When pressed, the kernels do not "give" as much as their more tender counterparts. According to Howard Hillman, the author of *Kitchen Science*

(Houghton Mifflin, 1989), trace amounts of calcium in salt toughen the kernel skin during cooking, just as a large quantity of salt prevents dried beans from softening as quickly.

Sugar-seasoned water brings out the natural sweetness of corn in the same way that salted water enhances the flavors of other vegetables. For most varieties of corn, boiling in lightly sweetened water works well. For some of the new sugar-enhanced varieties, however, extra sugar makes the corn too sweet.

Unlike corn cooked by other methods, boiled corn can be held in the cooking liquid for up to 10 minutes with very little flavor deterioration. (The same ear held at room temperature starts to wrinkle and dry out almost immediately.)

Corn steamed in a large pot or in a large soup kettle fitted with a collapsible steamer basket tastes every bit as good as the boiled. In addition, the mere inch of water comes to a simmer much faster than the gallon needed for boiling.

Boiling, however, works best if you are cooking for a crowd. When you steam more than eight ears at once, they cook unevenly, requiring some juggling. And you must serve steamed corn immediately or its kernels start to wrinkle and dry out.

For cooking fewer than six ears of corn, the microwave works best. Not only is this method fast, it's simple, too. Cover the ears of corn with plastic wrap, place them the microwave, set the timer and serve.

No other cooking method beats grilling when you want your corn to have an incomparably sweet, smoky flavor. You can grill corn three ways. If you prefer a muted smoky flavor, soak the unhusked ears in water while heating the grill. For a more pronounced taste, do not soak the corn—simply place the unhusked ears on the grill. For a more caramelized ear, husk the corn, brush with oil and grill until the kernels are spotty brown. Corn grills best on a medium-hot fire with an occasional turn.

In the Husk or Out?

Regardless of which cooking technique you use, corn that has not been shucked picks up some of the grassy flavor of the husk. The taste is pleasant, but it does compete with the pure sweetness of the kernels. Cooking corn in the husk has the advantage of simplicity, for you can serve it that way. Corn expert Betty Fussell is right: you don't need to remove the silk before cooking, for the silks and husks easily slip from the corn after it is done.

How to Identify Fresh, Ripe Corn

CORN-BUYING ETIQUETTE requires you to trust the farmer's expertise. It's not unusual to see signs asking customers not to pull down the husks before purchase. So what's a consumer to do? Organic farmer and food writer Cynthia Hizer says you can tell a great deal about an ear of corn without pulling down the husks. Feel the silk end of the ear. If plump and filled out, the corn should be ready. A hollow tip end is a good indication that the corn was picked too soon. Husk condition tells a lot too. According to Hizer, limp or dry husks usually mean dry kernels. Choose corn with fresh, perky husks.

Check the corn when you get home too. You can use the fingernail test to check ripeness the same way farmers spot-check corn in their fields. The kernel, when pricked with a fingernail, should be juicy but not milky; corn juice should explode from the pricked kernel. The kernels should be plump, with no space between the rows. Immature corn kernels are not filled out, and there are deep furrows between the rows. Kernels of overripe corn, on the other hand, will have started to dimple. When pricked with a fingernail, the covering of the kernel is tough and the kernel is dry and doughy, meaning that much of the sugar has already been converted to starch. If you're not happy with what you see, take the corn back and find a new source.

Ideally, corn should be eaten the same day it is picked. For those who need to refrigerate it for a few days, Dr. Charles McClurg, extension vegetable specialist at the University of Maryland, recommends doing so as soon as possible. Shuck it and silk it first because the husk can insulate the kernels and keep them too warm. "About the worst thing you could do," says McClurg, "is to buy corn at a farmer's market in the morning, toss the bag in the trunk and spend the next few hours shopping."

Boiled Corn on the Cob

SERVES 4

BOIL THE CORN in small batches. If you want to serve more than one ear per person, it's better to remove the cooked ears from the pot and cook the second batch while you eat the first. If the corn you are serving is one of the new supersweet varieties, you may want to omit the sugar from the water.

4 teaspoons sugar
4 ears corn, husked or not
Butter
Salt
Ground black pepper

Bring 1 gallon water to a boil with sugar in a large pot. Add corn, return to a boil and cook until corn is done, about 5 minutes. Drain and serve immediately with butter, salt and pepper to taste or with flavored butter (page 244).

Microwave Corn on the Cob

SERVES 4

WHEN COOKING SIX EARS or fewer, no method beats the microwave.

> 4 ears corn, husked or not
> Butter
> Salt
> Ground black pepper

Place corn on a large plate, cover tightly with plastic wrap and heat in a microwave on high power for 10 minutes. Leaving plate covered with plastic wrap, let corn stand 2 to 3 minutes more. Serve immediately with butter, salt and pepper or with flavored butter (page 244).

Steamed Corn on the Cob

SERVES 8

WHEN YOU DON'T FEEL LIKE heating up a big pot of water, steaming is the method of choice for six ears or more.

8 ears corn, husked or not
  Butter
  Salt
  Ground black pepper

Set a steamer basket into a large pot over about 1 inch of water. Bring to a boil; carefully place ears of corn on basket. Cover and steam over high heat until corn is tender, about 5 minutes. Remove from basket with tongs and serve immediately with butter, salt and pepper to taste or with flavored butter (page 244).

Grilled Corn on the Cob

SERVES 4

IF YOU WANT THE EARS OF CORN to steam over the grill, soak them in their husks in water for about 30 minutes before cooking. For an even smokier flavor, do not soak the corn. For a distinctly smoky, caramelized flavor, shuck the corn, brush it lightly with oil, then grill.

4 ears corn, husked or not, soaked or not
Butter
Salt
Ground black pepper

Build a medium-hot fire or preheat a grill to medium-high. Grill corn in husks, turning occasionally, for 12 to 15 minutes or shucked corn for 8 to 10 minutes, until kernels brown and caramelize. Serve immediately with butter, salt and pepper to taste or with flavored butter (page 244).

Salt and Pepper Butter

MAKES ABOUT ½ CUP

THIS SEASONED BUTTER saves diners from the three-step process of buttering, salting and peppering.

8 tablespoons (1 stick) unsalted butter,
softened but not melted
1 teaspoon salt
1 teaspoon ground black pepper

Mix butter, salt and pepper in a small bowl. Spread softened butter on hot corn.

Fresh Herb Butter

MAKES ½ CUP

THE FLAVORING HERBS in this butter represent just a few of the many possibilities. Try fresh dill, cilantro, tarragon or even thyme.

8 tablespoons (1 stick) butter, softened but not melted
1 teaspoon salt
½ teaspoon ground black pepper
2 teaspoons minced fresh parsley leaves
2 teaspoons minced fresh basil leaves
2 teaspoons minced fresh scallion greens or snipped chives

Mix butter, salt, pepper and herbs in a small bowl. Spread softened butter on hot corn.

Perfect Potato Salad

THERE ARE CERTAIN DISHES you grow up making, dishes that don't need measuring cups and spoons. Potato salad is one of those. Although I have probably never followed a recipe for potato salad in my life, when I did deviate from my rote formula, I learned that there's a good and a better way of making this seemingly straightforward favorite.

After analyzing well over a hundred recipes, I limited myself to French, German and American potato salads. Before compiling a shopping list for what still promised to be a massive project, I began to wonder what I had gotten myself into.

How many potato salad recipes would I have to test to determine the best way to make the dish? Was it possible to come up with a "best" salad in each category, or was this idea presumptuous, considering all the regional variations in the United States alone? As I put together the list, though, it wasn't nearly as long as I thought it would be. Though all the recipes seemed dramatically different, they all had four things in common: potatoes, of course; fat (whether bacon, olive oil or mayonnaise); flavorings to make the salad distinctive; and acid to perk up the dish.

So Many Questions, So Little Time

The issues boiled down to these:

What kind of potato is best for salad? Recipe writers seemed split down the middle between starchy and waxy potatoes—starchy potatoes were more absorbent, and waxy potatoes were sturdier.

How to cook that potato? I had always just boiled mine with the skins on, so I was surprised to find other cooks steaming, roasting, baking or using the microwave, leaving the skins on or with the potato peeled and cut up. One recipe suggested boiling the potatoes in chicken broth; another recommended milk. Would these liquids infuse and enrich the potato?

When to peel? On the assumption that hot potatoes are more absorbent, some writers thought it worth scorching fingertips to get the cooked potatoes peeled and cut immediately. Others were more casual: "peel when cool enough to handle." Still others instructed me to refrigerate the potatoes, then peel and cut them the next day. And of course, you might ask, "Is it really necessary to peel them at all?"

When to season? Do warm potatoes really absorb flavorings better? Is it worth the extra steps of seasoning the potatoes with vinegar and salt and pepper first? Or should you toss everything together at the same time?

High-Starch Spud: A Dud

After boiling, steaming, baking and microwaving four different varieties of potatoes—Red Bliss, russets, all-purpose and Yukon Golds—I chose boiling as the method of choice. The low-starch boiling potato—Red Bliss and new potatoes are in this category—was the preferred variety. Higher-starch potatoes—russets, all-purpose and Yukon Golds—are not sturdy enough for salad making. They fell apart when cut and looked sloppy in salad form.

But before giving up completely on high-starch potatoes for salad making, I wanted to test their absorption qualities, a selling point to many cooks. A number of French, German and American potato salad recipes suggested drizzling either vinegar or vinaigrette over the warm or hot potatoes so that they would taste thoroughly seasoned. I found that high-starch potatoes do indeed absorb better than the lower-starch varieties—

but to a fault. When tossed with the same amount of dressing, the high-starch potato salads tasted dry, sucking up all the dressing and asking for more. These potatoes are great for mashing or baking, but not for salad. In contrast, the low-starch boiling potatoes successfully absorb the vinegar and most of the oil and have a firm yet creamy texture.

Experiments on the Boil

To see if I could boost flavor at the cooking stage, I compared potatoes boiled in chicken broth to those boiled in water heavily seasoned with bay leaves and garlic cloves. (I ruled out simmering in milk—the idea of drizzling vinegar over milk-coated potatoes was unappetizing.) The chicken broth may as well have been water—there wasn't even a scent of evidence that the potatoes had been cooked in broth. The bay leaves and garlic smelled wonderful as the potatoes cooked, but although the potato skin smelled faintly of garlic, the potato itself was still bland.

I performed yet another experiment cooking two batches of potatoes—one in heavily salted water, the other in just plain water. I rinsed them quickly under cold running water and tasted. Sure enough, the potatoes cooked in heavily salted water tasted exactly like the potatoes cooked in the unsalted water. When cooking potatoes in their jackets, plain water is the sensible choice, because seasonings can't penetrate the skins.

Because potatoes that float close to the water's surface cook more slowly than potatoes at the bottom of the pan, covering the pot, as well as giving the potatoes a gentle stir once or twice during cooking, helps them to cook more evenly. Choose potatoes fairly equal in size so that they are fully cooked at about the same time.

To test for doneness, the thinner the utensil the better. A fork, frequently the quickest and simplest thing to grab, is actually the worst testing tool, for it visibly damages the potato and sometimes causes it to split. A thin-bladed knife or a metal cake tester works best.

Cool Them Down

Peeling boiled red potatoes is not necessary, for the peel isn't distracting and is pleasant to look at in what is often a monochromatic dish. To prevent the skin from tearing and separating, let the potatoes cool a bit before cutting them with a serrated knife—warm potatoes are just as absorbent as hot ones and hold together much better. If you need to cool the potatoes quickly, drain them and rinse them under cool running water for a bit.

Vinegar: In Moderation

Although I knew that warm potatoes absorbed vinegar, I wasn't necessarily sure where the acidity should be: in the potato, in the dressing or in both? I made three mayonnaise-based salads— one with all the vinegar drizzled on the potato; one with half the vinegar on the potato and the other half mixed with the mayonnaise; and a third version with all the vinegar mixed with mayonnaise. The results were clear. Sprinkling all the vinegar on the potatoes made them taste pickled. Putting it all in the mayonnaise produced a zesty salad dressing, but bland potatoes. Using vinegar in moderation on the potatoes and in the dressing provided the right balance.

Use low-starch potatoes, boil them in their skins, don't salt the water, don't peel the potatoes unless you really want to and use a serrated knife to cut them. While the potatoes are still warm, drizzle them with a splash of vinegar. Then proceed with the recipe. If you think I've left out the green pepper, Tabasco or white wine, you're right. That's where you take over.

Boiled Potatoes

YIELDS 2 POUNDS

To REMOVE SPECKS OF DIRT easily from any potato, scrub them with a clean soft-scrub kitchen sponge or vegetable brush.

2 pounds Red Bliss or new potatoes (about 6 medium
or 18 new), rinsed, scrubbed if not peeled

1. Place potatoes in a 4-to-6-quart pot; cover with water. Bring to a boil, cover, and simmer, stirring once or twice to ensure even cooking, until a thin-bladed paring knife or a metal cake tester inserted into potato can be removed with no resistance, 25 to 30 minutes for medium potatoes and 15 to 20 minutes for new potatoes.

2. Drain, rinse under cold water, and drain again. Cool potatoes slightly and peel, if you like. Cut potatoes (with a serrated knife if they have skins) while still warm. Proceed as directed with one of the following recipes.

French-Style Potato Salad with Tarragon Vinaigrette

SERVES 6

IF FRESH TARRAGON is not available, increase the parsley to 3 tablespoons and use tarragon vinegar.

Boiled Potatoes, peeled if desired,
and cut into ¼-inch-thick slices

¼ cup white wine vinegar

1 teaspoon kosher salt or ½ teaspoon table salt

½ teaspoon ground black pepper

1 tablespoon Dijon-style mustard

1 medium shallot, minced

6 tablespoons olive oil

2 tablespoons minced fresh parsley

1 tablespoon minced fresh tarragon

1. Layer warm potato slices in a medium bowl. Sprinkle with 2 tablespoons vinegar, seasoning with salt and pepper as you go. Let stand at room temperature while you prepare dressing.

2. Mix remaining 2 tablespoons vinegar, mustard and shallot in a small mixing bowl. Gradually whisk in oil so that mixture is somewhat emulsified. Pour over potatoes; toss lightly to coat. Refrigerate until ready to serve. Bring to room temperature; toss in parsley and tarragon, adjust seasonings and serve.

German-Style Potato Salad with Bacon and Balsamic Vinegar

SERVES 6

FOR GERMAN-STYLE SALADS, the smaller new potatoes are more attractive because the slices tend not to break up as they do with bigger potatoes. Balsamic vinegar gives this salad an appealing sweet-sour flavor.

> Boiled Potatoes (page 248), peeled if desired, and cut into ¼-inch-thick slices
> ¼ cup balsamic or cider vinegar
> 1 teaspoon kosher salt or ½ teaspoon table salt
> ½ teaspoon ground black pepper
> 4-5 thick slices (about 4 ounces) slab bacon, cut crosswise into ¼-inch strips
> 1 medium onion, cut into medium dice
> 2 tablespoons vegetable oil
> ½ cup beef broth
> ¼ cup minced fresh parsley

1. Layer warm potato slices in a medium bowl. Sprinkle with 2 tablespoons vinegar, seasoning with salt and pepper as you go. Let stand at room temperature while you prepare dressing.

2. Fry bacon in a medium skillet over medium heat until bacon is brown and crisp and fat is rendered, 7 to 10 minutes. Transfer with a slotted spoon to potatoes. Add onion to bacon drippings. Sauté until softened, 4 to 5 minutes. Add up to 2 tablespoons vegetable oil to yield 2 tablespoons unabsorbed fat. (If bacon is fairly lean, onion will absorb most of the drippings.)

3. Add beef broth and bring to a boil; add remaining 2 tablespoons vinegar. Pour broth-onion mixture over potatoes. Add parsley; toss gently to coat. Adjust seasonings; serve warm or at room temperature.

American-Style Potato Salad with Eggs and Sweet Pickles

SERVES 6 TO 8

IN A BLIND TASTING of seven different mayonnaises—Hellmann's, Hellmann's Light, Hellmann's Reduced Fat, Kraft, Kraft Light, Kraft Free and homemade— the potato salad dressed with Hellmann's Real Mayonnaise was the unanimous number one choice.

2 pounds Red Bliss or new potatoes, boiled, peeled if desired, and cut into ¾-inch cubes

2 tablespoons red wine vinegar

1 teaspoon kosher salt or ½ teaspoon table salt

½ teaspoon ground black pepper

3 boiled eggs, cut into small dice

2-3 scallions, sliced thin (about ½ cup)

1 small celery stalk, cut into small dice (about ½ cup)

¼ cup sweet pickle (not relish), cut into small dice

½ cup mayonnaise

2 tablespoons Dijon-style mustard

¼ cup minced fresh parsley

1. Layer warm potato cubes in a medium bowl. Sprinkle with vinegar, seasoning with salt and pepper as you go.

2. Mix in remaining ingredients. Refrigerate until ready to serve. Adjust seasonings and serve chilled.

Mashed Potatoes: The Best They Can Be

W E MAY EAT mashed potatoes less often than we did 30 years ago, but we seem to long for them more. Such special foods ought to be prepared with particular care.

What do great mashed potatoes taste and feel like? For me, they need to be rich, with the definite flavor of potato, light but substantial. I prefer silky smooth over chunky. Although I wasn't sure exactly what kind of potato and which cooking and mashing method would deliver my ideal, some of my preconceived ideas about making this dish were confirmed during testing. And, as always, I learned something new.

Baking Potatoes Boil Best

In order to determine which variety of potato and what cooking method delivered the best mashed potato, I prepared four types—russets, also called baking or Idaho potatoes; reds, known as boiling potatoes; all-purpose, or chef's, potatoes; and Yukon Golds—by boiling, steaming and baking. The russet potato mashed up best. Its dry, mealy texture,

while not ideal for salads and home fries, is perfect for absorbing liquid and swelling into light, fluffy mashed potatoes. Not surprisingly, most of the varieties responded best to boiling.

The real discovery for me was that baking potatoes were best boiled *skin on*, then peeled before mashing. After tasting mashed potatoes made from potatoes peeled before and after cooking, I was struck by the flavor and textural differences. Those made from potatoes peeled before boiling were more watery and grainy and had less potato flavor than those peeled after boiling. Nor is peeling potatoes after cooking more difficult than peeling them before. On the contrary, if grasped with a pot holder, a cooked potato is actually easier to peel than a raw one. While the raw skin must be scraped off with a vegetable peeler or paring knife, the cooked skin slips right off.

Because I knew that potatoes cooked with their skins on do not absorb salt from the cooking water, I worried that salting them after mashing might not be enough. My concerns were unfounded.

Boiled russets, skin on, made the best mashed potatoes, but other potatoes and cooking methods also worked well. The boiled red potatoes were pleasant, mashing up a little heavier, but very creamy and smooth. Unlike the russets, however, boiling potatoes were better peeled before cooking because, given their greater density, they did not seem to absorb their cooking liquid, and the boiled skins gave the mashed potatoes a subtle but detectable unripe, bitter taste.

Also a little more densely textured than Idahos, the Yukon Gold potatoes mashed up quite respectably. Mashed potatoes made from boiled all-purpose potatoes, however, were gummy and wet.

As for the other cooking methods, steaming produced inferior mashed potatoes. Baking did not help the potatoes, either. It consistently took longer than steaming or boiling, and much of the potato flesh is lost when stripping off the baked-on skin. Oddly, too much moisture evaporated from the russet potato during baking and the resulting mashed potatoes tasted more like twice-baked.

A Food Mill Mashes Best

I grew up on electric-mixer mashed potatoes but later switched to a ricer, while fellow cooks swore by a potato masher. None of these methods, however, is as simple or delivers as smooth a result as the food mill. In fact, if I were to make a list of 10 of the most worth-while kitchen gadgets, the food mill, which retails for about $20, would be near the top. It makes fast work of sifting whole potatoes into a light, snowy pile. Even better, you don't have to peel the potatoes before mashing because the food mill holds back the skin while pushing the flesh through.

Although potatoes from a ricer are as smooth as those from the food mill, it is an awkward little device. Because its bowl is so small, only one potato can be processed at a time. Depending on design, the ricer may leave up to a half a potato in its bowl, forcing you to lose it or push it through manually with a spoon or spatula.

Without a doubt, a potato masher is the simplest gadget for this task, but it does not deliver lumpless potatoes. The whisk attachment of the mixer turns the potatoes to wallpaper paste (as does a food processor fitted with the steel blade), while the paddle attachment leaves lumps. If faced with making mashed potatoes for more than 20 people, however, the paddle-fitted mixer is not a bad choice.

Once the potato is mashed, I prefer to incorporate the milk and butter with a rubber spatula, which mixes the ingredients well and easily scrapes the bowl's bottom and sides. Potatoes mixed with a whisk were lighter and fluffier, more like the potato purees frequently served in French restaurants.

Milk Before Butter

Prior to these tests, I had made my mashed potatoes by enriching them first with butter, then thinning with hot milk. Many recipes follow this pattern, reasoning that it's better to add butter to really hot potatoes. I found, however, that mashed potatoes in which milk had been added first were smoother and lighter than those in which butter had been added first. The butter-first potatoes were grainy and heavy by comparison; the butter seemed to have coated the potato starch and prevented it from absorbing the milk. It's also easier to incorporate butter into milk-thinned potatoes than just-mashed ones.

Although I tried a variety of liquids and enrichers to enhance my mashed potatoes, nothing worked as well as a combination of half-and-half or whole milk and butter. Cream made the potatoes too heavy, thick and rich, while sour cream made them taste like baked potato. Cream cheese, called for in a number of recipes, made the potatoes leaden and taste slightly off.

I also tried a number of fat-reducing ingredients—buttermilk, yogurt, skim milk, as well as reduced amounts of butter. Just as overly rich potatoes were heavy and filling, reduced-fat ones were lean and unsatisfying.

Simple Mashed Potatoes

SERVES 6

IF YOU DON'T HAVE A FOOD MILL, you can press the potatoes through a large single-mesh strainer with a rubber spatula, but it's messier and requires more muscle. If you prefer lumpy potatoes, use a potato masher. Though not quite as light as russets, Yukon Golds make good mashed potatoes. If you find yourself with only red boiling potatoes on hand, peel them, then boil. Your mashed potatoes will be heavier but very smooth and creamy.

2 pounds (6-7 medium) russet (Idaho) potatoes, scrubbed
   Salt
1 cup hot half-and-half or whole milk
4 tablespoons (½ stick) butter, softened
   Ground black pepper

1. Place potatoes in a large saucepan with cold water to cover. Bring to a boil over high heat, then simmer, covered, until potatoes are just tender when pricked with a thin-bladed knife, about 20 minutes. Drain.

2. For perfectly white mashed potatoes, peel them. Drop them, 1 or 2 at a time, into a food mill and process them back into warm, dry saucepan. Add salt to taste and half-and-half or milk. With a rubber spatula, beat potatoes until fluffy. (For a lighter, pureed texture, beat potatoes with a wire whisk.) Add butter; continue to beat until melted. Generously season with lots of pepper and serve. (Potatoes can be transferred to a heatproof bowl, loosely covered with plastic wrap, and set over a pan of simmering water for up to 30 minutes.)

Simple Mashed Potatoes
with Roasted Garlic

SERVES 6

T HIS RECIPE CALLS FOR one head of roasted garlic. While you're at it, though, you should certainly roast more than one and use them to flavor vinaigrettes, spreads, oils, dips or in any recipe where the flavor of raw garlic is too pronounced. Or spread them on toast rounds and serve as an appetizer topped with thin-sliced rare roast beef. Cook up to four heads in the milk quantity listed below.

1   head garlic, left whole
1   cup whole milk or half-and-half
2   pounds russet (Idaho) potatoes (6-7 medium), scrubbed
     Salt
4   tablespoons (½ stick) butter, softened
     Ground black pepper

1. Preheat oven to 350°F. Remove outer papery skin from garlic. Cut off about ½ inch from tip end of head, so that most clove interiors are exposed. Place garlic head in a small saucepan, cut side down, add milk or half-and-half and bring to a simmer. Cover and simmer until garlic softens slightly, about 10 minutes. Drain garlic, reserving milk and bringing amount back up to a full 1 cup. Wrap garlic in foil and bake until very soft, about 1 hour. Squeeze garlic puree from head; set aside.

2. Follow recipe for Simple Mashed Potatoes (page 255), using hot garlic-poaching milk in place of milk or half-and-half. Add garlic puree to potatoes and stir before adding hot milk.

◆ Mashed Potatoes with Horseradish

These potatoes are a natural with a nice juicy steak.

Follow recipe for Simple Mashed Potatoes (page 255), stirring 1 tablespoon prepared horseradish into finished potatoes just before adding pepper.

◆ Mashed Potatoes with Cheddar Cheese and Bacon

A pan-broiled hamburger—without the bun—is the perfect no-nonsense partner for these very straightforward mashed potatoes.

Follow recipe for Simple Mashed Potatoes (page 255), stirring ½ cup grated cheddar cheese and 4 slices bacon, fried and crumbled, into finished potatoes just before adding pepper.

◆ Mashed Potatoes with Porcini Mushrooms

Follow step 1 of recipe for Simple Mashed Potatoes (page 255). While potatoes cook, soak 1 ounce dried porcini mushrooms in 1 cup hot water for about 20 minutes, or until softened. Drain, reserving soaking liquid; finely chop mushrooms. Continue as directed, stirring 2 tablespoons mushroom liquid and chopped mushrooms into finished potatoes just before adding pepper.

Mashed Potatoes with Fresh Herbs

SERVES 6

ERBED MASHED POTATOES team up well with fish, such as seared salmon or swordfish or sautéed snapper or sole.

2 pounds (6-7 medium) russet (Idaho) potatoes, scrubbed
Salt
1 cup hot half-and-half or whole milk
4 tablespoons (½ stick) butter, softened
2 tablespoons minced fresh basil leaves
1 tablespoon minced fresh chives or scallion greens
1 tablespoon minced fresh parsley leaves
Ground black pepper

Follow recipe for Simple Mashed Potatoes (page 255), stirring basil, chives or scallion greens and parsley into finished potatoes just before adding pepper.

V

Bread Winners

Daily Bread

THOUGH MOST BAKERS say it can be a simple process, making bread is still like many of life's little disciplines, from exercising to reading the daily newspaper. Either it's important—you make time for it and perform the task faithfully—or it's not. Most committed bakers make bread at least once or twice a week. They have a recipe and a technique they've memorized, and they rarely deviate from it. The same is true of bread-machine owners: either the machine is still in the box, or the owner makes bread practically every day. With all of today's kitchen aids—food processors, microwaves and the dump-in-the-ingredients-and-start-it-up bread machine—the question is really not "Do I have the time?" but rather "Do I want to?"

My answer was yes: I wanted to develop a recipe for a French-style loaf that was so simple I could make it every day. That criterion ruled out any recipes that required starters or sponges. What I needed was a dough I could make without thinking, slash and form into myriad shapes and add different flours without having to chase down a whole new recipe. For a good sourdough loaf, I'd visit my local baker.

I also wanted this recipe to be bread-machine simple in the time and effort expended. So why not buy a bread machine? I knew bread-machine bread, and I didn't like its shape or the texture of its leathery crust. Given those drawbacks, I didn't think the machine was worth the precious counter space.

Which flour, yeast and kneading method would turn out a prizewinning loaf? Are pizza stones or quarry tiles necessary for a crisp bottom crust? Is a blast of moisture at the start essential to the rest of the loaf's thick, crisp crust? If so, what is the best and safest way to produce one? Some people daintily mist shaped loaves before popping them in the oven. (I had tried this trick and never found it very effective.) Others live more dangerously, plunging a heated brick into a pan of boiling water set in the oven. There had to be a safe method somewhere between the two extremes. And did I actually need to perform all those fancy stretches, tucks and folds to get a decent daily French loaf? Or was there a simpler way?

The Proof's in the Yeast

Yeast, the mysterious spores that give life to bread, seemed like a good place to start my quest. I made three loaves—one with cake yeast, one with active dry yeast and another with 50-percent-faster active dry yeast. The ripe, earthy smell gave the cake variety a slight edge in my mind, but speed of preparation was critical, so I was also rooting for the quick-rising yeast. And compared to the longer shelf life and convenience of the snip-and-pour packets of the active dry yeasts, cake yeast also required refrigeration and special handling.

Naturally, quick-rising yeast won the time race, delivering a swollen loaf ready for shaping in about an hour and forty-five minutes. The other two yeasts tied for second, both clocking in at about two hours and forty-five minutes. (I performed these tests during the winter in a kitchen that fluctuated between 68 and 70 degrees.)

All three loaves displayed good body, great texture and full flavor, regardless of yeast type. Although I knew that sponge-risen breads and those made with smaller amounts of yeast (and therefore much longer rising times) have a chance to develop more flavor, I opted for a bread with a shorter rising time.

Depending on its protein content, wheat flour can be hard (as in high-protein or bread flour) or soft (as in low-protein or cake flour) or a mix of the two (as in all-purpose). Many bread books suggested that the harder the wheat, the higher its gluten content, the stronger the dough's structure and the better the bread's body. To see if flour made all that much difference in my everyday loaf, I made three simple loaves of bread—one with bread flour, one with all-purpose bleached and one with all-purpose unbleached.

Bread Flour Power

Bread flour nosed by as the winner in both dough and bread form. It kneaded into a firm, elastic ball, rose into a perky, taut dough round and baked into a firm, shapely loaf. Compared to the other loaves, the bread-flour bread displayed better body. Although the bleached-flour loaf was lighter in color, a little flabby and a tad gummy, the loaf made with unbleached flour certainly rivaled the one made with bread flour. Most major flour companies these days make 5-pound bags of bread flour, but if you have trouble locating it or happen to be out, unbleached all-purpose flour, which traditionally has a higher percentage of hard wheat flour than does bleached flour, is a good second choice.

The biggest surprise for me was that machine-kneaded dough—which I tried in both a food processor and a standing mixer—was not inferior to hand-kneaded dough. The choice is personal. I opted for the food processor because it is the fastest method, and I found I could get my kneading fix satisfied by playing with the dough for a few minutes after it came out of the machine.

Many who favor the food processor method promote the plastic rather than the steel blade, cautioning that the steel blade can overheat the dough. Obediently I started with the plastic blade, but I quickly discovered that the machine struggled. I switched to the steel blade and tried Julia Child's technique of dissolving the yeast in a bit of warm water, then adding cold water to the bowl to compensate for the heat of the blade. With only 35 seconds of steel-blade kneading, I turned out a batch of dough that was as warm and smooth as a baby's bottom.

Oil the Bowl Sparingly

I hoped that greasing the rising bowls was unnecessary (I'm not fond of oily dough), but dough risen in an ungreased bowl does stick slightly. Fortunately, only a touch of oil is needed to coat the bowl and dough top. For this reason, I've come to like vegetable cooking spray.

While a damp towel absorbs accumulated moisture from the rising bread, plastic wrap traps it, leaving beads of water hanging on the plastic covering. Also, if the rising bowl is too small, the dough can stick to the plastic. If you use a plastic wrap covering, make sure the bowl is at least four times the size of the unrisen ball of dough. Plastic wrap has its advantages. Sealing the bowl holds in warmth, creating a moist, greenhouse environment. The extra heat causes the dough to rise slightly faster than dough risen in a bowl covered with a damp towel.

Shapely Loaves

The classic shaping technique for French bread ensures that the bread will not rise and bake fat and flat. While I didn't like the idea of severely oblate French bread, I wondered if it was worth the lengthy series of stretches, pulls, pinches, troughs and tucks, just for one supremely cylindrical loaf. After a number of tests, I developed a short-cut technique (see figures 1-3, page 266).

The way the dough is risen for the final time also contributes to the French loaf's shape. The most uniformly shaped loaves were those risen in French bread pans or in floured kitchen towels that had been shaped into a trough. (But French bread pans caused problems with the crust. Read on.) The kitchen-towel technique requires that after rising, the bread be rolled over onto a cornmeal-coated pizza peel or cookie sheet. Like the detailed shaping process, this method added extra time and steps I didn't want to deal with in my daily bread routine. By letting the dough rise right on the peel, I got a respectable-looking loaf, and I was virtually done with the process once the loaves were shaped.

Slashing the dough provides a way out for the trapped gases as the loaves rise. Some bakers advocate slashing before rising, others perform the task right before baking. If you slash before rising, the slash marks rise flush with the rest of the dough, and in many cases, the slash work becomes almost invisible. And slashing takes practice. Successful slashing begins with a razor-sharp blade used with courage. If you hesitate, the dough will stick to your blade like bubble gum to an innocent shoe. Call on your killer instincts—jab, slash, jab, slash. Quickly. Effortlessly. For those who have trouble, I've also found scissors to be successful slashers.

Cracker-Crisp Crust

The key to a crusty bottom is baking the bread on a hot surface. Lining the oven rack with quarry tiles is the best solution. Not only are these tiles great for bread, but they are perfect for pizza as well. I have since found that oven tiles not only crisp bread and pizza bottoms, they also temper the oven heat. Cakes and muffin bottoms that normally burn on the bottom rack bake to an even golden brown on a tile-lined rack.

Don't bother with a pizza stone. Even a large one won't hold more than one large country loaf, and often the tips of French baguettes stray over the edges. Line the whole oven rack and, depending on your oven size, you can bake four to six loaves at a time or two small to medium pizzas.

If you don't want to bother with the tiles, *heavy-duty* lipless cookie sheets, heated in the preheating oven, work quite well. Breads baked on hot heavy-duty cookie sheets and the quarry tiles produce cornmeal-coated bottoms worthy of display in a great bakery. The big disappointment came with the French-bread form, a pan designed especially for baking this bread. Although their top crusts gleamed, breads baked in these forms offered the least impressive bottom crusts—barely brown, hardly crisp. Perhaps the curved shape of the pans traps moisture, retarding the browning process.

Like a seasoned farmer identifying a juicy, ripe watermelon with a mere thump, some can judge a bread's doneness by tapping on the bottom crust. For those who have trouble hearing when bread is done, check it by inserting a meat thermometer in the bottom of the loaf. Bread is ready for the cooling rack when a meat thermometer plunged into the center of the loaf registers between 190 and 200 degrees.

Where There's Steam, There's Crust

Just as the human body benefits from the complementary effects of the steam room and sauna, so good bread demands both the moist and dry heat of the oven. Steam tames the scorching oven heat, allowing the dough to swell a bit longer before its yeast is killed. Moist heat also sets the starch on the dough's surface, giving it a satiny sheen, which is later transformed into a glazy crisp crust. Dry heat comes naturally in the oven; it's moist heat that you have to create. I placed a pan of water in a preheating oven; I threw handfuls of ice into the hot oven; I tossed cupfuls of water onto the hot oven floor. Many of these techniques worked fine. But again the criterion was "What's easiest?" Tossing water in worked well for me (I've been tossing cupfuls of water into my electric oven for four years now without a single call to the repairman). But because water thrown directly into gas units can extinguish the pilot light, an alternative for gas-stove owners—or anyone worried about oven damage—is to set an empty baking pan on the bottom rack of the preheating oven. As you put the bread on the rack directly above it, pour hot water into the heated pan.

As a result of my successful experiments, I now eat homemade bread at least two meals a day and freeze what my family can't eat. A freshly baked loaf is one of life's basic pleasures: when it's good it's great, and it's always more satisfying than store-bought.

Basic French Bread

MAKES TWO 14-OUNCE LOAVES

BREAD RECIPES don't get more basic than this one. This 4-cup flour recipe makes a dough that you can easily knead in a food processor with a 2-quart capacity. If you have a smaller work bowl, halve the dough recipe or make it in a standing mixer with a dough hook attachment. If you don't have a food processor or a standing mixer, you can knead the dough by hand until it's smooth and satiny, 8 to 10 minutes. If you are using quick-rising yeast, simply mix it into the flour mixture, add 1½ cups tepid water and process in the food processor.

> 1 envelope active dry yeast, regular or quick-rising
> 4 cups bread flour or all-purpose unbleached flour
> 2 teaspoons salt
>   Cornmeal or semolina for dusting peel

1. Sprinkle yeast over ½ cup warm water. (If using quick-rising yeast, see note above.) Let stand until yeast dissolves and starts to swell, about 5 minutes. Meanwhile, mix flour and salt in a food processor fitted with a steel blade. Add 1 cup cold water to yeast mixture, then add yeast mixture to dry ingredients. Process until mixture forms a rough ball. (If mixture is wet and sticky, add about 1 tablespoon flour to mixture; add about 1 tablespoon water if dough feels stiff and tight.) Then continue to process until dough is smooth and elastic, about 30 seconds more.

2. Turn dough onto a lightly floured work surface and knead by hand for a few seconds until dough is satiny and smooth. Form dough into a round and place in a large bowl coated with vegetable oil spray or a very light film of oil. Turn top of dough in bowl to barely coat with oil. Turn dough right side up, then cover with plastic wrap. Set in a warm place until dough doubles, 1½ to 3 hours, depending on room temperature and type of yeast.

3. Punch dough down and turn out onto a work surface. Halve dough; set 1 piece aside and cover to keep it from drying out and developing a "skin." Press and stretch remaining piece of dough into a 16-by-6-inch rectangle. With long edge facing you, fold dough into thirds lengthwise; pinch to seal (see illustrations, page 266). With side of hand, punch a trough lengthwise down center of dough. Pinch

SHAPING FRENCH BREAD

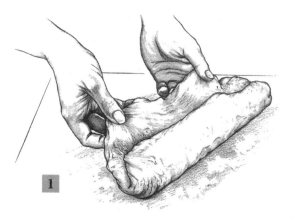

1. With the long edge of the dough facing you, fold the dough into thirds lengthwise; pinch to seal.

2. With the side of your hand, punch a trough lengthwise down the center of the dough.

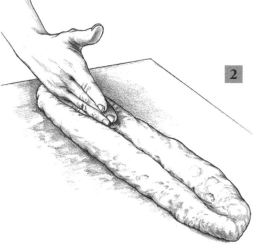

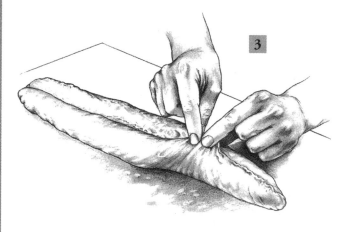

3. Pinch the dough on both sides of the trough together to form a tight cylinder.

dough together on both sides of trough to form a tight cylinder. Repeat with remaining piece of dough.

4. Transfer shaped dough, seam side down, to a cornmeal-coated pizza peel. Cover shapes with a barely damp, lightweight kitchen towel. Set pizza peel in a warm place; let dough shapes rise until *almost* doubled in size, 45 minutes to 1½ hours, depending on room temperature and type of yeast. (The initial burst of oven heat will help dough finish its rise.)

5. About 45 minutes before baking, line bottom rack of oven with quarry tiles and preheat oven to 450°F. (Tiles should be hot when you add loaves.) If oven is gas or you prefer not to throw water directly onto your oven floor, set a small baking pan on tiles or on oven floor.

6. Make 3 or 4 long, diagonal slashes about ½ inch deep across top of each risen loaf.

7. Slide loaves from peel onto tile-lined rack. Carefully toss ¾ cup water onto oven floor or into pan and close oven door. Bake until crust is brown and meat thermometer inserted into bread registers 190 to 200°F, about 30 minutes. Cool bread on a wire rack. (Bread can be wrapped in plastic wrap and stored at room temperature for a day or two or wrapped and placed in a zipper-lock plastic bag and frozen for up to 1 month. Reheat room-temperature bread in a 300°F oven for 5 to 10 minutes and frozen bread for 10 to 15 minutes.)

♦ French Rolls

MAKES 1 DOZEN

1. Follow steps 1 and 2 in recipe for Basic French Bread (page 265). After dough has doubled, punch it down and turn onto a lightly floured work surface.

2. For round rolls: Divide dough into 12 equal pieces. Keeping remaining dough rounds covered, form 1 piece of dough into a rough round. With cupped palm, roll dough until it is smooth and perfectly round. Place on cornmeal-coated pizza peel. Repeat with remaining balls of dough. With scissors or a sharp blade, slash a cross on each risen dough round.

For oval rolls: Using fingertips, roll dough rounds back and forth to form oval shapes and slash with scissors or a sharp blade.

3. Continue with step 4, rising rolls and baking as directed in step 7, reducing baking time to about 20 minutes.

♦ Whole Wheat Bread

MAKES TWO 14-OUNCE LOAVES

1   envelope active dry yeast, regular or quick-rising
2   cups bread flour or all-purpose unbleached flour
2   cups whole wheat flour
2   teaspoons salt
    Cornmeal or semolina for dusting peel

Follow recipe for Basic French Bread (page 265), adding whole wheat flour to bread flour or all-purpose flour in step 1.

Large Round Loaves

MAKES TWO 14-OUNCE LOAVES

1. Follow steps 1 and 2 in recipe for Basic French Bread (page 265). After dough has doubled, punch it down and turn onto a lightly floured work surface.

2. Divide dough into 2 equal pieces. Work with 1 piece of dough at a time (keep second piece of dough covered with a damp cloth while you work with first). With fingers positioned underneath piece of dough and thumbs on either side of it, turn dough clockwise, tucking excess dough underneath (see figure 1). Then with one hand, turn dough bottom side up and with other hand pinch excess dough to form a ball (figure 2). Place dough on work surface, rough side down. With palms of hands on either side, pat and rotate ball clockwise until it is smooth and round (figure 3).

3. Continue with step 4, rising and baking loaves as directed.

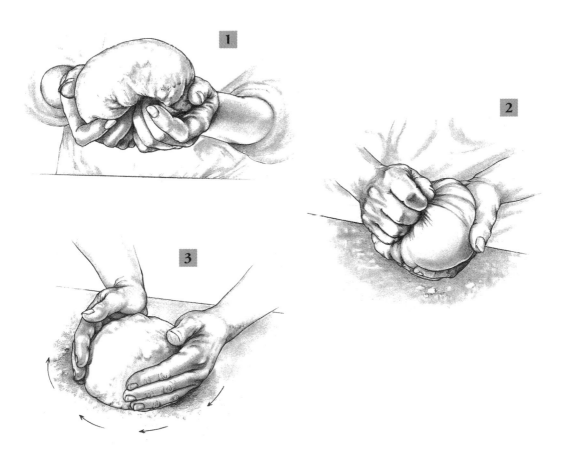

♦ Soy, Millet, Corn, Rice, Buckwheat or Barley Bread

MAKES TWO 14-OUNCE LOAVES

1   envelope active dry yeast, regular or quick-rising
3¼ cups bread flour or all-purpose unbleached flour
¾   cup soy flour, millet flour, corn flour, rice flour,
      buckwheat flour or barley flour
2   teaspoons salt
      Cornmeal or semolina for dusting peel

Follow recipe for Basic French Bread (page 265), adding any specialty flour listed above to bread flour or all-purpose flour in step 1.

Breadsticks

MAKES 12 DOZEN

IF YOU'RE TIRED of paying $5 for a little box of imported breadsticks, make your own with a manual pasta machine fitted with the fettuccine attachment.

This technique was developed by my friend and colleague Michele Scicolone in *The Antipasto Table* (William Morrow, 1991).

1. Follow recipe for Basic French Bread (page 265), adding ½ cup grated Parmesan to flour-salt mixture in step 1, and adding 2 to 3 tablespoons olive oil, if desired, when you add water-yeast mixture to food processor. Divide dough into 6 equal pieces. Preheat oven to 350°F.

2. Working with 1 piece of dough at a time and keeping remaining pieces of dough covered with a damp cloth, press dough into a 6-by-4-inch rectangle on a well-floured work surface. (Make sure dough is well coated with flour or dough strips will stick together as they come out of machine.) Run dough through a manual pasta machine fitted with fettuccine attachment.

3. Separate dough into strips and place them ½ inch apart on a cornmeal-coated heavy-duty cookie sheet. Bake in batches until crisp and golden brown. (Breadsticks can be stored in an airtight container for up to 1 month.)

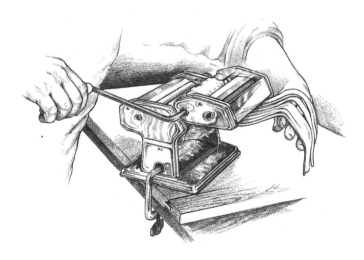

New-Style Southern Corn Bread

ALTHOUGH I'VE LIVED most of my adult life in the Midwest and the Northeast, I grew up in a small town on the Florida Panhandle, a short 60 miles from the Alabama border and not much farther from the Georgia line. Usually we ate southern-style, which meant there was hardly a noon or evening meal without a couple of long-simmered vegetables, which we ate with fork in the right hand, corn bread in the left. These, then, are my credentials. I know Southern corn bread. I've eaten the full range of it—a hunk so dry only a good pot likker could save it; a wedge so crisp and moist I could hardly resist eating half a skillet of it.

Having lived north of the Mason-Dixon Line for 20 years, I've sampled lots of northern corn bread as well. Although the ingredient lists may look similar, the corn breads of the North and the South are as different as Boston and Birmingham. Northern-style corn breads start with yellow cornmeal and a hefty scoop of all-purpose flour. The bread is unmistakably sweet and is usually moistened with milk, enriched with butter and leavened with baking powder. It's almost always baked in a baking pan or muffin tin. Northern corn bread is sweet, fine-textured and pale golden brown.

Proudly Southern

For southern-style corn bread, white cornmeal, not yellow, is the choice. There are only trace amounts of flour, if any, in the mix. Very few southern corn bread recipes call for sugar. Those that do treat it like salt, measuring it out in teaspoons rather than by the cup. Buttermilk moistens, bacon drippings enrich, and a combination of baking powder and soda gives the bread a lift. Classic southern corn bread batter is poured into a greased, scorching hot cast-iron skillet, which causes it to develop a thin, shattery-crisp crust as it bakes. At its best, this bread is moist and tender, with the warm fragrance of a cornfield and the subtle flavor of dairy in every bite.

Each style has its appeal, but to my mind, southern corn bread, with its savory, moist interior and crisp exterior, makes a superior accompaniment to soups, salads, chilis and stews. To make my favorite corn bread, I had always used the family recipe of cornmeal, salt, buttermilk, baking soda, baking powder, egg and vegetable oil (or bacon drippings when I had them). After looking at scores of recipes in addition to my own, I began to wonder if white cornmeal was really worth seeking out over yellow. Was this style of corn bread better off without *any* sugar or flour? Was milk, cream, sour cream or yogurt—used individually or in some combination—better than buttermilk? Could I get just as good a crust pouring the batter into a cold skillet or muffin tins and baking it a little longer? And finally, because I make more muffins and corn sticks than skillet bread these days, was it possible for the same batter to perform well in a variety of baking vessels?

Yellow is Better

To explore the significant differences among cornmeals, I began by testing 11 different types in a simple southern corn bread recipe, trying as many national and regional brands as possible—Quaker, Indian Head, Martha White and Arrowhead Mills—as well as those from major mail-order houses: Walnut Acres, King Arthur and Hoppin' John. I was primarily interested in flavor differences between the yellow and white

meals, but I was also curious about whether the growing conditions (organic versus unorganic) and production methods (stone-ground versus steel cut; whole-grain versus degerminated) made much difference in the bread. (See page 274 for a clarification of terms.)

Before the tests, I would have bet that color was a regional idiosyncrasy, having little to do with flavor. But my tasting proved otherwise. Corn breads made with yellow cornmeal have a more potent corn flavor than breads made with white cornmeal. Less surprising, breads made with stone-ground, whole-grain cornmeals are better textured and better flavored than those made with steel-cut and degerminated grains. Whether organically grown corn results in superior cornmeal is debatable, but coincidentally, my two favorite meals—Walnut Acres and King Arthur—are yellow, whole-grain, stone-ground *and* organic. The Walnut Acres breads taste of fresh corn, the King Arthur breads more like corn husk. Of the white cornmeals, Hoppin' John, a whole-grain, stone-ground meal, takes top honors.

More mass-produced steel-cut cornmeals, such as Quaker or Martha White, certainly make pleasant enough breads. But after tasting breads made from whole-grain, stone-ground cornmeals, I now make the effort to find these cornmeals, many of which are available in grocery or health-food stores.

UNDERSTANDING THE TERMS

♦ **Steel-Cut Cornmeal** has been processed between steel rollers, which break the corn kernels, resulting in a grittier meal. The major brands—Quaker and Martha White—are processed in this way.

♦ **Stone-Ground Cornmeal** is ground or "mashed" between stones, resulting in a softer-textured meal. Most of the meals I preferred were made like this.

♦ **Water-Ground Cornmeal** has been stone-ground at a mill powered with water rather than electricity. This process has no effect on flavor.

♦ **Bolted Cornmeal** is ground whole, with larger pieces of meal—usually the bran—sifted out.

♦ **Enriched Cornmeal** has had nutrients—thiamin, niacin and riboflavin—added.

♦ **Unenriched Cornmeal** does not contain added nutrients.

♦ **Whole-Grain Cornmeal** is ground whole, resulting in a meal made up of the bran, germ and endosperm. Because the bran and germ contain the oil, this meal is more flavorful but also more perishable than degerminated meal. It should therefore be refrigerated or even frozen.

♦ **Degerminated Cornmeal** is the opposite of whole-grain cornmeal. It has been stripped of its bran and germ before milling. It is drier and less flavorful than whole-grain meal.

♦ **Organic Cornmeal** is milled from corn that has been grown in a field that is certified to be organic.

Just a Spoonful of Sugar

Testing corn breads with ratios of all-purpose flour and cornmeal ranging from 1 part flour and 16 parts cornmeal to equal parts flour and cornmeal made it clear that flour lightens the bread and gives it a finer crumb. The more flour, however, the less corn flavor. I began with a 4-to-1 ratio of cornmeal to flour—¾ cup cornmeal for every 3 tablespoons flour.

Sugar was a big surprise. Although I didn't want my corn bread to taste like dessert, I wondered whether a little sugar might enhance the corn flavor. I made three batches of breads: one with no sugar, one with just a teaspoon, and one with a full tablespoon. The corn bread made with a teaspoon tasted fuller-flavored than the sugarless one. The corn bread with more sugar, on the other hand, was noticeably sweet. Using a smaller amount of sugar indeed enhances the natural sweetness of the corn without calling attention to itself.

Dairy Decisions

Although most southern-style corn bread batters are made with straight buttermilk, I found other recipes calling for the full range of acidic and sweet dairy products. I tested them all—buttermilk, sour cream, yogurt, milk and cream—both individually and many of them in combination.

Of the various moisteners, I loved the pure, straightforward flavor of the buttermilk-based corn bread, but breads made with sour cream and a combination of sour cream and milk were also tasty. With very little added fat and flavor, the distinct taste of yogurt clouded the clear corn flavor I wanted. The corn breads moistened with milk and milk-cream were less impressive than those made with sour cream and buttermilk, and the thicker dairy products made particularly good-looking muffins.

Now I was starting to become a little uneasy about where I was taking this bread. A couple of tablespoons of flour were forgivable; I could overlook a teaspoon of sugar; but yellow cornmeal was a big blow, and my sour cream leanings seemed to cross the border.

Southern Again

I had also come upon a much leaner corn bread recipe that wasn't much more than a baked cornmeal mush. I stirred boiling water into the meal, along with modest amounts of milk, egg, butter, salt and baking powder, and baked it. The formula was so simple, so lean, so humble, that I was tempted to pass it over. One bite, however, completely changed my direction. Unlike anything I had tasted so far, the crumb of this bread was incredibly moist and fine and bursting with corn flavor, all without flour and virtually no fat.

Because the foundation of this bread

is cornmeal mush, it's not surprising that the crumb itself was actually a bit mushy. After a few unsuccessful attempts at fixing the texture, I was becoming frustrated. As a last effort, I tried the recipe again, making cornmeal mush out of half of the cornmeal and mixing the remaining cornmeal with the baking powder.

To my relief, this method much improved the bread. Decreasing the ratio of cornmeal mush even further—from a half to a third of the cornmeal—gave me exactly what I was looking for. I made the new, improved corn bread with buttermilk in place of milk and tinkered with the leavenings, adding some baking soda, and it tasted even better. Although I still preferred yellow cornmeal and liked a sprinkle of sugar, I had achieved a moist, tender, fine-crumbed all-corn bread from a batter that could be made into shapely muffins without using sour cream.

With my new recipe in hand, I performed a few final tests. I made corn bread with vegetable oil, peanut oil, shortening, butter and bacon drippings, as well as a batch with no fat at all. The corn bread with no added fat was as moist and delicious as the other breads. Butter and bacon drippings, however, are certainly pleasant flavor additions.

After tasting breads baked on the bottom rack of a 475-degree oven, I found that a dark brown crust makes bitter bread. When I moved the rack up a notch and reduced the oven temperature to 450 degrees, the bread baked to golden brown perfection.

Although corn bread will not be as crisp in an unheated pan, heating the skillet before adding the batter is not strictly necessary because the bread will ultimately brown with a longer baking time. For confirmed southerners, however, as well as those who are southern at heart, at least when it comes to corn bread, preheating is the only way to go.

Southern-Style Corn Bread

MAKES ONE 8-INCH SKILLET OF BREAD

THE ONLY TRICKY PART of this recipe is making sure that the cornmeal mush is the right texture. If the water is not boiling when you add it to the cornmeal or your mixing bowl is too large, causing the water to cool down too quickly, a mush will not form. On the other hand, if the mush is too stiff, you'll need to work in an extra teaspoon or two of hot water before adding the buttermilk. For additional flavoring, you can add ½ teaspoon coarsely ground black pepper to the dry ingredients or ½ teaspoon seeded and minced jalapeño pepper.

4 teaspoons bacon drippings (or 1 teaspoon
    vegetable oil and 1 tablespoon butter, melted)
1 cup yellow cornmeal, preferably stone-ground
1 teaspoon sugar
½ teaspoon salt
1 teaspoon baking powder
¼ teaspoon baking soda
¾ cup buttermilk
1 large egg, lightly beaten

1. Adjust oven rack to lower-middle position and preheat oven to 450°F. Preheat an 8-inch cast-iron skillet (measured at the top) with all bacon drippings or, if using butter, with 1 teaspoon oil, in oven.

2. Measure ⅓ cup cornmeal into a medium bowl; set aside. Measure remaining ⅔ cup cornmeal, along with sugar, salt, baking powder and baking soda, into a small bowl.

3. Pour ⅓ cup boiling water all at once into the ⅓ cup cornmeal; stir to make a stiff mush. Stir in buttermilk until mush is smooth, then stir in egg. When oven is preheated and skillet is hot, stir dry ingredients into cornmeal mush. Remove skillet from oven and pour hot bacon drippings (or melted butter, if using) into batter, then quickly pour batter into heated skillet. Bake until golden brown, about 20 minutes. Remove skillet from oven and immediately turn corn bread onto a wire rack. Let cool for 5 minutes, then serve immediately.

♦ Southern-Style Corn Muffins

MAKES 6 MUFFINS

YOU CAN DOUBLE THIS RECIPE to make an even dozen.

1. Follow step 1 of recipe for Southern-Style Corn Bread (page 277), heating a dry heavy-gauge 6-muffin cup mold (each mold measuring ½ cup) instead of a skillet; do not grease mold.

2. Continue as directed in steps 2 and 3, removing muffin mold from oven and generously brushing cups with 4 teaspoons bacon drippings or 4 teaspoons vegetable oil (omit butter). Continue as directed, filling muffin cups almost to rim with batter. Bake until golden brown, about 20 minutes.

Big, Beautiful Muffins

I T'S RARE THAT A MUFFIN tastes as good as it looks, or looks as good as it tastes. Big bakery-style muffins often entice but seldom satisfy. Many muffin recipes don't deliver either. I know because over the years I have tried scores of them. Some came out flat-topped or misshapen. Other batches were either rich and leaden or dense and dry. The best were pleasant but not outstanding. I wanted a muffin that was both irresistibly beautiful and delicious.

My standards, admittedly, were high. I wasn't looking for a healthy muffin I could make part of my daily diet. I wanted a really great weekend muffin— one that would make brunch guests covet the recipe. This muffin had to have it all. It needed rich, full flavor with a thin crust protecting its fragile, tender crumb. It had to be a real looker: I would settle for nothing less than a perfect, round, mushroomlike cap with a pronounced, crisp overhang.

After looking at dozens of recipes, I started with a fairly common, but rather lean 6-cup muffin formula, reasoning that I could increase and adjust ingredients as testing progressed:

2	tablespoons butter
2	tablespoons sugar
6	tablespoons milk
1	large egg
1	cup flour
1½	teaspoons baking powder
¼	teaspoon salt

Mix It Up

Before focusing on individual ingredients, I decided to investigate mixing techniques. There are basically three methods of mixing muffin batter. The simplest, most common technique requires measuring wet and dry ingredients separately, pouring wet into dry, then mixing them together as quickly as possible. Most quick-bread batters are made this way.

A second method, more common to cake making, starts with creaming the butter and sugar, adding eggs and flavorings, then alternately mixing the dry and liquid ingredients into the creamed fat.

A final method draws from the biscuit and pie dough mixing tradition. Fat is cut into the dry ingredients. When the mix is the texture of cornmeal and contains pea-size pieces, the liquid is added and quickly mixed in.

The creaming method worked best, producing a more tender-crumbed muffin than the competitors.

My success with this method left me a bit puzzled. The technique called for beating the batter after flour had been added with an electric mixer for up to two minutes, depending on the recipe. But overbeating causes gluten development, so why were the muffins made according to this method more tender? The reason, according to the food scientist Shirley Corriher, is that the butter and eggs coat the flour and keep it from forming gluten. Then the remaining flour and liquid ingredients are mixed in, which stimulates a portion of the flour's gluten. (Some gluten must be activated, or the muffin would have no structure at all.) Creaming the butter and sugar together aerates the butter and provides lift. In the quick-bread method, by contrast, the wet ingredients and fats are added all at once, preventing the flour from receiving a fat coating.

I naturally questioned why the quick-bread method couldn't be adapted to approximate the creaming method of coating the fat with flour first. So I made a batch of muffins, mixing the dry ingredients with a whisk, then adding melted butter and a small portion of the wet ingredients to disperse the fat. When the flour was sufficiently coated, I stirred in the remaining wet ingredients. The muffins were as tender as those made by the creaming method, but because the batter had not been aerated by the mixer, they lacked the height of the mixer muffins. When you're short on time, you can achieve more tender muffins by simply mixing the butter and part of the liquid ingredients into the flour. When perfection counts, get out the mixer.

All-Purpose Flour Is Best

With the mixing method decided, I moved on to testing individual ingredients. Because my original formula was too dry and needed more sweetness, I increased the butter and sugar by 1 tablespoon each and the milk by 2 tablespoons. Starting with flours, I made muffins with cake flour, unbleached flour, bleached flour and a combination of half cake flour and half all-purpose.

The batter made with cake flour was noticeably loose compared to the other batters. The resulting muffins were squat, wet and greasy, and they lacked a distinct crisp outer crust. Muffins baked with half cake and half all-purpose flour were a step up but their texture was somewhat wet, and they didn't achieve the beautiful shape of the muffins made entirely with all-purpose flour. The muffins made with all-purpose bleached and unbleached flour were excellent. After settling on the flour, I decided that the formula still needed more sugar, so I increased the sugar by an additional tablespoon.

Plain Yogurt Offers Flavor and Texture

To come up with the best liquid addition, I made muffins with low-fat milk, whole milk, half-and-half, cream, powdered milk mixed with water, buttermilk, yogurt and sour cream, adjusting the leavenings accordingly in the case of buttermilk, yogurt and sour cream. As I had expected, the thin liquids—low-fat milk, whole milk, powdered milk and half-and-half—produced thin batters that baked into smooth-topped muffins that looked like cupcakes. Low-fat-milk muffins were shaped like soufflés, with straight sides and flat tops.

The thicker liquids—cream, buttermilk, yogurt and sour cream—delivered thicker batters and baked into muffins with rounded, textured tops. The higher-fat muffins, particularly those made with sour cream and cream, were squatty, dense, heavy and wet. Buttermilk muffins were good, but the yogurt-enriched were even better, producing a rough-textured, rounded top, a sweet-tangy flavor and a light, tender crumb.

The Big Muffin

Most recipes that yield a dozen muffins call for 2 to 2½ cups of flour. Multiplying my formula with those flour quantities gave me muffins with beautiful rounded tops, but there wasn't enough batter to produce the overhang that I wanted. Tripling the recipe was the answer. The resulting muffins were just right, rising enough for the batter to rise over onto the rim and set, then continuing to rise into a perfectly round top.

Having formulated a working base, I started adding fruits and flavorings, which led me to two additional recipe adjustments. Although the sugar level seemed right in the plain muffin, with the addition of tart fruit and other ingredients, the muffins were not sweet enough. I found that adding 2 tablespoons of sugar to the 3-cup recipe helped immensely. I also found that 1 more tablespoon of butter produced just the right tenderness without weighing down the muffin.

Muffin Papers Get a Poor Grade

A few recipes advised against muffin papers, warning that the muffins would not rise as high; others recommended greasing the bottom but not the sides of the muffin cups. I tested three batches of muffins—one baked in papers, one baked in greased cups and a final batch baked in cups that had only the bottoms greased.

The muffin-paper versions were, indeed, not as tall as those baked in the cups. I disliked the papers for other reasons. When peeling them off, I lost a good portion of the muffin. Muffin papers also keep the muffins' sides from browning as well as those baked right in the cups.

Muffins baked in fully greased cups looked no different from those that had been baked in cups with only the bottoms greased. It's much less fussy to coat the whole cup, and vegetable cooking spray is the fastest and easiest way to accomplish that.

Basic Muffins

MAKES 1 DOZEN LARGE MUFFINS

IF YOU'RE SHORT ON TIME, you can melt the butter, mix it with the eggs and stir into the dry ingredients. After the batter is thoroughly mixed, beat in the yogurt and proceed with the recipe.

Vegetable cooking spray
3 cups all-purpose flour
1 tablespoon baking powder
½ teaspoon baking soda
½ teaspoon salt
10 tablespoons (1 stick plus 2 tablespoons) butter, at room temperature
1 cup minus 1 tablespoon sugar
2 large eggs
1½ cups plain yogurt

1. Adjust oven rack to lower-middle position and preheat oven to 375°F. Coat a 12-cup muffin tin (with standard-size molds that have ½ cup capacity) with vegetable cooking spray.

2. Mix flour, baking powder, baking soda and salt in a medium bowl; set aside.

3. Beat butter and sugar with an electric mixer at medium-high speed until light and fluffy, about 2 minutes. Add eggs, one at a time, beating well after each addition. Beat in half of dry ingredients. Beat in one-third of yogurt. Beat in half of remaining dry ingredients, alternating with one-third of remaining yogurt, and repeat until fully incorporated.

4. Use a large ice cream scoop to divide batter evenly among muffin cups. Bake until muffins are golden brown, 20 to 25 minutes. Set on a wire rack to cool slightly, about 5 minutes. Remove muffins from tin and serve warm.

Cinnamon-Sugar Topping

Enough for 1 dozen muffins

THIS CINNAMON-SUGAR COATING is optional with the plain muffins or many of the less-sweet variations that follow.

- ½ cup sugar
- 2 teaspoons ground cinnamon
- 4 tablespoons (½ stick) butter, melted

Mix sugar and cinnamon in small bowl. Dip each warm muffin in melted butter, then in cinnamon sugar and serve immediately.

♦ Cranberry-Walnut Orange Muffins

MAKES 1 DOZEN LARGE MUFFINS

WIDELY AVAILABLE YEAR-ROUND, dried cranberries are excellent in these muffins as well. If using dried cranberries, reduce the amount to 1 cup.

Follow recipe for Basic Muffins (page 284), creaming butter-sugar mixture with 1 teaspoon orange zest in step 3 and folding 1½ cups coarsely chopped cranberries (fresh or frozen) or ¾ cup dried and ¾ cup walnut pieces into finished batter. Continue as directed.

♦ Lemon Blueberry Muffins

MAKES 1 DOZEN LARGE MUFFINS

USING DRIED BLUEBERRIES instead of fresh will contribute an intense blueberry flavor without leaking juice into the batter. If using dried blueberries, reduce the amount to 1 cup.

Follow recipe for Basic Muffins (page 284), creaming butter-sugar mixture with 1 teaspoon lemon zest in step 3 and folding 1½ cups blueberries tossed with 1 tablespoon flour into finished batter. Continue as directed and dip in Cinnamon-Sugar Topping, if desired.

♦ Lemon Poppy Seed Muffins

MAKES 1 DOZEN LARGE MUFFINS

1. Follow recipe for Basic Muffins (page 284), adding 3 tablespoons poppy seeds to dry ingredients in step 2 and creaming 1 teaspoon grated lemon zest with butter-sugar mixture in step 3. Continue as directed.

2. Topping: While muffins are baking, heat ¼ cup sugar and ¼ cup lemon juice in a small saucepan until sugar dissolves and mixture forms a light syrup, 3 to 4 minutes. Brush warm syrup over warm muffins and serve.

♦ Carrot-Cinnamon-Raisin Muffins

MAKES 1 DOZEN LARGE MUFFINS

THESE MUFFINS can also be made with grated apple.

Follow recipe for Basic Muffins (page 284), adding 1 teaspoon ground cinnamon to dry ingredients in step 2 and folding 1½ cups grated carrots and ¾ cup dark or golden raisins into finished batter. Continue as directed.

♦ Pineapple Ginger Muffins

MAKES 1 DOZEN LARGE MUFFINS

CRYSTALLIZED GINGER IS AVAILABLE in Asian markets and in the spice section of most supermarkets.

Follow recipe for Basic Muffins (page 284), adding 1 teaspoon ground ginger to dry ingredients in step 2 and folding ¾ cup drained crushed pineapple and ¼ cup minced crystallized ginger into finished batter. Continue as directed.

♦ Apricot-Almond Muffins

MAKES 1 DOZEN LARGE MUFFINS

DRIED PEACHES OR PEARS, cut into small dice, are equally good fruit choices in these muffins. Dried cherries are also wonderful.

Follow recipe for Basic Muffins (page 284), creaming 1 ounce (2 tablespoons) almond paste with butter and sugar in step 3 and folding 1½ cups finely diced dried apricots into finished batter. Sprinkle muffin tops with ½ cup sliced almonds and bake as directed.

♦ Raspberry-Almond Muffins

MAKES 1 DOZEN LARGE MUFFINS

THESE MUFFINS are one of my daughter's favorites. To ensure that the jam does not run out of the muffin, make a little indention with a small spoon in the batter in each cup before spooning in the jam. We love raspberry jam for these muffins, but you can use any jam, preserves or marmalade.

1. Follow recipe for Basic Muffins (page 284), creaming 1 ounce (2 tablespoons) almond paste with butter and sugar in step 3.

2. In step 4, spoon a half portion of batter into each muffin cup. Spoon 1½ teaspoons raspberry jam into each cup and fill with remaining batter. Bake as directed.

♦ Mocha Chip Muffins

MAKES 1 DOZEN LARGE MUFFINS

MINIATURE CHOCOLATE CHIPS, if you have them on hand, are perfect for these small cakes.

Follow recipe for Basic Muffins (page 284), dissolving 3 tablespoons instant coffee granules in yogurt in step 3 and folding 1 cup chocolate chips into finished batter. Continue as directed.

Banana-Walnut Muffins

MAKES 1 DOZEN LARGE MUFFINS

TOASTING THE NUTS before adding them to the batter makes all the difference in amplifying their flavor.

¾	cup walnuts, chopped
3	cups all-purpose flour
1	tablespoon baking powder
½	teaspoon baking soda
½	teaspoon salt
½	teaspoon grated nutmeg
10	tablespoons (1 stick plus 2 tablespoons) butter, softened
1	cup packed light brown sugar
2	large eggs
1½	cups plain yogurt
1½	cups finely diced bananas (3 small)

1. Toast walnuts in a small skillet over medium heat until fragrant, 3 to 4 minutes, stirring frequently.

2. Follow recipe for Basic Muffins (page 284), adding nutmeg to dry ingredients in step 2.

3. In step 3, cream butter with brown sugar. Fold bananas and walnuts into finished batter. Continue as directed.

Perfect Pancakes

PANCAKES ARE A FAST and simple breakfast, but if they are also to be good, there are a few things you have to get right. First, the batter has to be the proper texture. Runny batters cook into crepes. Thick batters—particularly those made with buttermilk—can cook up wet and heavy. Second, the pan must be the correct temperature. An overly hot skillet produces a scorched exterior and raw interior, while a cool one makes for a hard crust and a dry interior. Finally, one of the most critical issues is getting the leavening right. Too much baking powder or soda in a batter can result in metallic- or soapy-flavored pancakes—the taste equivalent of fingernails scraping across a blackboard.

Before working on this pancake story, these leaveners were a bit of a mystery to me. After performing extensive tests, I know one thing: many recipes call for far more baking powder and baking soda than is needed.

Variations on a Formula

My simple pancake formula started out with the following ingredients:

1 cup all-purpose flour
1 tablespoon sugar
1 teaspoon baking powder (if using milk) or ½ teaspoon baking soda (if using buttermilk)
½ teaspoon salt
1 cup milk or buttermilk
1 large egg
2 tablespoons melted butter

I began the tests with flour, trying the original formula (using milk and baking powder) with all-purpose flour, cake flour and a combination of the two. Batters made with cake flour were significantly thinner than those made from regular all-purpose flour. None of the pancakes rose nearly as high as they should have, and the cake-flour pancakes were particularly crepelike. Although the all-purpose pancakes looked and tasted flat, they were nevertheless more substantial, yet tender.

From past experience, I was certain that buttermilk was the easiest way to boost flavor, so I substituted buttermilk and baking soda (to neutralize the buttermilk's acid) in the original formula for the milk and baking powder. The batter was so thick that it had to be spooned, rather than poured, onto the griddle. Even after I thinned it with a little milk, the cooked pancakes were still too wet and lacked the subtle tang of buttermilk.

I was certain that the baking powder and baking soda were responsible for the heavy texture and had obscured the flavor of the buttermilk.

Leavener Lessons

To figure out just which leavener or what combination of leaveners would work best with buttermilk, I made three batches of batter: one with 2 teaspoons baking powder and no baking soda, another with no baking powder and ½ teaspoon baking soda and a final batch with 1 teaspoon baking powder and ¼ teaspoon baking soda.

Pancakes made from all three batters rose beautifully on the griddle. The all-baking powder pancakes were pale and very fine—almost gummy. Compared to the other two varieties of pancakes, they were tough. They tasted salty (probably from acid salt, which is contained in baking powder) and had a tinny aftertaste. The buttermilk flavor came through but was almost too strong. Rather than tasting mildly tangy, these pancakes were almost sour.

The all-baking soda pancakes were more yellow. They were tender, with a coarser crumb, and weren't nearly as salty as the baking powder pancakes, but they tasted flat.

The combination of baking powder and baking soda offered a good balance, displaying the best qualities of the other batches, without any of the negatives. The small amount of baking soda gave pancakes the right crumb and made them light and tender, while a little baking powder helped with the rise and let the buttermilk flavor come through.

Fluffy, Springy Pancakes

Although my pancakes were relatively light, they weren't exactly fluffy. The batter was still too thick, and the resulting pancakes were still a little wet. I wanted my pancakes to look like the ones on the Bisquick box—the kind that spring back into shape when cut. I tried fixing the problem by thinning the batter with milk. Using ¾ cup buttermilk and ¼ cup milk lightened the batter and gave me fluffy pancakes.

I discussed the results with a colleague, who suggested that I could perhaps get away with even less baking powder. It was good advice. I made a final batch of pancake batter with the baking soda but reduced the baking powder to ½ teaspoon. The pancakes rose as beautifully as if they had been made with the full teaspoon, they looked light and fluffy and they tasted great.

Easy Mixing

Although I was pleased with my new recipe, I wanted to run a final few tests with eggs and butter to determine the fastest way to mix up a lumpless batter.

A number of pancake recipes call for separating the egg: first mix the yolk into the batter and then whip and fold in the white. This method made a stiff batter that had to be spooned onto the griddle, but it produced airy and tender pancakes.

Although some recipes insist that the egg and milk be brought to room temperature before making the batter, I found that pancakes made from refrigerator-temperature eggs and milk were fine. The only problem was that the cold milk and egg caused the melted butter to harden and turn the mixture lumpy. So instead of stirring the whole egg into the milk, I separated the egg, added the white to the milk and then whisked the yolk into the melted butter before stirring it into the milk, greatly reducing the size of the butter pieces.

The quickest way to incorporate the wet ingredients into the dry ingredients of the pancake batter is to dump the milk mixture all at once into the flour mixture, then quickly whisk. This method guarantees a virtually lumpless batter within seconds every time.

Light and Fluffy Pancakes

MAKES ABOUT EIGHT 3-INCH PANCAKES, SERVING 3 TO 4

YOU MAY WANT TO DOUBLE this recipe when making it on the weekend, when breakfasts tend to be larger. If you use salted butter, you may want to cut back a bit on the salt.

> 1 cup all-purpose flour
> 2 teaspoons sugar
> ½ teaspoon salt
> ½ teaspoon baking powder
> ¼ teaspoon baking soda
> ¾ cup buttermilk
> ¼ cup milk, plus 1 tablespoon more if necessary
> 1 large egg, separated
> 2 tablespoons unsalted butter, melted
>   Vegetable oil for brushing pan

1. Mix flour, sugar, salt, baking powder and baking soda in a medium bowl. Pour buttermilk and ¼ cup milk into a 2-cup liquid measuring cup. Whisk in egg white. Mix yolk with butter, then add to milk mixture. Dump wet ingredients into dry ingredients all at once; whisk until just mixed.

2. Meanwhile, heat a griddle or large skillet over strong medium heat. Generously brush pan with oil. When water splashed on surface sizzles, pour batter, about ¼ cup at a time, onto griddle, making sure not to overcrowd. When pancake bottoms are brown and top surfaces start to bubble, 2 to 3 minutes, flip pancakes and cook until browned, 1 to 2 minutes more. Serve hot.

BUNDLE 'EM UP

THERE'S NO GETTING AROUND IT. Pancakes are best served right off the griddle. I'd rather dole them out, one per customer, than try to hold and serve them all at once. But sometimes—whether you're cooking for a crowd or you can't get everyone to the table at one time—making them a little in advance is unavoidable. Wrapping the pancakes in a clean kitchen towel and placing them in a warm oven works fairly well. But pancakes do pick up the scent of the towel, so be careful not to use one that smells of laundry detergent or dryer sheets.

To wrap pancakes, line a large baking pan with a clean scent-free kitchen towel. Place the cooked pancakes in the pan in a single layer and cover with a kitchen towel. Place them in a 200-degree oven. Repeat, making sure that each layer of pancakes is covered with a layer of toweling. The pancakes can hold for about 15 minutes.

♦ Blueberry Pancakes

MAKES ABOUT EIGHT 3-INCH PANCAKES,
SERVING 3 TO 4

Follow recipe for Light and Fluffy Pancakes (page 294), pouring a little less than ¼ cup batter at a time onto griddle in step 2. Immediately drop about 7 blueberries onto top of each pancake (you will need about ½ cup blueberries total). Continue and cook as directed.

♦ Whole Wheat Pancakes

MAKES ABOUT EIGHT 3-INCH PANCAKES,
SERVING 3 TO 4

Follow recipe for Light and Fluffy Pancakes (page 294), substituting ½ cup whole wheat flour for ½ cup all-purpose flour in step 1. Continue as directed.

VI

Be-All and End-All
Desserts

Mix-and-Match Fruit Cobblers

COBBLERS HAVE BEEN my standard casual company dessert for many years. Enriched with whipped cream or ice cream, they taste as good as a fruit pie and can be assembled much more quickly. I had been eyeing this group of desserts for a while, thinking it just might be possible to develop an all-purpose formula that would work for whatever fruit, ingredients and time I had. Because I prepare these desserts so often during the summer, I wanted a recipe that fit into a simple 8-inch pan (or, doubled, fit the equally common 13-by-9-inch size). Even ill-supplied vacation houses usually have one of the two, and if not, disposables are always available in both sizes at the grocery. Finally, in honor of their humble, friendly roots, I wanted to make sure these desserts remained easy to make and simply flavored, neither excessively lean nor overly rich.

Paging through large stacks of recipes, I isolated three cobbler styles that made sense for my plan. Pastry, biscuit and butter cookie dough all looked like possible mix-and-match toppings for most any prepared fruit. Although very different in character, fruit baked in a batter of some sort offered a fourth style I thought might round out the selection.

Before refining the toppings, I wanted to understand the fruit. Would a given amount, regardless of variety, bake up more or less the same under the crust? Did the fruit need to be thickened, sweetened or flavored?

First Fruits

In order to develop a fruit chart, I needed to check the juice and sugar level of each baked fruit. I tested a variety of both fresh and frozen fruits—apples (Winesaps, Granny Smiths, McIntoshs and Empires), peaches, nectarines, plums, dark sweet and sour cherries, strawberries, blueberries, pears, blackberries, rhubarb and raspberries—lightly sweetening a small portion of each and baking it until fully cooked.

Most of the fruits produced a nice quantity of slightly thickened juices. Two fruits, however, responded very differently. Cobblers made with apples, at one extreme, were so dry that I ultimately added water to make them juicy enough. At the other end, cobblers made with sour cherries were too watery, their juices lacking the natural body of peach, pear and berry juices. Cherries demand more thickener than the other fruits.

To my surprise, most of the frozen fruits made respectable cobblers. As a matter of fact, frozen blueberries held their shape and flavor better than pricey out-of-season Chilean imports. Strawberries, rhubarb, blackberries, raspberries and cherries all worked well, with a few exceptions. Frozen peach slices lacked the juiciness and perfume of fresh, ripe ones. Frozen dark sweet cherries were sweet and flavorless when baked, but so were the fresh ones. Sour cherries, fresh or frozen, are more suited to baking.

Sweeteners, Thickeners and Flavorings

Baked fruits need sugar, because sweet cobbler toppings and ice cream only accentuate their tartness. Not only is sugar necessary for flavor, but it also doubles as a light thickener. After a number of tests with each fruit, I came up with a formula (see page 303). Because fruit varies in sweetness, however, taste before adding sugar. Add the lower of the suggested amounts, then taste and increase as needed. When sweetening,

remember that sugar ultimately cooks into the fruit. But because it clings to the surface before you bake it, you may want to sweeten a little more than seems necessary.

Even though sugar helped thicken the juice, it wasn't quite sufficient. All fruits benefit from a little thickener, which not only gives the juice body and sheen, but also tones down the intensely sweet-tart flavor of the baked fruit.

Which starch to use? For a natural thin, silky syrup, I preferred cornstarch, arrowroot or potato starch. I ultimately used small quantities, so I found it difficult to detect much difference among the three, as all worked equally well at unobtrusively thickening the juices. Unlike fruit pie, where a good clean cut is important, cobblers are moist and messy. Instant tapioca, which is great for thickening pie fruit, gave the cobbler fruit too jellylike a texture. Flour, in contrast, turned the cobbler juices a little cloudy. The riper the fruit, the lower its pectin level, so you may want to add more starch if your fruit is very ripe.

I knew that minced apple is often used for its natural pectin to thicken fruit jams, so I tried this thickening method as well. I minced apple chunks with sugar in the food processor, then cooked the mixture until the apples softened and the sugar formed a syrup. The "syrup" coated the fruit nicely before the cobbler was baked, and it thickened the

CAN'T KEEP THEM STRAIGHT?

FOR THOSE WHO can't keep remember the difference between a pandowdy and a buckle, the following definitions will help.

DESSERTS WITH BISCUIT TOPPING

♦ **Cobbler**—The fruit is covered with a biscuit dough—either rolled out, stamped out or dropped. The dessert is baked until the biscuit is golden brown.

♦ **Grunt**—The fruit is topped with a drop biscuit dough, *covered* and baked. The biscuits steam rather than bake.

♦ **Plate Cake**—The fruit is covered with rolled biscuit dough and baked. When the dessert is done, it is flipped, and the topping becomes the bottom crust.

♦ **Fruit Roll**—Biscuit dough is rolled and fitted into a loaf pan. Fruit is added, and dough encases the fruit. The dessert is baked, then sliced.

DESSERTS WITH PASTRY TOPPINGS

♦ **Deep-Dish Pie**—The fruit is covered with a pastry dough and baked. This dessert can also be called a cobbler.

♦ **Pandowdy**—The fruit is covered with pastry dough and partially baked. The crust is cut and pressed into the fruit, and the dessert is returned to the oven and baked until the crust crisps again.

DESSERTS WITH CRUMB TOPPING

♦ **Crisp**—The fruit is topped with a mixture of butter, sugar, flour and nuts, then baked.

♦ **Crumble**—The fruit is topped with a mixture of butter, sugar, flour and oatmeal, then baked.

♦ **Betty**—The fruit is topped with buttered bread crumbs and baked. (Crumbs are also scattered in between layers of the fruit.)

FRUIT DESSERTS WITH CAKE BATTER TOPPING

♦ **Buckle**—The fruit is topped with a simple yellow cake batter and baked.

fruit ever so slightly. The method showed promise, but it was more complicated and less effective than starch.

In the spirit of cobbler, I kept flavorings simple. I liked the way vanilla extract quietly rounded out and deepened flavors. To some of the milder fruits, I added a pinch of clove or cinnamon, but many of the stronger-flavored berries needed nothing. In some cases, a tablespoon of liqueur or cognac enhanced the cobbler, but all flavorings are optional, depending on your taste.

Four Choices
for the Topping

While exploring fruits, I developed various toppings, all of which worked well. I knew I wouldn't find a better pastry topping than two parts fat to one part flour. This dough, sprinkled generously with sugar and baked over any of the suggested fruits, makes a delicious cobbler.

After testing a number of biscuit toppings, I opted for a rich, sweet shortcake dough to help anchor the assertive fruit. Buttermilk and baking powder-style biscuits were too fluffy and savory for this dessert. I modeled my cookie-dough topping after a favorite blueberry cobbler recipe published in *Cook's* magazine. It bakes up soft and rich underneath and delicately crisp on top.

Finding a batter-based cobbler was more difficult. Fruit baked in rich yellow cake batter was technically a buckle, but the dessert looked and tasted too much like cake. Fruit baked in a lean, sweet pancakelike batter resembled coarse quick bread. Both batters absorbed the fruit's excess juice. Stiffer batters, dropped by the tablespoonful onto the fruit, baked into mediocre cobblers that couldn't compete with the other winners. Finally, I discovered Nathalie DuPree's recipe for peach cobbler in *New Southern Cooking* (Knopf, 1986). She calls it "the best peach dessert there is." After making it with mixed berries, I wholeheartedly agree.

The result of all my tests is a fruit cobbler that can be made year-round. The following recipe, with its various toppings and fruit choices, is really at least 40 desserts all in one.

Fruit Cobbler

ENOUGH FOR ONE 8-INCH SQUARE
OR ONE 9-INCH ROUND PAN, SERVING 4 TO 6

YOU CAN MIX ANY of the fruits on the following page together. If sugar quantities for fruits you selected are different, simply average the two amounts. Individually quick frozen (IQF) fruits make good cobblers, especially compared to those made with out-of-season fresh fruit. Preparation is embarrassingly simple—just snip the bag and dump it in the bowl. Cobblers made with frozen fruit need a little extra oven time, so bake them for a good 55 minutes. Match with any of the toppings on the following pages.

> **Butter Cookie Dough Topping (page 304),**
> **Rich Shortcake Topping (page 305),**
> **Flaky Pastry Topping (page 306)**
> **or Batter Fruit Cobbler (page 308)**
> **Fruit of choice (see following page)**

1. Prepare topping for fruit. Refrigerate shortcake or pie dough while preparing fruit.

2. Adjust oven rack to lower-middle position and preheat oven to 375°F. Mix sugar and cornstarch and any dry spices together in a medium bowl. Add prepared fruit and liquid flavorings; toss to coat.

3. Place prepared fruit in an 8-inch square or 9-inch round baking pan. Cover with selected topping and bake on a cookie sheet until golden brown, 45 to 55 minutes. Let cool slightly before serving.

FRUIT CHOICES

BLUEBERRIES

2 pints fresh berries (or 20 ounces
  frozen), rinsed and picked over
½-⅔ cup sugar
2 teaspoons cornstarch
½ teaspoon ground cinnamon
  1 teaspoon vanilla extract

BLACKBERRIES

2 pints fresh berries
  (or 20 ounces frozen), rinsed
⅓-½ cup sugar
1 tablespoon cornstarch
1 teaspoon vanilla extract

STRAWBERRY OR
STRAWBERRY-RHUBARB

2 pints fresh berries (or 20 ounces frozen)
  or 10 ounces each rhubarb and
  strawberries, stemmed and rinsed: small
  or medium berries left whole; halved if
  large; rhubarb cut into ⅓-inch chunks
⅓-½ cup sugar
1 tablespoon cornstarch
1 teaspoon vanilla extract

RASPBERRIES

2 pints fresh berries
  (or 20 ounces frozen), rinsed
½-⅔ cup sugar
1 tablespoon cornstarch
1 teaspoon vanilla extract

ITALIAN PLUMS

1¾ pounds plums, pitted, seeded
  and quartered
½-⅔ cup sugar
2 teaspoons cornstarch
½ teaspoon ground cinnamon

SOUR CHERRIES

1¾ pounds fresh cherries (or 20 ounces
  frozen), stemmed and pitted
⅔-¾ cup sugar
1½ tablespoons cornstarch
1 tablespoon kirsch, ½ tablespoon
  almond extract

APPLES

1¾ pounds tart, firm apples, peeled,
  quartered, cored and thickly sliced
⅓-½ cup sugar
2 teaspoons cornstarch dissolved in
  ¼ cup water
½ teaspoon ground cinnamon, 1 teaspoon
  vanilla extract, 1 tablespoon brandy

PEARS

1¾ pounds pears, peeled, quartered,
  cored and thickly sliced
⅓-½ cup sugar
2 teaspoons cornstarch
¼ teaspoon ground ginger or nutmeg,
  1 teaspoon vanilla extract

APRICOTS

1¾ pounds apricots, pitted and halved
½-⅔ cup sugar
2 teaspoons cornstarch
1 teaspoon vanilla extract, ½ teaspoon
  almond extract

PEACHES OR NECTARINES

1¾ pounds fruit, peeled, pitted, and
  thickly sliced
⅓-½ cup sugar
2 teaspoons cornstarch
Pinch ground cloves, 1 teaspoon vanilla
  extract, 1 tablespoon brandy

Butter Cookie Dough Topping

ENOUGH FOR ONE 8-INCH SQUARE
OR ONE 9-INCH ROUND PAN

THIS TOPPING, from the May 1990 issue of *Cook's* magazine, makes one of the best cobblers you'll probably ever eat. Because the cookie dough is quite sweet, use the smaller amount of sugar suggested in the fruit chart on page 303.

½   cup all-purpose flour
¼   teaspoon baking powder
     Pinch salt
8   tablespoons (1 stick) unsalted butter, softened
½   cup sugar
½   large egg or 1 yolk
¼   teaspoon vanilla extract

1. Mix flour, baking powder and salt in a small bowl; set aside.

2. Beat butter and sugar until well blended. Beat in egg and vanilla. Add flour mixture; stir until just combined.

3. Drop cookie dough by heaping tablespoons onto prepared fruit in step 2 of recipe for Fruit Cobbler (page 302). Bake, following instructions in step 3.

Rich Shortcake Topping

ENOUGH TO COVER ONE 8-INCH SQUARE
OR ONE 9-INCH ROUND PAN

SINCE THE BISCUIT easily absorbs juices, this topping is particularly nice with berries. If you want to top the cobbler with individual biscuits, increase the recipe by half, roll the dough to ¾ inch thick and sprinkle the dough rounds with sugar. Or, for a more cobbled look, increase the recipe by half, break off golf-ball-size pieces of biscuit dough and simply drop them onto the fruit.

>   1   cup all-purpose flour
> 1½   teaspoons baking powder
>   ¼   teaspoon salt
>   4   tablespoons (½ stick) unsalted butter,
>   chilled and cut into ¼-inch pieces
>   2   tablespoons vegetable shortening, chilled
>   7   tablespoons milk
>   1   tablespoon sugar

1. Mix flour, baking powder and salt in a food processor fitted with a steel blade. Scatter butter pieces over flour mixture, tossing to coat butter with a little flour. Cut butter into flour with five 1-second pulses. Add shortening; continue cutting in until flour is pale yellow and resembles coarse cornmeal, with butter bits no larger than small peas, about 4 more 1-second pulses. Turn mixture into a medium bowl.

2. Pour 6 tablespoons milk into flour mixture. Toss with fork until mixture forms large clumps, adding remaining 1 tablespoon milk if dough does not clump. Turn mixture onto a work surface; lightly knead until mixture just comes together. Place dough on a sheet of plastic wrap and press into either a square or a disk, depending on pan shape. Refrigerate while preparing fruit. (Shortcake can be refrigerated for up to 2 hours before baking.)

3. Roll dough into a 10-inch square or circle. Lay dough over prepared fruit in step 2 of recipe for Fruit Cobbler (page 302); tuck excess in between pan side and fruit. Brush dough with remaining tablespoon of milk; sprinkle with sugar. Cut 4 air vents in top of dough and follow baking instructions in step 3.

Flaky Pastry Topping

ENOUGH TO COVER ONE 8-INCH SQUARE
OR ONE 9-INCH ROUND PAN

YOU CAN EFFORTLESSLY ACHIEVE a soft and crisp-textured crust by tucking the pastry between the fruit and pan wall. The fruit juices keep the side crust tender, while the dry oven heat crisps the top. To turn your cobbler into a pandowdy, when the crust has fully set but has not browned (about 30 minutes into baking), remove the dessert from the oven and score the crust lengthwise and crosswise to form 2-inch squares. Using a large spoon or metal spatula, press the partially baked crust down into the fruit. Continue to bake until the crust is set and golden.

    1   cup all-purpose flour
    ¼   teaspoon salt
    2   tablespoons sugar
    6   tablespoons (¾ stick) unsalted butter,
        chilled and cut into ¼-inch pieces
    2   tablespoons vegetable shortening, chilled

1. Mix flour, salt and 1 tablespoon sugar in a food processor fitted with a steel blade. Scatter butter pieces over flour mixture, tossing to coat butter with a little flour. Cut butter into flour with five 1-second pulses. Add shortening; continue cutting in until flour is pale yellow and resembles coarse cornmeal, with butter bits no larger than small peas, about 4 more 1-second pulses. Turn mixture into a medium bowl.

2. Sprinkle 2 tablespoons ice water over mixture. Using a rubber spatula, fold water into flour mixture. Press down on dough mixture with broad side of spatula until dough sticks together, adding up to 1 tablespoon more ice water if necessary. Place dough on a sheet of plastic wrap and press into either a square or a disk, depending on pan shape. Refrigerate while preparing fruit according to step 2 of recipe for Fruit Cobbler (page 302). (Topping can be refrigerated for up to 2 days before baking.)

3. Roll dough into a 10-inch square or circle. Lay dough over prepared fruit; tuck excess dough in between pan side and fruit. Brush dough top lightly with water and sprinkle with remaining 1 tablespoon sugar. Cut four 2-inch air vents in top of dough and bake following instructions in step 3 of recipe for Fruit Cobbler (page 302).

Batter Fruit Cobbler

SERVES 4 TO 5

ADAPTED FROM A RECIPE in Nathalie DuPree's *New Southern Cooking* (Knopf, 1986), this cobbler is one of the best in its category.

    4   tablespoons (½ stick) unsalted butter
    ¾   cup all-purpose flour
    ¾   cup plus 1 tablespoon sugar
    1   teaspoon baking powder
    ¼   teaspoon salt
    ¾   cup milk
    2   cups prepared fruit or berries
        (not sweetened or thickened)

1. Adjust oven rack to lower-middle position and preheat oven to 350°F. Put butter in an 8-inch square or 9-inch round pan; set in oven to melt.

2. Whisk flour, ¾ cup sugar, baking powder and salt in small bowl. Add milk; whisk until just incorporated into dry ingredients. When butter has melted, remove pan from oven. Pour batter into pan, then arrange fruit over batter. Sprinkle with remaining 1 tablespoon sugar. Bake until batter browns, 40 to 50 minutes. Cool slightly and serve.

Strawberry Shortcake

I<small>T'S CURIOUS</small> that although I grew up in the heart of biscuit country, I didn't eat a biscuit-based strawberry shortcake until I was in my twenties and living in Chicago. Just about everybody I knew down South spooned strawberries over pound cake or angel food cake. Maybe they thought cake was more manageable because it could be made ahead, whereas last-minute biscuits were inconvenient. Perhaps my sweet-toothed family and friends preferred sweet cake to the more savory biscuit. Or maybe because biscuits were so common at our supper table, my crowd just couldn't conceive of them as suitable for dessert.

Having since enjoyed strawberries over all sorts of pastries and cakes, I've become a fan of biscuit-based shortcakes. Cakes and other pastries just don't offer the contrasts of cool berries sandwiched between warm, tender-crisp biscuit and chilled softly whipped cream on top.

Strawberry season is short, and I make shortcake once or twice a year when strawberries are at their prime. For the last several years, I've used a standard baking powder biscuit with a tablespoon of sugar mixed into the dry ingredients. But I wondered if it was really the best base for my strawberries and whipped cream.

To find out, I started the tests by baking four very different sweetened biscuits—one made with baking powder, one with buttermilk, the third with light cream and the fourth with egg. After sampling each one, I determined that the egg-enriched biscuit had the advantage. Even with the added sugar, the baking powder and buttermilk biscuits seemed more at home in a bread basket than on a dessert plate. The cream biscuits were good-looking but gummy inside. Though still very much a biscuit, the egg- and cream-enriched shortcakes were finer and more cakey.

2 cups cake flour
½ teaspoon salt
4 teaspoons baking powder
3 tablespoons sugar
8 tablespoons (1 stick)
   unsalted butter
1 large egg, beaten
⅓ cup milk or cream

I tested three batches of biscuits, one with all-purpose bleached flour, another with a mix of all-purpose and cake flour and a final one with all cake flour. I placed my bet on the cake flour to deliver the best tender biscuit. Defying the odds, the cake flour biscuit came in last, with a powdery dry texture. The flour did not have enough gluten to support the fat. Shortcakes made with bleached all-purpose flour were my favorites—tender, moist and cakey.

With the flour issue resolved, I moved to the bottom of the ingredient list, making biscuits with milk, half-and-half and heavy cream. Biscuits made with cream were squat and dense. The half-and-half and milk biscuits were tall and light-textured. Though both were good, those made with milk were comparatively flat-tasting for my dessert biscuit. Because of their good looks and rich flavor, the half-and-half biscuits were my favorites.

Biscuits made with 4 teaspoons of baking powder tasted slightly metallic. By reducing the baking powder to 1 tablespoon, I lost the off flavor but not the height. In a quick test of different sugars, biscuits made with granulated sugar were my favorites. Brown sugar biscuits tasted fine, but they looked as if they had been made with whole wheat flour. Confectioners' sugar did nothing to improve the biscuits.

The unresolved issues that remained concerned methods of mixing, cutting, baking and brushing the cakes.

Cutting in the Butter

Each mixing method—pastry cutter, food processor, fingertips—has its assets and liabilities. A pastry blender works well, but cutting the butter into small cubes beforehand can be a problem. If the butter is soft enough to cut easily, then it's too soft for the pastry (and it tends to stick to the knife). It must be refrigerated or frozen. If the butter is hard enough for the pastry, it's difficult to cut.

I like the food processor for big jobs, but it works less well for a quick task like cutting butter into flour for six shortcakes. Some cooks have cold fingertips, but I usually soften the butter too much in the process of getting it to pea size.

My favorite method is one I picked up from a fellow cook. I grate a frozen stick of butter on the large holes of a box grater right into the flour mixture, then finish the job with the pastry cutter. The hardened butter is the perfect texture for grating, and after a few cuts with the pastry cutter, the butter is fully incorporated.

Although hand-formed biscuits look attractive and rustic, they are easy to overwork, and a pair of warm hands can cause the dough's surface butter to melt. Using a biscuit cutter requires less handling, and dough rounds cut with a biscuit cutter develop a natural crack around the circumference during baking, making them easy to hand-split. You don't need to use a rolling pin. Patting the dough to a ¾ inch thickness on a floured work surface is fast and simple. In reforming the dough scraps to make additional rounds, it's necessary to knead the scraps lightly back together. Biscuits made from scraps tend to crack on top, losing their nice uniform shape.

After testing several biscuit glazes, I opted for brushed egg white drizzled with a little sugar. Not only does it give the cake a nice, glossy sheen, it helps crisp the top crust. My next favorite— milk and cream—had a semigloss finish, perfectly acceptable when sprinkled with sugar. Brushed egg yolk made the biscuits too yellow, and those dipped in or brushed with butter were dull and greasy.

At what temperature should the shortcakes be baked? I tested oven temperatures ranging from 375 degrees to 500 degrees. Biscuits baked on the lower-middle oven rack at 425 degrees were perfect. Those baked at higher temperatures tended to brown too much on the bottom before getting done. Those baked at lower temperatures tended to dry out before browning.

Split Apart

Some people butter the split biscuits before topping them with strawberries, perhaps to keep strawberry juices from making the biscuit soggy or to enrich the dessert. Regardless, I found the butter unnecessary. It didn't keep the juice from penetrating the biscuit, and it took away from the freshness of the berries and gave them a greasy taste.

Quartered or sliced strawberries on strawberry shortcake slip and slide, remaining separate and having to be chased with the fork. A crushed berry topping is less attractive. I found a happy compromise by slicing a majority of the berries and crushing just a few to unify the mixture. Although strawberries are classic, a mix of berries— blueberries, blackberries and raspberries, as well as ripe peaches—can stand in for them throughout the summer and into the fall.

Rich and Tender Shortcakes with Strawberries and Whipped Cream

SERVES 6

Serve this strawberry shortcake with pasteurized cream, rather than the more common ultrapasteurized, if possible. Ultrapasteurized cream is heated to a higher temperature during processing and has a less fresh flavor than pasteurized.

3 pints strawberries, hulled: 1 pint crushed
   with a potato masher or fork; 2 pints quartered
6 tablespoons sugar

Shortcakes

2 cups all-purpose bleached flour
½ teaspoon salt
1 tablespoon baking powder
5 tablespoons sugar
1 stick (8 tablespoons) unsalted butter, frozen
1 large egg, beaten, plus 1 egg white, lightly beaten
½ cup half-and-half

1 cup chilled heavy cream, whipped to
   soft peaks with 1 tablespoon sugar

1. Mix crushed and quartered berries with sugar in a medium bowl; set aside while preparing biscuits.

2. Shortcakes: Adjust oven rack to lower-middle position and preheat oven to 425°F. Mix flour, salt, baking powder and 3 tablespoons sugar in a medium bowl. Grate butter into dry ingredients. Toss butter with flour to coat. Use a pastry cutter to finish cutting butter into flour. Or scoop up coated butter with both hands, then quickly rub it into dry ingredients with fingertips until most butter pieces are the size of split peas.

3. Mix whole egg and half-and-half and pour into flour mixture. Toss with a fork until mixture forms large clumps, adding more half-and-half if mixture seems dry. Turn mixture onto a work surface and lightly knead until dough comes together.

4. Press dough out to a ¾ inch thickness. Dip a 2½-inch biscuit cutter into flour and cut as many dough rounds as possible. Gather scraps and gently knead. Repeat cutting process to form 6 rounds. Place 1 inch apart on a small ungreased baking sheet. Brush dough tops with egg white and sprinkle with remaining 2 tablespoons sugar. (Shortcakes can be covered and refrigerated for up to 2 hours before baking.) Bake until golden brown, 12 to 14 minutes. Place baking sheet on a wire rack and cool until warm, about 10 minutes.

5. Split each shortcake crosswise and spoon a portion of berries over each cake bottom. Spoon a dollop of whipped cream over berries. Cap with cake top and serve immediately.

♦ Citrus Shortcakes

Follow recipe for Rich and Tender Shortcakes, adding ½ teaspoon lemon or orange zest to dry ingredients in step 2. Continue as directed.

♦ Ginger Shortcakes

Follow recipe for Rich and Tender Shortcakes, adding ½ teaspoon ground ginger and 1 tablespoon minced candied ginger to dry ingredients in step 2. Continue as directed.

An Even Better Apple Pie

EVER MADE ONE of those mile-high apple pies with fruit mounded so tall there was barely enough dough to stretch over the heap? As you peer through the oven door, you're filled with pride. You can't believe you've made such a beautiful pastry. The pie comes out of the oven looking as full and shapely as it did going in. But as you peek expectantly through the steam pouring from the air vents, you discover that the impressive mountain of apples has shrunk to ground level, while the crust has set in the clouds. Cutting the pie, you carefully saw through the crust, but with no filling for support, it collapses and crumbles. That looker of a pie turns into a cobbled-up mess on the plate.

How to fix the shrinking apple problem was only one of a number of questions I had about this classic American dessert. I wanted to know which apple varieties keep their shape as well as their flavor after an hour in the oven. Although I had seen recipes calling for all kinds of thickeners, I wondered which one is best for apple pie, and how much of it to use?

Finally, although flavorings are a matter of individual taste, I wanted to try a range of spices, extracts and zests to find out if any of them could compete with just plain cinnamon.

Considering that there are some 7,000 apple varieties in the world, I decided to limit my tests to 11 common types found at my local grocery stores at the peak of the fall season (I disqualified Red Delicious, based on its poor performance in my previous baking experiences): Jonagold, Fuji, Golden Delicious, Winesap, Braeburn, Rome Beauty, Granny Smith, Macoun, Cortland, McIntosh and Empire.

Testing the Apple Varieties

To qualify, the apple needed to hold its shape, soften without turning mushy or leathery and retain its distinct, perfumey flavor during cooking. Granny Smiths held their shape well, but lacked the perfumey apple flavor of the McIntosh, Macoun and Empire (another Mac offspring). On the other hand, the McIntosh apples, although wonderfully fragrant, fell apart at the first sign of heat. Jonagolds, Braeburns and Romes scored fairly high in both texture and flavor.

(See page 319 for more detailed results.)

A friend had told me that her grandmother used a variety of apples to make her pie, always including a soft-textured McIntosh. Since I had a hodgepodge of apples left over from testing, I selected a group of the firmer apples, as well as a McIntosh. During baking, the firm apples held up well, while the McIntosh softened, acting as a binder to further thicken and unify the filling. The pie made with a mix turned out to be the best one of all.

Harvest Time

After testing this recipe in both fall and spring, I've found that spring apples, after several months in storage, are drier and less flavorful than freshly harvested fall ones. In the fall, the softer apples such as McIntosh fell apart and helped unify the apples. In the spring, however, they dissolved after only a few minutes of heat. For that reason, it's best to save apple pie making for its traditional season: fall and early winter, when apples are at their peak.

The Right Flavorings

Apple pie flavorings are personal, and I happen to be a cinnamon fan. To decide if there was anything that could lure me away from the classic pairing, I made several small pies with a variety of flavorings and spices. After tasting a dozen or so, I didn't find another spice or spice combination—cloves, allspice and ginger included—that I preferred.

Even though citrus juice and zest add flavor and prevent fruit discoloration, I left both out of the final recipe. The citrus-spiked apples tasted clean, fresh and perky, but I craved a richer, more luxurious flavor. Rose water, a common ingredient in heirloom recipes, made the apples smell sweet, yet taste savory. Vermouth and nutmeg were savory influences as well—perfect for apples with pork but not for pie. Almond extract, a natural with peaches and pears, clashed with apples. Vanilla, on the other hand, enhanced and rounded out the apple fragrance, while cognac offered depth and richness. I ended up with a simple trio of flavorings—cinnamon for flavor, vanilla for smoothness and cognac for depth.

Sweeteners

Sugar is the most commonly used sweetener, but a number of recipes recommended others. After tasting pies with honey, dark brown sugar, light brown sugar and a mix of equal parts brown and granulated sugar, I decided to stick with granulated. Most of the more distinctly flavored sweeteners interfered with the apple flavor, especially dark brown sugar and honey. In addition, both types of brown sugar turned the apples a dirty brown.

Thickening Techniques

My next set of tests, although designed to address the issue of apple shrinkage in the pie shell, solved a number of other problems as well. There were three potential solutions offered by cookbooks: I could drain, sauté or stew the apples to shrink them before, not after, they hit the pie shell.

The recipes that advocated draining called for tossing the apples with sugar and flavorings and setting them in a colander over a bowl. The recipe writers differed, however, in their handling of the drained apple liquid. One simply added the liquid along with the apples to the pie shell. Another boiled the liquid to a syrup, then tossed it in. A third reduced the drained liquid to a syrup and added this syrup to the apples through a vent hole after the pie was baked. After trying each of these methods, I found that none went far enough to prevent apple shrinkage, and the recipe that added the syrup to the pie after baking was abnormally juicy.

The sautéed apple recipe required a full 5 pounds of apples to fill the pie. To sauté this quantity properly, I had to cook, flavor and enrich the apples in three separate batches—a time-consuming effort. Although this method took care of the gap—the crust rested perfectly over the apples in this pie—the apples didn't meld together to form a unified filling, but instead were tough, leathery and slippery.

The winning technique came from the baking expert and cookbook author Nick Malgieri, whose Ultimate Apple Pie appears in *Nick Malgieri's Perfect Pastry* (Macmillan, 1989). The apples are cooked, covered, in butter and sugar until their juices release. The pan is uncovered, and the apples continue to cook until the juices reduce to a thin syrup. The hot apples are then cooled to room temperature before being turned into the pie shell. (This step doesn't take long if the apples are spread out on a baking sheet, and on a cold day, they'll cool outside in less than 15 minutes.) Not only did I find that this method solved the shrinkage problem, but I also discovered that the juices thickened enough to eliminate the need for thickener.

For those who prefer to bake their apples in the shell, I tested thickeners too—flour, cornstarch, arrowroot, potato starch, instant tapioca and tapioca flour. I was surprised to prefer flour. Arrowroot, cornstarch and potato starch all performed similarly, producing nicely thickened apple pies with clean, clear juices. Instant tapioca made the apple filling too thick and jellylike, while the tapioca flour-thickened pie was quite dry; both tapioca pies also had a distinct grain flavor. Interestingly, the day-old tapioca pies developed an unpleasant sourness. I liked the richness and hominess of the flour-thickened juices as compared to the clean, clear juices of the other thickeners.

The Crust

As for the crust, my friend and colleague Chris Kimball had done my homework for me. Having made scores of crusts to come up with the winning pie dough combination, Chris determined that two parts all-purpose flour to one part fat makes a wonderfully flavored, beautifully textured crust. For the fat, a high proportion of butter (for flavor) is coupled with a smaller amount of shortening (for flakiness). When working with a high-fat dough such as this one, there are a few tricks to getting the dough mixed, rolled, into the pan and baked (see page 318).

PIE CRUST PRINCIPLES

♦ Butter and shortening should be well chilled. If they are not, the dough will be difficult to work with and the resulting crust will not be flaky. When making pie dough, I quarter a stick of refrigerated butter lengthwise, cutting the long quarters crosswise into small pieces. I put these butter pieces into the freezer while making ice water and measuring the flour. Because I usually keep a couple of sticks of shortening in the freezer, I simply cut off the amount needed for the dough.

♦ A food processor is the best tool to cut fat quickly into flour. Because chilled butter is much harder than chilled shortening, it is better to pulse the butter into the flour a few times before adding the shortening. Overprocessing causes the butter and flour to break down too much, resulting in a less-than-flaky crust. Make sure to leave lots of pea-size or larger pieces of butter in the flour.

♦ Before adding the ice water, pour the fat-flour mixture into a bowl rather than continuing in the food processor. This extra step ensures that the dough will not be overprocessed.

♦ Always refrigerate the dough before rolling it out. It needs a chance to relax. If you skip this step, the dough will most likely shrink when baked.

♦ Because a really cold dough is difficult to work with, you may need to let it sit at room temperature for 10 minutes or so before rolling it out.

♦ For a foolproof method of rolling, place the disk of dough in a 2-gallon zipper-lock plastic bag and roll it to the desired circumference. When you are ready to put the dough into the pan, cut down the sides of the bag with scissors and remove the top of the bag, exposing the dough. Flip the dough into the pie pan. Peel off the remaining piece of plastic and discard.

♦ To ensure that the dough is well chilled before baking, place the filled pie in the freezer for 10 to 15 minutes while preheating the oven.

THE RIGHT MIX OF APPLES

FOR A PIE, you need a fairly large quantity of apples that hold their shape during cooking and a smaller number of soft apples that fall apart and unify the rest. This list includes the most common grocery store varieties. To test an apple variety for pie for yourself, simply sauté the slices and see if they stay firm or fall apart.

APPLES THAT HOLD THEIR SHAPE

♦ **Braeburn**—Great texture. Soft but holds its shape. A little on the sweet side, so you may want to use less sugar.

♦ **Golden Delicious**—Holds its shape fairly well but on the mushy side. Very juicy. Flavor has no complexity.

♦ **Granny Smith**—Holds its shape fairly well. Not as appley tasting as the others, but fine when teamed with a perfumey, softer apple.

♦ **Jonagold**—Medium juicy, pale golden yellow, good texture. Tastes like a really good golden delicious apple. Great flavor.

♦ **Rome Beauty**—Very nice texture—soft but hold its shape nicely. Quite juicy. Old fashioned, multidimensional flavor. A little sweet, so cut back on sugar.

♦ **Winesap (Stayman)**—Fairly tart, the right juiciness and texture, but without complex apple flavor. Best teamed with a more flavorful variety.

APPLES THAT SOFTEN

♦ **Cortland**—Good complex flavor, with well-rounded sweetness.

♦ **Empire**—Fairly juicy. Quite tart and perfumey.

♦ **Macoun**—Not very juicy. Nice, soft pink color. Great flavor.

♦ **McIntosh**—Turns to applesauce when cooked. Pretty pink hue. Quite sweet.

APPLES NOT RECOMMENDED FOR PIE BAKING

♦ **Fuji**—Very flat in flavor with a texture like that of reconstituted dehydrated apple.

♦ **Red Delicious**—Flavorless when baked. Save this one for brown-bag lunches.

Blue Ribbon Apple Pie

MAKES ONE 9-INCH PIE, SERVING 8

FOR BEST RESULTS, make this pie from late summer through late fall, when apples are fresh. After that, apples are put into storage, where they dehydrate and lose their fresh flavor and crisp texture.

Pie Dough

2¼	cups all-purpose flour
1	teaspoon salt
2	tablespoons sugar
11	tablespoons (1 stick plus 3 tablespoons) unsalted butter, chilled and cut into ¼-inch pieces
7	tablespoons vegetable shortening, chilled

Apple Filling

4	tablespoons (½ stick) unsalted butter
3½	pounds apples that hold their shape during baking (page 319), peeled, quartered, cored and sliced ¼ inch thick
½	pound McIntosh or other apples that soften and thicken pie (page 319), peeled, quartered, cored and sliced ¼ inch thick
¾	cup sugar
¾	teaspoon ground cinnamon
2	tablespoons cognac, brandy or applejack
1	teaspoon vanilla extract
1	egg white
1	tablespoon sugar

1. Pie Dough: Mix flour, salt and sugar in a food processor fitted with a steel blade. Scatter butter pieces over flour mixture, tossing to coat butter with a little flour. Cut butter into flour with five 1-second pulses. Add shortening and continue pulsing until flour is pale yellow and resembles coarse cornmeal, with butter bits no larger than small peas, about 4 more 1-second pulses. Turn mixture into a medium bowl.

2. Sprinkle 5 tablespoons ice water over mixture. With a rubber spatula, use a folding motion to mix. Press down on dough with broad side of spatula until dough sticks together, adding up to 1 tablespoon more ice water if necessary.

3. Divide dough into 2 balls, one slightly larger than other. Flatten each into 4-inch-wide disk. Dust lightly with flour, wrap in plastic and refrigerate for at least 30 minutes. (Dough can be refrigerated overnight.)

4. Apple Filling: Meanwhile, heat butter in a large (11-to-12 inch) skillet over medium-high heat. Add apples slices, sugar and cinnamon, and when they start to sizzle and steam, reduce heat to low. Cover pan and simmer until apples soften and release their juices, about 8 minutes. Uncover, increase heat to medium-high and cook, stirring frequently, until softer apples start to fall apart and juices thicken to thin syrup consistency, about 5 minutes longer. Transfer apples to a jelly roll pan; refrigerate or set in a cool place until apples cool to room temperature. Stir in cognac, brandy or applejack and vanilla extract.

5. Adjust oven rack to lowest position and preheat oven to 400°F. Remove larger dough disk from refrigerator. (Let stand to soften slightly if refrigerated for longer than 30 minutes.) Roll disk out on a lightly floured surface into a 12-inch circle, about ⅛ inch thick. Transfer and fit dough into a 9-inch ovenproof glass pie pan, leaving any overhanging dough in place. Turn cooled apples into pie shell.

6. Roll smaller dough disk out on a lightly floured surface into a 10-inch circle. Lay it over fruit. Trim top and bottom edges to ½ inch beyond pan lip. Tuck this rim of dough underneath itself so that folded edge is flush with pan lip. Flute dough or press with fork tines to seal. Cut 4 vents at right angles on top of dough to allow steam to escape. Brush pie top with egg white and sprinkle with sugar. Freeze pie for 15 minutes.

7. Place pie on a baking sheet and bake until top crust is golden, about 15 minutes. Reduce oven temperature to 350°F and continue baking until crust is golden brown and juices bubble, 30 to 35 minutes. Transfer to a wire rack; cool slightly. Serve warm.

Apple-Cranberry Pie with Crumble Topping

MAKES ONE 9-INCH PIE, SERVING 8

THIS BROWN-SUGAR crumble topping is a great match for the tart cranberries.

Pie Dough

- 1¼ cups all-purpose flour
- ½ teaspoon salt
- 1 tablespoon sugar
- 6 tablespoons (¾ stick) unsalted butter, chilled and cut into ¼-inch pieces
- 4 tablespoons vegetable shortening, chilled

Crumble Topping

- 9 tablespoons all-purpose flour
- 6 tablespoons packed light brown sugar
- 6 tablespoons sugar
- ½ cup quick rolled oats
- 1 stick (½ cup) unsalted butter, chilled and cut into 1-inch pieces
- ½ cup chopped walnuts

Apple-Cranberry Filling

- 4 tablespoons (½ stick) unsalted butter
- 3½ pounds apples that hold their shape during baking (page 319), peeled, quartered, cored and sliced ¼ inch thick
- ½ pound McIntosh or other apples that soften and thicken pie (page 319), peeled, quartered, cored and sliced ¼ inch thick
- ¾ cup sugar
- ¾ teaspoon ground cinnamon

2   tablespoons cognac, brandy or applejack
1   teaspoon vanilla extract
¾   cup picked-over cranberries (fresh or frozen)

1. Pie Dough: Follow steps 1 and 2 of recipe for Blue Ribbon Apple Pie (page 320), to make a single pie shell, adding 3 to 4 tablespoons ice water to flour mixture and flattening and refrigerating as directed in step 3.

2. Crumble Topping: Mix flour, sugars, oats and butter in a food processor fitted with a steel blade; pulse to combine. Add walnuts; pulse until pea-size crumbs form; set aside.

3. Apple-Cranberry Filling: Follow step 4, adding cranberries to cooled apple mixture.

4. Continue as directed in step 5, crumbling topping over apples in place of top portion of dough. Bake until topping begins to brown, 20 to 25 minutes. Reduce heat to 350°F and continue to bake until topping is rich dark brown, about 25 minutes more. Cool and serve as directed.

◆ Sour Cream Apple Pie

Use either double crust in Blue Ribbon Apple Pie (page 320) or Crumble Topping in Apple-Cranberry Pie. Follow recipe for Blue Ribbon Apple Pie, stirring ½ cup sour cream into cooled apples in step 4. Continue as directed.

◆ Apple Pie with Cheddar Cheese

Follow steps 1 to 5 of recipe for Blue Ribbon Apple Pie, sprinkling 1 cup (3 ounces) grated cheddar cheese over apples in pie shell. Top with remaining dough and continue as directed.

Infallible Lemon Meringue Pie

MOST EVERYBODY loves lemon meringue pie —at least the bottom half of it. The controversial part is the meringue. Of all the people I've talked to, I know only one person who admits to adoring the meringue. Most consider it penance for the pleasures of the filling and crust. For cooks, meringue falls into the category of unsolvable culinary mysteries. On any given day, it can shrink, bead, puddle, deflate, burn, sweat, break down or turn rubbery. Most cookbooks don't even attempt to deal with this dilemma but simply run the standard meringue topping recipe: sugar and cream of tartar beaten slowly into the egg whites. After making 30 lemon meringue pies, I'm not sure I blame anyone for skirting the issue.

My goals in developing the ultimate lemon meringue pie were clear. I wanted a pie with a crisp, flaky crust. I wanted a filling rich enough to balance the airy meringue without compromising the clear lemon flavor; soft but not runny; firm enough to cut but not stiff and gelatinous. And I wanted to develop a meringue that didn't break down and puddle on the bottom, waterlogging the crust or developing teardrops on top, even on rainy days.

A Formula for the Filling

For at least the last century, the main ingredients of the lemon filling have remained pretty much constant: sugar, water (sometimes milk), cornstarch (sometimes part flour), egg yolks, lemon juice (and usually zest) and a little butter. To start, I analyzed about 50 recipes and developed a formula that was representative:

> 1½ cups sugar
> 6 tablespoons cornstarch
> ¼ teaspoon salt
> 2 cups water
> 3 large egg yolks
> ½ cup lemon juice and 2 teaspoons zest
> 2 tablespoons unsalted butter

I preferred the clear, straightforward lemon flavor of the water-based filling, but it was one-dimensional, lacking depth. The milk-based filling, a Key lime cousin, was rich, mellow and delicious, but the lemon flavor was too subdued. I thought a water-milk combination might be the answer. To my surprise, though, the fillings made with this mixture were the color of butterscotch. The flavor was fine, the color totally unacceptable. While trying to fix the color, I also wanted to improve the pie's texture. The original was thick in a gelatinous way. I now had two other choices for enriching the pie—eggs and butter. I had less faith that butter would solve this problem, so I focused on eggs.

Because I wanted a tidy formula—the same number of whites in the meringue as yolks in the filling—I at first limited the filling to three yolks, which would also keep the meringue to a minimum. But after making pies with four, five and six yolks, I finally realized that the pies tasted progressively richer with each yolk, without compromising the lemon flavor. The eggs also reinforced the pie's yellow color.

Focusing on the sugar, I found that the fillings made with 1½ cups sugar were significantly softer textured than the pies made with 1 cup. By decreasing the sugar and increasing the egg yolks, both of which firmed up the pie, I was able to cut back on cornstarch. These changes gave me the firm yet tender filling I was looking for.

Graham-Cracker Crisp

I tried four different methods to keep the pie shell crisp. I baked one shell until almost fully cooked, brushed it with beaten egg white, then returned it to the oven until fully cooked. I baked another shell exactly the same way, brushing it with beaten yolk instead of white. I brushed a third fully baked shell with seedless raspberry jam, as suggested by a few southern-style lemon meringue pie recipes.

The jam was completely ineffective. The filling, which must be poured into the shell while it's piping hot to keep the meringue from weeping, heats up the jam, causing it to bleed. Although the yolk-brushed crust was crisper and drier than the white-brushed crust, neither was as impressive as the one I produced from a technique suggested in *Pie Marches On* by Monroe Boston Strause (Ahrens Publishing, 1939), a book I would never have discovered without the help of Nahum Waxman, owner of Manhattan's Kitchen Arts and Letters, a bookstore devoted to food and wine.

Although this book is geared primarily to the food service industry of a half century ago, Strause's tip of rolling both sides of the pie dough in graham cracker crumbs enlightened this nineties cook. The trick not only promotes browning and therefore crisps the crust, it also adds a wonderful graham flavor that complements the lemon, and it keeps the pie shell from shrinking and losing its shape during baking.

Meringue Without Tears

With each filling and crust experiment, I tried a new meringue topping. Long after I had settled on the perfect filling and crust, I was still defeated by meringue. I couldn't find a consistently perfect recipe. Stormy weather during the first two days of testing blew me off course. I attributed all the weeps and tears to the weather. After almost settling for a less-than-perfect meringue, I called the food scientist Shirley Corriher, who convinced me that the problems with meringue topping were not weather-related. According to Corriher, the puddling that forms underneath the meringue is the result of undercooking, as the undercooked whites break down and return to their liquid state. The beading on top of the pie, in contrast, is caused by overcooking, which causes the proteins in the egg white to coagulate, squeezing the moisture to the surface of the baked meringue.

To prevent undercooking, Corriher said, the filling must be piping hot, and she urged me to make the meringue first, then the filling. Through the course of all my testing, once the filling was cooked, I had covered its surface with plastic wrap to insulate it while making the meringue. Sometimes my meringues puddled; sometimes they didn't. When I followed Corriher's suggestion, I found that the delicate meringue deteriorated by the time the filling was made. I tried another strategy. I made the filling and covered it as usual, but during the final minute or so of beating the meringue, I returned the filling just to a simmer over low heat. I poured this superhot filling into the shell and promptly topped and sealed it with meringue and immediately placed the pie in the oven to bake. I followed this procedure with a number of differently prepared meringues, none of which puddled or wept.

To solve the problem of overcooking, Corriher suggested that the whites in the meringue needed to be stabilized, making them more heat-tolerant. Cornstarch, the yolk stabilizer in the filling, could also be used to strengthen the whites. I mixed cornstarch and water and cooked them together until thick. Then I gradually beat this paste into the soft-peak meringue until firm peaks formed.

I found that this cornstarch mixture did not adversely affect the flavor or texture of the meringue. After a bit more tinkering with the oven time and temperature, I finally got the cornstarch-stabilized meringue to produce a virtually tearless pie, even on a hot, humid day.

The Ultimate Lemon Meringue Pie

MAKES ONE 9-INCH PIE, SERVING 8

AFTER MAKING THE MERINGUE, reheat the lemon filling before pouring it into the pie shell, so that the meringue does not weep. Beating the cornstarch mixture into the meringue not only prevents beading, but also keeps the meringue from shrinking.

Graham Cracker-Coated Pie Shell

- 1¼ cups all-purpose flour
- 1 tablespoon sugar
- ½ teaspoon salt
- 6 tablespoons (¾ stick) unsalted butter, chilled and cut into ¼-inch pieces
- 4 tablespoons vegetable shortening, chilled
- ½ cup graham cracker crumbs

Lemon Filling

- 1 cup sugar
- ¼ cup cornstarch
- ⅛ teaspoon salt
- 6 large egg yolks
- 1 tablespoon zest from 1 lemon
- ½ cup juice from 2-3 lemons
- 2 tablespoons unsalted butter

Meringue Topping

- 1 tablespoon cornstarch
- ¼ teaspoon cream of tartar
- ½ cup sugar
- 4 large egg whites
- ½ teaspoon vanilla extract

1. Pie Shell: Mix flour, sugar and salt in a food processor fitted with a steel blade. Scatter butter pieces over flour mixture, tossing to coat butter with a little flour. Cut butter into flour with five 1-second pulses. Add shortening; continue cutting in until mixture resembles coarse cornmeal with butter bits about the size of small peas, about 4 more 1-second pulses. Turn mixture into a medium bowl.

2. Sprinkle 3 tablespoons ice water over mixture. Using a rubber spatula, fold water into flour mixture. Press down on dough mixture with broad side of spatula until dough sticks together, adding up to 1 tablespoon more ice water if necessary. Shape dough into a ball with your hands, then flatten into a 4-inch-wide disk. Dust lightly with flour, wrap in plastic, and refrigerate at least 30 minutes before rolling.

3. Generously sprinkle an 18-inch work surface with 2 tablespoons graham cracker crumbs. Remove dough from wrapping; place disk in center of crumbs. Scatter a few more crumbs over disk top. Roll dough from center to edges into a 9-inch disk, rotating dough a quarter turn after each stroke and sprinkling additional crumbs underneath and on top as necessary to coat dough heavily. Flip dough and continue to roll, but not rotate, to a 13-inch disk, just under ⅛ inch thick.

4. Fold dough in quarters; place dough point in center of a 9-inch ovenproof pie pan. Unfold dough to cover pan completely, with excess dough draped over pan lip. Lift edge of dough with one hand and press dough into pan bottom with other hand; repeat process around circumference of pan to ensure that dough fits properly in pan and is not stretched in any way. Trim dough to ½ inch beyond lip all around. Tuck overhanging dough back under itself so folded edge is flush with lip of pan; press to seal. Flute dough by pressing thumb and index finger about ½ inch apart against outside edge, then use index finger or knuckle of other hand to poke a dent on inside edge through space created by other fingers. Repeat fluting around perimeter of pie shell.

5. Refrigerate dough until firm, about 30 minutes; prick shell at ½-inch intervals. Press a doubled 12-inch square of aluminum foil inside pie shell. Prick again to keep dough from ballooning during baking. Freeze pie shell while oven is preheating.

6. Adjust oven rack to lowest position and preheat oven to 375°F. Bake shell, checking occasionally to make sure it is not ballooning, pricking it if necessary, until shell is firmly set, about 15 minutes. Remove foil and continue to bake until shell is crisp and rich brown, about 10 minutes more.

7. Lemon Filling: Whisk sugar, cornstarch and salt together in a large, nonreactive saucepan. Add egg yolks, then immediately but gradually whisk in 1½ cups water. Bring mixture to a simmer over medium heat, whisking occasionally at beginning and more frequently as mixture begins to thicken, 8 to 10 minutes. Whisk in zest, then lemon juice and finally butter. Bring mixture to a good simmer, whisking constantly; simmer for 1 minute. Remove from heat, place plastic wrap directly on surface of filling to keep hot and to prevent a skin from forming.

8. Meringue Topping: Mix cornstarch and ⅓ cup water in a small saucepan. Bring to a simmer, whisking occasionally at beginning and more frequently as mixture thickens. When mixture starts to simmer and turn translucent, remove from heat.

9. Preheat oven to 325°F. Mix cream of tartar and sugar together. Beat egg whites with vanilla until frothy. Beat in sugar mixture, 1 tablespoon at a time, until sugar is incorporated and whites form soft peaks. Drop in warm cornstarch mixture, 1 tablespoon at a time, and continue to beat meringue to stiff peaks. Return saucepan of filling to very low heat during last minute or so of beating meringue to ensure that filling is hot.

10. Immediately pour filling into pie shell. Promptly distribute meringue evenly around edge, then center of pie, with a rubber spatula to keep it from sinking into filling and making sure it attaches to pie shell to prevent shrinking. Use back of a spoon to create peaks all over meringue. Bake until meringue is golden brown, about 20 minutes. Transfer to a wire rack and cool to room temperature. Serve.

Incredible Cream Pies

CHOCOLATE, banana, coconut and butterscotch—everyone has a favorite cream pie. Virtually no one can resist their allure. My mission in achieving perfection was to isolate the pie's four components—the filling, the crust, the flavoring ingredients and the whipped cream—and make certain that each was the best it could be. The filling required the greatest effort. What cooking method and thickener guarantees a substantial yet velvety filling? What combination of ingredients is unobtrusive enough to complement the richness of the crust and whipped cream, yet lush and irresistible on its own?

Equally important is a crisp crust. Some recipes instructed bakers to pour hot filling into the cooked pie shell. But wouldn't steam from the hot filling dampen the crust? Others suggested cooling the filling to warm, while still others required completely chilling the pie, uniting the filling with the crust shortly before serving.

Then there were flavoring questions. Does a great chocolate cream pie require bittersweet chocolate, cocoa or both?

Does the best coconut cream pie demand fresh coconut, or is sweetened, flaked coconut just as good? Should it be toasted? For banana cream pie, where do the bananas go—on the bottom, in the middle, on top or mashed and folded in? How can they be kept from turning brown?

Finally, once the pie is assembled, can the whipped cream hold up for several hours without any help or does it have to be whipped with gelatin, corn syrup, confectioners' sugar or anything else to keep it from disintegrating?

Filling First

After examining a range of cream-pie fillings, I developed a basic recipe consisting of milk, egg yolks, sugar, cornstarch, butter, vanilla flavoring and a pinch of salt. Some recipes were lean, using skim milk and whole eggs, while others were extravagant, with heavy cream and yolks. To find out just how rich the filling needed to be, I started by testing the range of milks, making the filling with skim milk, 2-percent, whole milk, half-and-half, evaporated milk and cream.

Because skim milk is translucent, the

yolks colored the filling a vivid yellow, but the filling tasted thin and lacked the creaminess that is desirable in pudding. I liked the fillings made from 2-percent and whole milk; 2-percent offered just enough fat to enrich without masking other flavors, and whole milk offered a slightly fuller flavor. Both the half-and-half- and the cream-enriched fillings were too much of a good thing, especially when teamed with a butter-rich crust, a generous mound of whipped cream and flavoring ingredients like coconut, bananas or chocolate.

Evaporated milk, the dark horse in this little series of tests, showed promise. Although the filling made with straight evaporated milk revealed its presence too distinctly, its rich caramel flavor had potential. I finally reduced the evaporated milk to ½ cup for every 2 cups of regular milk. Compared to a filling made with all milk, the evaporated milk-enriched filling has a deeper color and rounder, subtly caramelized flavor.

Deciding on the number of eggs or yolks was a fairly simple exercise. The fillings made with whole eggs were grainy and characterless, lacking the smooth, velvety texture and richness of the all-yolk fillings. An excessive amount of yolks turned my pie filling into a pastry cream, more appropriate for a tart. A generous five yolks produced the silky texture I sought.

Cornstarch Works Better Than Flour

I wanted a cream pie filling that was soft and creamy, yet stiff enough to cut cleanly. Flour gave me a soft, gummy result, producing a messy cut. Gelatin required additional thickeners, and although it certainly gave a clean cut, it was at the cost of a rubbery texture. Tapioca did not work: quick-cooking tapioca contributed its distinctive fish-eye texture, while tapioca flour produced a filling with the texture of stewed okra. A combination of flour and cornstarch made a filling that was too soft to cut properly. I returned to cornstarch for thickness, coupled with yolks for softness and creaminess.

At this point, my pie filling had the right texture, richness and creaminess, but it was still dependent on extra ingredients like coconut and bananas to become notable. Switching from vanilla extract to vanilla bean and adding a touch of brandy nudged a mediocre filling into the realm of greatness.

I had two choices for the filling procedure. Some cooks heat the sugar, cornstarch and milk to a simmer, gradually add a portion of this mixture to the yolks, then add the yolks to the simmering milk. My other choice was to dump everything (except the flavorings and the butter) into a saucepan and cook, stirring fairly constantly, until the thickened mixture began to bubble. Because starch prevents eggs from curdling, I opted for the latter, simpler method.

The Right Temperature, Flavorings and Topping

To determine how the crust would respond to fillings of various temperatures, I made three pies. The first shell contained hot filling straight from the saucepan. The second pie shell held filling that had cooled for 30 minutes. I refrigerated these pies for three hours. Finally, I spooned chilled filling into the third crust and refrigerated it for an hour.

To my surprise, neither the hot nor the warm fillings dampened their shells. The warm filling, having had a chance to set a bit, mounded when poured into the shell, whereas the hot filling settled more evenly. When cut, the denser, hot filling tended to fall apart. The pie with warm filling sliced more neatly, standing peaked and tall.

The chilled filling—the one you might think would work best—turned soupy and moistened my once-crisp crust. You can cool the filling a bit, but once the filling has set, don't stir it.

Because cocoa and chocolate differ from brand to brand, chocolate cream pie was the most difficult to perfect. I ultimately determined that a good filling needs a little cocoa and a little semisweet or bittersweet chocolate, the former for a lingering chocolate flavor, the latter for intensity.

I soon discovered that cream pie made with fresh coconut is not worth the effort. I preferred the fine long shreds of store-bought sweetened flaked coconut to the coarser, woody texture of the fresh variety. The difference between toasted and untoasted coconut in a cream pie is dramatic. Untoasted coconut offers little more than texture, while toasted coconut brings the pie to life.

For banana cream pie, simply sandwich the banana slices between layers of filling. If you place them over the pie shell, they tend to moisten the crust. If you place them over the filling or mash and fold them into it, they turn brown. Slice them with a very sharp knife; a dull one causes them to turn brown faster.

Whipped cream requires no special tricks to hold up on the pie overnight. I thought confectioners' sugar would be my sweetener of choice, but after the cream was whipped, I could tell no difference between creams whipped with different sugars. But if you have a choice between pasteurized and ultrapasteurized cream, choose the former. Although it has a shorter shelf life, it tastes noticeably fresher than ultrapasteurized.

Vanilla Cream Pie

MAKES ONE 9-INCH PIE, SERVING 8

ANY LEFTOVER PIE can be refrigerated and eaten the next day, but it is best eaten the day it is made.

Graham Cracker-Coated Pie Shell (page 327)

Vanilla Filling

- 10 tablespoons sugar
- ¼ cup cornstarch
- ⅛ teaspoon salt
- 5 large egg yolks, lightly beaten
- 2 cups milk
- ½ cup evaporated milk
- 1 1½-inch-long vanilla bean, split lengthwise
- 2 tablespoons unsalted butter
- 1 teaspoon brandy

Cream Topping

- 1 cup heavy whipping cream
- 2 tablespoons sugar
- ½ teaspoon vanilla extract

1. Pie Shell: Follow steps 1 to 6 in recipe for the Ultimate Lemon Meringue Pie (page 327).

2. Vanilla Filling: Whisk sugar, cornstarch and salt in a medium saucepan. Add yolks, then immediately but gradually whisk in milk and evaporated milk. Drop in vanilla bean. Cook over medium heat, stirring frequently at first, then constantly, as mixture starts to thicken, 8 to 10 minutes. Once mixture begins to simmer, continue to cook, stirring constantly, for 1 minute more. Remove vanilla bean, scrape out seeds and whisk them back into pudding along with butter and brandy.

3. Pour filling into a shallow pan (a pie pan works well). Put plastic wrap directly over surface to prevent a skin from forming; cool until just warm, about 30 minutes. (If filling cools for too long, it can turn soupy once transferred into pie shell.) Pour warm filling into fully baked pie shell and place a sheet of plastic wrap over filling surface. Refrigerate until completely chilled, at least 3 hours.

4. Cream Topping: Whip cream to soft peaks. Add sugar and vanilla; continue to whip to barely stiff peaks. Spread over filling and refrigerate until ready to serve.

♦ Chocolate Cream Pie

Follow recipe for Vanilla Cream Pie (page 333), adding 2 tablespoons unsweetened cocoa to cornstarch mixture in step 2 and stirring 4 ounces chopped semisweet or bittersweet chocolate in with butter. Substitute 1 teaspoon vanilla extract for vanilla bean. Continue as directed.

♦ Coconut Cream Pie

1. Adjust oven rack to lower-middle position and preheat oven to 300°F. Scatter 1¼ cups sweetened flaked coconut in a 9-inch square pan. Bake, stirring occasionally, until evenly golden brown, 20 to 25 minutes. Cool to room temperature.

2. Follow recipe for Vanilla Cream Pie (page 333), stirring 1 cup toasted coconut into filling once butter has melted in step 2. Continue as directed, sprinkling remaining ¼ cup toasted coconut over whipped cream topping.

♦ Banana Cream Pie

Follow recipe for Vanilla Cream Pie (page 333), spooning half of warm filling into baked and cooled pie shell. Peel, then slice, 2 medium bananas over filling. Top with remaining filling. Continue as directed, garnishing with a few banana slices, if you like.

Butterscotch Cream Pie

MAKES ONE 9-INCH PIE, SERVING 8

ALTHOUGH THE PROCESS of caramelizing the sugar makes this pie a bit more work than the others, it is one of my favorites. Don't worry if the sugar lumps a little when you pour the milk into it; it will dissolve as the milk heats.

Graham Cracker-Coated Pie Shell (page 327)

Butterscotch Filling

- ¼ cup cornstarch
- ¼ teaspoon salt
- ½ cup evaporated milk
- 5 large egg yolks
- 6 tablespoons unsalted butter
- 1 cup packed light brown sugar
- 2 cups whole milk
- 1 teaspoon vanilla extract

Cream Topping (page 333)

1. Pie Shell: Follow steps 1 to 6 of recipe for the Ultimate Lemon Meringue Pie (page 327).

2. Butterscotch Filling: Dissolve cornstarch and salt in evaporated milk; whisk in eggs and set aside.

3. Meanwhile, heat butter and brown sugar in a medium saucepan over medium heat until a candy thermometer registers 220°F, about 5 minutes. Gradually whisk in whole milk. Once sugar dissolves, gradually whisk in cornstarch mixture and continue cooking until mixture comes to a boil. Cook for 1 minute more. Off heat, stir in vanilla.

4. Continue as directed in steps 3 and 4 of recipe for Vanilla Cream Pie (page 333).

Exquisite Cheesecake: One Recipe, Three Textures

SOME DISHES have universal standards of perfection. Cheesecake, however, does not fall into this category. For most fans, perfect cheesecake has more to do with texture than flavor. Some cheesecakes are firm and dense; others are rich, lush and creamy. Still others are as light and airy as meringue.

Because it was clear from the beginning of my research that there would be no single perfect cheesecake recipe, my goal was to develop a basic cheesecake whose texture could be altered by changing one ingredient or by altering the baking method. To understand better what influences cheesecake's texture, I tested the key ingredients—cream cheese, eggs, cream and sour cream, as well as a variety of baking methods and temperatures. After three days of testing, not only had I come up with the creamy version I preferred, I had also figured out how to lighten the texture as well as how to make it more dense.

In order to determine the role of each ingredient, I made all my cheesecakes using 1 pound of cream cheese, sugar, eggs, vanilla and a little lemon zest. I baked all the cheesecakes in disposable 8½-inch cake pans in a 300-degree oven until the perimeter jiggled and the center was not quite set. Once I had developed the basic formula, I switched to a 2-pound cream cheese recipe and to springform pans in order to determine the best baking methods, times and temperatures.

Regular Cream Cheese, Please

Because cream cheese is the key ingredient, I started testing cheesecakes made with both fresh cream cheese and Philadelphia brand cream cheese (because I could not test every regional grocery store brand of cream cheese, I settled on this nationally available one). In addition, I tested cakes with Philadelphia brand's Neufchâtel (one-third less fat), light (50 percent less fat) and no-fat cream cheeses.

Fresh cream cheese was not available locally, so I resorted to mail order at $5.50 per pound, plus overnight shipping charges. Although this softer, creamier, tangy cheese was my first choice for spreading on a bagel, it proved too unstable for baking. Unlike any of the other cheesecakes, the one made with fresh cream cheese was grainy after baking and had curdled slightly.

Real cream cheese melts like butter in the mouth, but low-fat and no-fat varieties cling to the tongue. The cakes made from these cheeses also baked differently from those made with regular cream cheese. The Philly Neufchâtel brand, which is whiter, softer and more watery than regular cream cheese, baked more quickly. Even though I pulled it from the oven 10 minutes sooner than any of the other cheesecakes, it cracked. The cake made with this cheese was harder and more crumbly than the cheesecake made with the regular cream cheese.

The Philadelphia brand no-fat cream cheese cake developed a rubbery skin and several muddy shallow cracks during baking. Underneath the skin, the cake was soft and chalky, with an unpleasant artificial taste. Of all the cheesecakes I made, it was the only one I threw away. Although not nearly as bad as the no-fat cream cheese version, the light cream cheese cake tasted artificial as well. It was deceptively creamy at first, but an unmistakable dustiness lingered on the tongue.

The regular Philadelphia cream cheese, which is firmer and denser than fresh cream cheese, resulted in a cheese-cake that was uniformly smooth and creamy.

One Egg, Two Eggs, Three Eggs or Four

To see just how many eggs a cheesecake needs, I tried virtually every sensible combination, starting with a cheesecake made with all egg whites and ending with one made with all yolks. What I learned is that a good cheesecake needs a combination of egg whites and yolks. The all-egg-white cheesecake was dry, while the all-yolk cheesecake and the ones made with whole eggs plus extra yolks tasted more like custard. Two whole eggs (per 1 pound cream cheese) made the cake creamy and tender without tasting overly rich and custardy.

It made sense that folding whipped egg whites into the batter would lighten the cheesecake's texture. So during my egg tests, instead of beating whole eggs in, I separated them, beating the yolks into the cream cheese and sugar, then folding in the whipped whites just before baking. Though my recipe was still in process, I could see that this technique would deliver a rich, creamy, yet light cheesecake.

Indispensable Cream

These simple cheesecakes were perfect for testing individual ingredients, but their relatively dry texture needed softening and their flat flavor needed rounding out. My next set of tests—adding different ratios of sour cream and heavy cream to the batter—made me realize the importance of these two supporting ingredients.

Heavy cream gives cheesecake its signature velvety, smooth texture. Too much, though, and the distinctive cream cheese flavor starts to fade. And while sour cream supports the underlying tang of the cream cheese, it can easily become the dominant flavor. You need a little of each: heavy cream for texture and sour cream for flavor. Topping the cheesecake with sour cream rather than incorporating it into the batter seemed an extra step designed exclusively for hiding those unsightly, center cracks. My plan was to lose the cracks, not cover them up.

Water Bath, Right Path

I already knew that a water bath protects cheesecake from harsh, direct heat that can cause the cake to overcook, crack and sink. But I also knew that this method has its drawbacks. The springform pan must be lined with heavy-duty foil. If the water level exceeds that of the foil lining or if the foil rips, water seeps between foil and pan, and the cake can become waterlogged. Is there an easier way? Does baking the cake over a pan of water work just as well as a water bath? Does baking at a lower temperature without a water bath turn out a velvety cheesecake?

I baked three different cheesecakes at 325 degrees for 1 hour, the first cake in a dry oven; the second at the same temperature over a pan of water on the rack below, and the third in a water bath. The dry-baked cheesecake souffléd, developing hairline cracks around the perimeter toward the end of baking. As it cooled, it developed that familiar center crack. I tasted it: a large area around the perimeter was as grainy as a broken hollandaise—the eggs had clearly overcooked. Only the very center was smooth and creamy.

The cheesecake baked over the pan of water was a step up. It, too, had developed hairline cracks around the perimeter. It had souffléd throughout, not just around the edges. As it cooled, it developed only a tiny center crack. Its surface was off white with a few brown spots. The very outer edges of the cake were overcooked, but the large center area was soft and creamy.

The cake baked in the water bath was perfect—no cracks, no sinking, no spotting. The texture of the outer edges was just as creamy as the center.

For a Dense Cheesecake, a Dry Oven

I knew that moist heat could not deliver a dense cheesecake, which needed gentle, dry heat to evaporate some of the cake's moisture without overcooking the eggs. I tried baking cheesecakes for less time and at lower temperatures. Reduced oven time still delivered cracked cakes. Lower oven temperatures produced cakes that were neither creamy enough to compete with my soft, lush cakes nor dense enough to offer a contrast.

During my research, I had come across an odd baking method in James Villas's *Villas at Table* (Harper and Row, 1988). In his recipe for Lindy's Cheesecake, Villas instructs the cook to bake the cake dry in a blistering 500-degree oven for the first 12 minutes, then at 200 degrees for one hour longer. I followed Villas's instructions and, after 10 minutes, peered in at a beautifully puffed cake. I held the oven door open until the oven temperature was reduced to 200 degrees and baked the cheesecake for another hour. It was beautiful. The high heat had caused the graham cracker crumbs to brown nicely and the eggs to puff. The low heat had gently cooked the cake, keeping the eggs from overcooking, and the dry heat had allowed the cake to slowly dehydrate, creating the dense yet creamy texture I was looking for.

I had developed a creamy cheesecake, a light and fluffy one and a crack-free, smooth-textured dense cheesecake—all from one set of ingredients. The result: cheesecakes with textures to satisfy everyone.

Rich and Creamy Cheesecake

SERVES 12 TO 16

A NUMBER OF CHEESECAKE RECIPES instruct the cook to leave the cake in a turned-off oven once it has cooked. If you turn off the oven when the cheesecake is still slightly underdone in the center, it will slowly and gently set without overcooking.

To avoid having cheesecake stick to the knife every time you cut a slice, you can do one of two things. Dipping the knife in a glass of warm water before each swipe will keep the cheesecake from sticking. You can also get a nice cut using clean dental floss or fishing line.

  1 tablespoon unsalted butter, melted
  3 tablespoons graham cracker crumbs
  2 pounds regular cream cheese
1¼ cups sugar
  4 large eggs
  1 teaspoon zest from 1 small lemon
  2 teaspoons vanilla extract
  ¼ cup heavy cream
  ¼ cup sour cream
    Fresh Berry Sauce with Grand Marnier (optional; page 343)

1. Adjust oven rack to middle position and preheat oven to 325°F. Place foil over bottom disk of a 9-inch springform pan, tucking excess underneath disk; assemble pan. Pull up foil around pan sides. Brush interior of pan with butter. Sprinkle graham cracker crumbs into pan, tilting it in all directions to coat evenly with crumbs. Cover exterior of pan with a sheet of *heavy-duty* foil and set in a large roasting pan. Bring a kettle of water to a boil for water bath.

2. Meanwhile, beat cream cheese with an electric mixer until smooth. Gradually add sugar and beat on medium speed until it is fully incorporated, about 3 minutes. Add eggs, one at a time, beating until just incorporated and scraping down bowl after each addition. (If you don't scrape down bowl after each egg, any cream cheese sticking to sides will make batter lumpy.) Add zest and vanilla and beat until just incorporated. Stir in cream and sour cream by hand.

3. Pour batter into springform pan. Set roasting pan on oven rack, set spring-form pan in it, and pour in enough boiling water to come about halfway up the side of springform pan. Bake until perimeter of cake is set but center jiggles when pan is tapped, 55 to 60 minutes. Turn off heat and leave oven door ajar, using a long-handled kitchen fork or spoon if necessary to hold it open for 1 hour. Remove spring-form pan from water bath and set on a wire rack; cool to room temperature. Cover and refrigerate until chilled, at least 4 hours. Cheesecake can be refrigerated for up to 4 days.

♦ Light and Airy Cheesecake

Follow steps 1 and 2 of recipe for Rich and Creamy Cheesecake, but separate eggs and add egg yolks, rather than whole eggs, in step 2. Continue with step 2 as directed, stirring cream and sour cream into batter. Beat egg whites to soft peaks. Fold whites into batter, pour batter into prepared pan and bake, reducing cooking time to 45 to 50 minutes. Continue as directed.

♦ Dense and Firm Cheesecake

Follow steps 1 and 2 of recipe for Rich and Creamy Cheesecake, but preheat oven to 500°F. In step 3, omit water bath. Bake cake for 10 minutes. Reduce temperature to 200°F, open oven door and leave open until temperature reduces to 200°F. Close door and bake until perimeter is set, but center jiggles when pan is tapped, about 1 hour more. Turn off heat and leave oven door ajar, as directed. Cool on a wire rack to room temperature and then chill as directed.

♦ Mocha Cheesecake

Follow steps 1 and 2 of recipe for Rich and Creamy Cheesecake, dissolving 3 tablespoons instant coffee granules in heavy cream in step 2 and stirring 2 ounces finely chopped bittersweet or semisweet chocolate (or miniature semisweet chocolate chips) into finished batter. Continue as directed.

♦ Ginger Cheesecake

Follow steps 1 and 2 of recipe for Rich and Creamy Cheesecake (page 340), dissolving 1 tablespoon ground ginger in heavy cream in step 2 and stirring ¼ cup minced candied ginger into finished batter. Continue as directed.

♦ Lemon Cheesecake

Follow steps 1 and 2 of recipe for Rich and Creamy Cheesecake (page 340), stirring 6 tablespoons lemon juice and 4 teaspoons finely grated lemon zest into finished batter. Continue as directed.

♦ Orange Cheesecake

Follow steps 1 and 2 of recipe for Rich and Creamy Cheesecake (page 340), stirring 3 tablespoons orange liqueur (Cointreau, Triple Sec or Grand Marnier) and 4 teaspoons finely grated orange zest into finished batter. Continue as directed.

♦ Chocolate Marble Cheesecake

Follow steps 1 and 2 of recipe for Rich and Creamy Cheesecake (page 340), pouring 2 cups finished batter into a small bowl. Stir 4 ounces melted bittersweet or semisweet chocolate into same bowl. Pour half of white batter into springform pan. Drop half of chocolate batter by tablespoonfuls over white batter. Repeat with remaining batters. Use a chopstick or a wooden spoon handle to pull chocolate batter through white batter to create a swirled effect. Continue as directed.

Fresh Berry Sauce with Grand Marnier

MAKES 2½ TO 3 CUPS

SERVE THIS FRESH FRUIT SAUCE with any of the plain cheesecakes on pages 340-341, or with the Lemon or Orange Cheesecake.

> 2 pints berries (blueberries, strawberries, raspberries), rinsed (stemmed, if using strawberries)
>
> 4-6 tablespoons sugar
>
> 2 tablespoons orange liqueur (Cointreau, Triple Sec or Grand Marnier)

1. Put 1 pint berries in a medium bowl. Use a pastry cutter, fork or potato masher to mash berries coarsely.

2. Puree remaining berries with 4 tablespoons sugar in a food processor fitted with a steel blade. Mix with mashed berries, along with liqueur. Adjust flavorings, adding more sugar if necessary.

3. Let stand at room temperature to allow flavors to blend, at least 30 minutes. (Sauce can be covered and refrigerated for up to 4 hours.)

A Fudgy, Chewy, Cakey Brownie

OF ALL THE RECIPES in this book, brownies was one of the most difficult. With so many excellent published recipes out there—complete books have been written on the subject, for heaven's sake—why all the struggle? There are three different brownie camps—those who like them chewy and gooey, those who prefer them dense and fudgy and a third crowd who like them frosted and cakey. I gave myself the seemingly impossible task of trying to please everyone.

After making a batch of each—chewy, fudgy and cakey—I observed that each brownie style had assets. Cakey brownies offered structure and crumb but lacked the intense chocolate hit of the other two styles. Fudgy brownies packed a lot of chocolate flavor, but their heavy, dense, candylike structure needed a lift. Chewy brownies exhibited an irresistible gooey quality but needed a little crumb definition. I had my marching orders: to develop an intense, rich, chocolatey brownie, with just enough structure and definition.

As always, I started with a composite formula, a common, classic fudgy brownie recipe baked in an 8-inch pan:

    2 ounces unsweetened chocolate
    1 stick unsalted butter
    1 cup sugar
    2 large eggs
    1 teaspoon vanilla extract
    ½ cup all-purpose flour
       Pinch salt

I made batches with lesser and greater amounts of all-purpose flour, and substituted cake flour as well. I tried varying the formula using cocoa or semisweet chocolate, making the necessary sugar and butter adjustments. I made brownies with greater and lesser quantities of each chocolate and combinations of them all. I used various sweeteners—brown sugar and corn syrup—in place of the granulated sugar. I made a batch with baking powder, another with a smaller amount of butter and others with more and less eggs. Although many of the brownies from these initial tests were certainly good, none was outstanding. They were either too dense, too gooey, too dry or too bitter.

To determine whether my original formula was at fault, I made a few off-beat recipes that relied on less common brownie ingredients like cream cheese, sour cream, large quantities of ground nuts or liquor. Though interesting, none was familiar and satisfying.

Brownie Breakthroughs

Although I was a long way from the ultimate recipe, these initial tests did provide some important clues. I discovered that baking powder gives fudgy brownies a lift. A combination of bittersweet and unsweetened chocolate tastes intense without the harsh aftertaste I had often noticed when I used only unsweetened chocolate.

One day I finally got a break when I tasted Mrs. Fields's brownies. Better for Mrs. Fields begins with bigger. My original formula, doubled, follows here in parentheses for comparison with hers:

6 ounces unsweetened chocolate (4 ounces)

2 sticks (16 tablespoons) unsalted butter (2 sticks)

4 large eggs (4 eggs)

2 cups granulated sugar (2 cups)

1 tablespoon vanilla extract (2 teaspoons)

½ cup all-purpose flour (1 cup)

Baking twice the batter in the same size pan solved the height problem. This new recipe also called for a third more chocolate yet only half the flour of the original—a combination I hadn't tried. With the small amount of flour and no leavener, these brownies were a little too fudgy, so I gave them some more structure by increasing the flour to ¾ cup and adding ¾ teaspoon baking powder.

Mrs. Fields's brownies were towering—so much so that I found it difficult to bake them through before the outer edges overcooked. And when cut into small squares, the brownies threatened to topple over. I revised the recipe, diminishing the proportions a bit, until I got a brownie of the perfect height.

After trying the recipe with both bittersweet and unsweetened chocolate, making the necessary sugar and butter changes, I found that the brownies made with unsweetened chocolate alone were drier and more crumbly, with a slightly bitter finish. On the other hand, the brownies made with only bittersweet or semisweet chocolate were too gooey. I made the recipe with half bitter-sweet chocolate and half unsweetened chocolate. The result was exactly what I wanted: borderline decadent with a hint of structure.

Fudgy, Chewy, Cakey Brownies

MAKES 16 BROWNIES

KNOWING WHEN to pull a pan of brownies from the oven is the only difficult part of baking them. If you wait until a toothpick inserted comes clean, they're overcooked. Check your brownies even before the suggested minimum baking time. If a toothpick inserted in the middle comes up with really fudgy crumbs, it's time to take the brownies out and put them on a wire rack for cooling.

⅔ cup all-purpose flour
½ teaspoon salt
½ teaspoon baking powder
Vegetable cooking spray
2 ounces unsweetened chocolate
4 ounces bittersweet or semisweet chocolate
10 tablespoons (1 stick plus 2 tablespoons) unsalted butter
1¼ cups sugar
2 teaspoons vanilla extract
3 large eggs
¾ cup toasted walnuts, pecans, macadamia nuts
   or peanuts (optional)

1. Adjust oven rack to lower-middle position and preheat oven to 325°F.

2. Whisk flour, salt and baking powder in a small bowl; set aside. Spray an 8-inch baking pan with vegetable cooking spray. Fit a 16-by-8-inch sheet of foil in pan and up 2 sides, so you can use foil overhang as a handle to pull cooked brownies from pan. Spray sheet of foil with vegetable cooking spray.

3. Melt chocolates and butter in a medium bowl over a pan of simmering water. Remove from heat; whisk in sugar and vanilla. Whisk in eggs, one at a time, fully incorporating each one before adding the next. Continue to whisk until mixture is completely smooth and glossy. Add dry ingredients; whisk until just incorporated. Stir in nuts, if desired.

4. Pour batter into prepared pan; bake until a toothpick or cake tester inserted into center comes out with wet crumbs, 35 to 45 minutes.

5. Cool brownies in pan on a wire rack for 5 minutes. Use foil handles to pull brownies from pan. Completely cool brownies on rack, at least 3 hours. Cut into squares and serve. If not serving immediately, do not cut brownies. (Whole brownie cake can be wrapped in plastic wrap, then foil, and refrigerated for up to 5 days.)

Fudgy Brownies
with Raspberry-Cream Cheese Swirl

MAKES 16 BROWNIES

WITH THE ADDED CREAM CHEESE, these brownies are a little taller than Fudgy, Chewy, Cakey Brownies (page 346). You may decide to cut them a bit larger, so that they are at least as wide as they are tall.

Raspberry-Cream Cheese Swirl

- ¼ cup sugar
- 8 ounces cream cheese
- 1 large egg yolk
- ½ teaspoon vanilla extract

Brownies

- ⅔ cup all-purpose flour
- ½ teaspoon salt
- ½ teaspoon baking powder
- 2 ounces unsweetened chocolate
- 4 ounces bittersweet or semisweet chocolate
- 10 tablespoons (1 stick plus 2 tablespoons) unsalted butter
- 1¼ cups sugar
- 2 teaspoons vanilla extract
- 3 large eggs

- ¼ cup raspberry jam

1. Raspberry-Cream Cheese Swirl: Mix sugar, cream cheese, egg yolk and vanilla in a small bowl until smooth. Set aside.

2. Brownies: Follow steps 1 to 3 of recipe for Fudgy, Chewy, Cakey Brownies (page 346), omitting nuts. In step 4, pour half of brownie batter into prepared pan. Spread cream-cheese mixture evenly over batter, then top with remaining brownie batter. Spoon raspberry jam by teaspoonful over batter. Use a tablespoon to gently swirl jam, batter and cream cheese filling for a marbled effect.

3. Bake until a toothpick or cake tester inserted in center comes out with wet crumbs, 35 to 40 minutes. Cool as directed.

Just-Right Rolled Cookies

Each holiday season, most food magazines do an obligatory decorated cookie story. To rekindle annual interest, they usually include trendy shapes or the latest decorating techniques. Although I'm attracted to these centerfold cookies as much as the next baker, I find they're more fun to think about than to bake. I wanted a cookie that was simple to make and crisp, tender, light, sturdy and buttery.

Tenderizing ingredients like cornstarch can make cookies fragile. Leaveners like baking powder and soda can lighten cookies, but too much can impart a distinct metallic taste. Egg whites and sugar make for crisp cookies, but an excess of either can turn cookies brittle and hard. Developing the perfect holiday cookie was like walking a culinary tightrope.

Success with Simplicity

What kind of flour? Granulated or confectioners' sugar? Butter, shortening, oil or a combination of some sort? In order to understand the role of each of these ingredients, I developed the following formula:

¾ cup all-purpose flour
¼ cup sugar
¼ cup unsalted butter
1 large egg yolk
½ teaspoon vanilla extract
  Pinch salt

I substituted different flours, sugars and fats, as well as varying quantities of each. Following the formula, I also made doughs with different leaveners, as well as with milk, cream and sour cream standing in for part of the egg. Curious about whether a fresh vanilla bean might make a more flavorful cookie, I scraped flecks of vanilla into a batch. Finally, in an attempt to lighten the cookies without using chemical leaveners, I tried cutting the butter into the flour rather than creaming it with the sugar.

From these initial tests, I learned that my simple formula wasn't far off the mark. Although the recipe needed refining, none of the extra ingredients I had added to the recipe was necessary. Cake flour, cornstarch and smaller quantities of flour as well as confectioners' sugar all made the cookies too tender and fragile. Cookies made with shortening and oil were sandy and lacked flavor.

Although baking powder and soda helped lighten the cookies, their flavors were distracting. Whole egg, rather than all yolk, made the cookies brittle rather than crisp. Adding milk and cream for part of the egg resulted in moist, difficult doughs, and the cookies tasted hard and stale, while sour cream neither helped nor hurt. The flavor of the vanilla bean was disappointingly imperceptible.

Bleached Flour, an Egg Yolk and Superfine Sugar

The cookies made with all-purpose bleached flour were better than those made with unbleached flour. The unbleached flour cookies were chewier, denser, tougher and not nearly as buttery-tasting. Other than that, the formula was still butter, sugar, flour, eggs, vanilla and salt.

To refine the formula as a recipe, I quadrupled the proportions to 3 cups flour, ¼ teaspoon salt, 1 cup butter, 1 cup sugar and 2 teaspoons vanilla. Working in larger quantities allowed me to try a whole egg plus two yolks, rather

than four yolks. Made with that amount of flour, the cookies tasted dry and not very buttery. To solve this problem, I reduced the flour to 2½ cups and eliminated the yolks to compensate for the loss of the dry ingredients. The flavor was excellent, but the whole egg alone still made the cookies brittle and hard.

Adding the egg yolk back into the cookie made it more tender, and increasing the salt to ½ teaspoon rounded out the sugar. Cookies made with even 2 tablespoons less sugar compromised the tender-crisp texture and once again accentuated the flour taste of the dough.

After I described my cookie project to my friend and colleague Gail Naegel-Hopkins, she volunteered that her grandmother always used superfine sugar in her cookies. Using the food processor, I turned my granulated sugar into superfine and made another batch of cookies. They were flavorful, light and fine enough to satisfy the most perfectionistic baker, but durable and sturdy enough to roll into a variety of shapes.

All-Purpose Butter Cookies

MAKES ABOUT 7 DOZEN 2½-INCH COOKIES
ROLLED TO ⅛ INCH THICK

ROLL DOUGH SCRAPS UP just once to avoid toughening cookies.

16   tablespoons (2 sticks) unsalted butter,
        at cool room temperature
1   cup superfine sugar (or granulated sugar,
        processed to fine texture in a food processor)
½   teaspoon salt
1   egg yolk, plus 1 whole egg
2   teaspoons vanilla extract
2½   cups bleached all-purpose flour
        Decorating Glaze (optional; page 356)

1. Cream butter, sugar and salt with an electric mixer at medium speed until light and fluffy. Add yolk, beat well, then add whole egg and vanilla; continue beating until well incorporated. Add flour and beat on low speed until flour is just mixed. Divide dough in half and wrap in plastic. Refrigerate until firm, at least 1 hour. (Dough can be refrigerated for up to 2 days or double-wrapped and frozen for up to 1 month.)

2. Adjust oven racks to upper and lower-middle positions and preheat oven to 375°F. Line 2 baking sheets with parchment paper. Remove one disk of dough from refrigerator and cut in half. Return unused portion to refrigerator. Lightly flour work surface; roll dough to ⅛ inch thick, using a spatula to loosen dough and lightly sprinkling work surface with flour as needed. Using a cookie cutter, cut dough into desired shapes. Place ½ inch apart on cookie sheets. Or form dough into balls, using about 1 tablespoon for each, and flatten with a greased bottom of a glass, dipped in flour from time to time.

3. Bake cookies, rotating sheets halfway through baking, until golden brown, 6 to 8 minutes. Use a thin-bladed spatula to transfer them immediately to a cooling rack. Cool to room temperature. Repeat rolling, cutting and baking with remaining dough. Decorate cooled cookies, if desired, and transfer to an airtight container where they can be stored for up to 3 weeks.

♦ Cornmeal-Citrus Cookies

Follow recipe for All-Purpose Butter Cookies, adding 1 teaspoon finely grated lemon or orange zest to creamed butter and sugar in step 1 and substituting 1 cup fine cornmeal for 1 cup flour. Continue as directed.

♦ Chocolate-Cinnamon Cookies

Follow recipe for All-Purpose Butter Cookies, adding 1 ounce melted and cooled unsweetened chocolate to creamed butter and sugar in step 1. Substitute ¼ cup cocoa for ¼ cup flour, and mix in ¼ teaspoon cinnamon to flour-cocoa mixture. Continue as directed.

♦ Lemon or Orange Butter Cookies

Follow recipe for All-Purpose Butter Cookies, adding 2 teaspoons finely grated lemon zest or 1 teaspoon finely grated orange zest to creamed butter and sugar in step 1. Continue as directed.

♦ Lemon-Poppy Seed Cookies

Follow recipe for All-Purpose Butter Cookies, adding 2 teaspoons finely grated lemon zest to creamed butter and sugar in step 1 and stirring 2 tablespoons poppy seeds into finished dough. Continue as directed.

♦ Orange-Nut Cookies

Follow recipe for All-Purpose Butter Cookies (page 352), adding 1 teaspoon finely grated orange zest and 1 cup finely ground walnuts, pecans or toasted skinned hazelnuts to creamed butter and sugar in step 1. Continue as directed.

♦ Ginger Cookies

Follow recipe for All-Purpose Butter Cookies (page 352), adding 1 teaspoon ground ginger to flour in step 1 and stirring 6 tablespoons minced candied ginger into finished dough. Continue as directed.

♦ Butterscotch Cookies

Follow recipe for All-Purpose Butter Cookies (page 352), substituting 1 cup packed light brown sugar for superfine sugar.

♦ Coconut Cookies

Follow recipe for All-Purpose Butter Cookies (page 352), stirring 1 cup toasted flaked, sweetened coconut into finished dough.

♦ Peanut Butter Cookies

Follow recipe for All-Purpose Butter Cookies (page 352), creaming ⅔ cup peanut butter with butter and sugar in step 1. Continue as directed.

Spice Cookies

16 tablespoons (2 sticks) unsalted butter,
 at cool room temperature
1 cup packed light brown sugar
½ teaspoon salt
1 egg yolk, plus 1 whole egg
2 teaspoons vanilla extract
2½ cups bleached all-purpose flour
¾ teaspoon ground cinnamon
½ teaspoon ground ginger
¼ teaspoon ground nutmeg
¼ teaspoon ground allspice
⅛ teaspoon ground cloves
 Decorating Glaze (optional; page 356)

Follow recipe for All-Purpose Butter Cookies, substituting brown sugar for superfine sugar in step 1 and adding cinnamon, ginger, nutmeg, allspice and cloves to flour. Continue as directed.

♦ Raisin or Currant Spice Cookies

Follow recipe for Spice Cookies, stirring ½ cup minced raisins or ½ cup dried currants into finished batter. Continue as directed.

Decorating Glaze

MAKES ABOUT ¾ CUP

To GLAZE COOKIES, you can spread glaze on each cookie with a knife or drizzle it onto the cookies from the tines of a fork or fit a pastry bag with a writing tip and pipe the glaze over each cookie in a pattern. If you decide to color the glaze, cut back a bit on the liquid, unless you are using color pastes.

    1   cup confectioners' sugar
5-6   teaspoons milk, or lemon or orange juice

Mix sugar and liquid in a small bowl, adding just enough liquid to make a spreadable or pourable glaze. Use immediately or cover with a sheet of plastic wrap placed directly on surface of glaze to keep it from hardening.

All-Purpose Chocolate Glaze and Frosting

MAKES ½ CUP

BECAUSE THIS GLAZE HARDENS as it cools, you may need to warm it several times during decorating.

    4   ounces bittersweet or semisweet chocolate
    4   tablespoons (½ stick) unsalted butter
    1   tablespoon corn syrup

Melt chocolate and butter in a medium bowl set over a pan of almost simmering water. Stir in corn syrup. Proceed with decorating.

INDEX